DRAWING FOR BEGINNERS

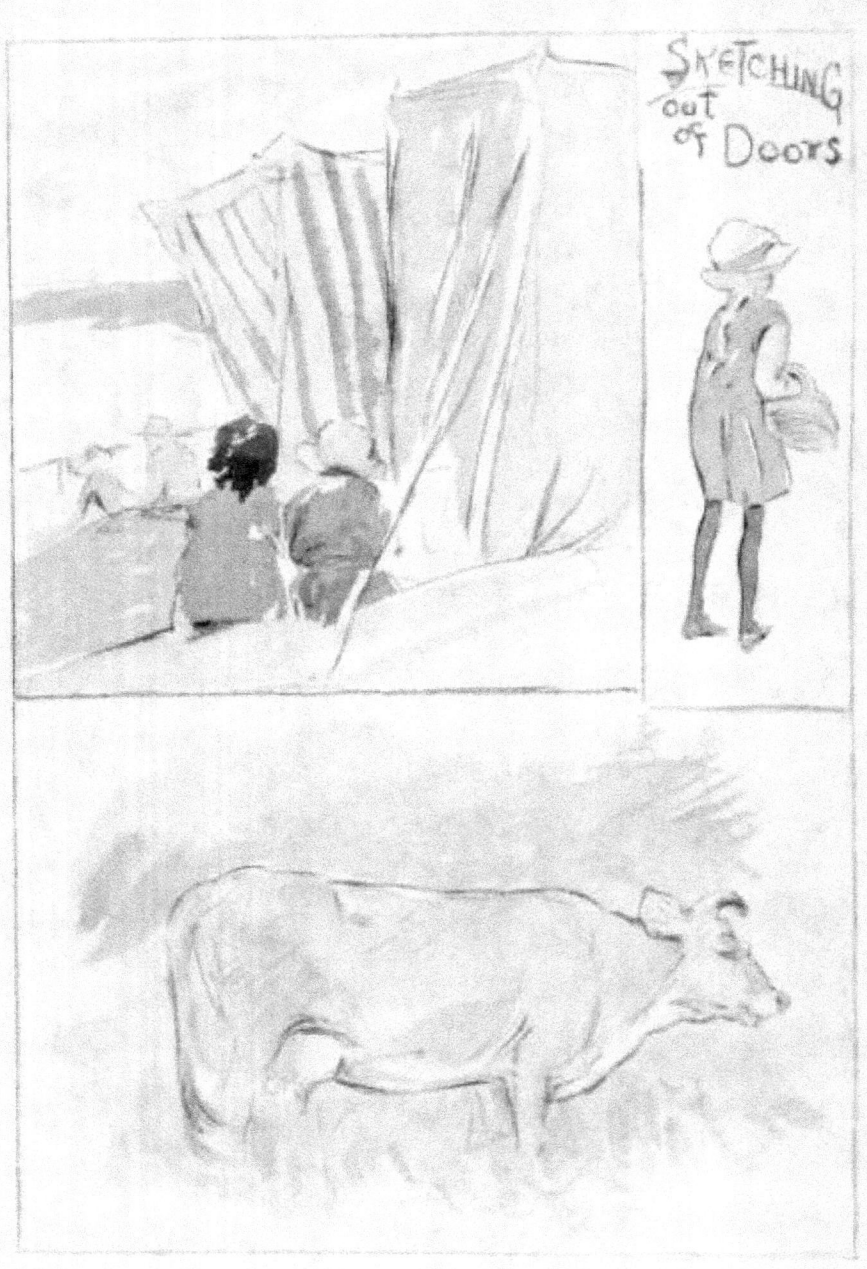

Fig. 1. A Page from a Sketch-book.

DRAWING
FOR BEGINNERS

BY

DOROTHY FURNISS

PUBLISHED BY
BRIDGMAN PUBLISHERS
BY SPECIAL
ARRANGEMENT
WITH GEORGE G.
HARRAP & CO. LTD.
LONDON

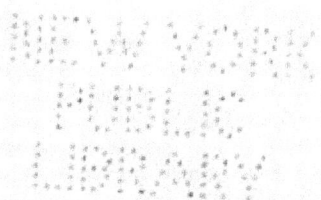
BRIDGMAN PUBLISHERS
PELHAM   NEW YORK

Printed in Great Britain
by Turnbull & Spears, Edinburgh

TO

MY FATHER HARRY FURNISS

And all ike breeze of Fancy blows. And every dew-drop paints a bow. The wizard lightnings deeply glow.

And every thought breaks out a rose.

Tennyson

FOREWORD

HAVE you heard the reply given by a small boy to a query, " How do you draw ? " " I think," he said, " and then I draw round my think."

It is an excellent answer to a very difficult question.

Many an artist could not give as lucid a reply. As far as I can judge, and I have been peculiarly fortunate in meeting many artists, the great artist would probably say :

" How do I draw ? Here—give me a paint-brush "—and if he were inclined to be brutally frank—" don't ask me fool questions ; watch— this is how it is done." And he would proceed with a few swift strokes to paint something, at which you would gasp and feel no wiser than before. It would look perfect. It would be perfect. But how was it done ? He thought, and then drew round his thought. The great artist speaks with his tools ; more often than not he is a man of few words.

We are told that when a Japanese artist wishes to paint a flower he watches its growth from bud to blossom and then to seed. After a little time has elapsed he takes up his brush and paints his remembrance of the flower. Whether he could describe the manner in which he intends to paint that flower is doubtful.

We must think with the brush and the pencil; we must think first and then draw round our ' think.'

I hope that this book may help you to arrange your thoughts.

It is but a helping hand on the broad highway that leads to the great world of art.

D. F.

CONTENTS

DRAWING FOR BEGINNERS

INTRODUCTION

A Few Technical Hints

Drawing with the Lead Pencil

A PENCIL has many excellent qualities. It is a clean tool and easy to handle. It can be carried in the pocket and pressed into service whenever required. Beyond sharpening, it requires no attention.

To sharpen a pencil you should pare the wood in small shavings with a sharp knife. When a small portion of the lead is exposed place the lead on a piece of paper and whittle down to a firm and not very thin point. A very sharp point is a mistake. With such a point we are inclined to dig into the paper, and thus to add to our difficulties when erasing. A thin point, moreover, snaps easily, needs constant sharpening, and therefore leads to much wasting of valuable lead.

A word or two about the position of the pencil when drawing.

We hold it, of course, as we do the pen, between the thumb and the first two fingers, and half-way up the shaft.

There is a modern fashion of holding the pen between the second and third fingers, and whatever may be said for this position in writing nothing could be advanced in its favour for drawing.

An overwhelming argument for holding the pencil between the thumb and the first two fingers is this: the hand never tires.

I have never heard an artist complain of a tired hand, though his work extended from early morning till late at night; the reason lies in the perfect balance of the tool in his hand.

Take the pencil between the first finger and the thumb

Drawing for Beginners

and hold it lightly. Is it not perfectly balanced ? Does not the point respond to the slightest motion of the two fingers ? Raise the thumb. If you are holding the pencil correctly, it remains resting against the two fingers and the root of the first finger. The little finger is the pivot of the hand. The hand sweeps round in curves from the tip of the finger with perfect freedom.

Practise various touches with your pencil. For light, feathery, gossamer lines hold the pencil lightly and half-way up the shaft; for rich firm effects hold the pencil firmly and lower on the shaft, rubbing the lead to and fro without removing the point from the paper; for minute or detailed drawing it will probably be desirable to hold the pencil lower still.

A medium HB pencil is generally useful. B or BB for textures, rough-coated animals, etc.

A firm-surfaced paper such as cartridge is useful both for pencil and water-colour. A polished card is not advisable, neither is a paper with a rough ' toothed ' surface ; the latter is apt to lend a tricky effect which is alluring, but dangerous. It is wiser to employ straightforward methods. Then you know exactly the various stages of your progress.

Do not use patent pencils with metal holders or decorated tops. The ordinary plain wooden pencil is the best tool.

Drawing with Black Chalk

Black chalk, in the shape of a pencil, is a pleasant medium, but it has one disadvantage, it is very difficult to erase. Therefore the use of chalk necessitates a certain amount of confidence and experience. In other words, do not begin your studies with chalk in preference to lead, but reserve it for your later work.

Chalk gives a rich velvety tone and never a greasy shine, the drawback of blacklead. It is delightful for quick sketches, for materials of a coarse or rough texture, for the sketching of animals, buildings, trees, and landscapes.

Chalk crumbles and breaks more easily than lead, and it 14

Introduction

white chalk gives the highest Hghts, and the paper itself forms the middle tone.

I know of nothing more interesting than sketching animals, dogs, rabbits, and goats with these three mediums.

White chalk needs very little pointing. It crumbles and breaks with the slightest encouragement, and the small pieces are often useful for sharpening up the edges, or touching in the brightest light.

Drawing with Coloured Chalks

Coloured chalks are very simple mediums. Often the baby begins with a box of coloured chalks as a step toward the colour-box.

Chalk does not trickle about the paper like water-colour, and is, moreover, a very direct medium.

A red berry demands red chalk ; a blue bead demands blue chalk ; a skein of mixed silk or wool of blue, green, and yellow demands blue, green, or yellow chalk.

By placing yellow against blue, or blue against green, or red against brown, we obtain a degree of shading, a mixing of tints, which teaches us to blend our colours. Chalks should not be applied to the paper too heavily, but laid on with a ligV^: touch. There is no need to point the chalks. By rolling the chalk in the fingers we can usually find a sharp little edge. Rub the chalk on a piece of waste paper, and on one side only ; that will give a flattened side for sharp and decided drawing.

Drawing with the Brush

Drawing with the brush is more difficult than with the pencil, but you should accustom yourself to the use of both.

It is far better to paint a picture from the very beginning with a brush. Drawing first with a pencil and then with a brush necessitates changing one's tool, and readjusting one's mind. We look at a model, pencil in hand, very differently from the way we regard the same object when holding a brush.

Drawing for Beginners

If you accustom yourself to the use of the brush you will soon find it an adaptable tool.

The artist holds the brush in the same way as he holds the pen or the pencil, and he shifts the position according to the demands of the subject.

For instance, if we are applying a broad wash of colour we should hold the brush with freedom, and fairly high on the shaft. One with a fair point, full and firm, will be necessary for drawing. A long hairy point will give a feeble line, and one too short and blunt no line at all.

A brush that is at its thickest the size of an ordinary lead pencil is a useful tool. A very small brush will prove inefficient, for in drawing with a brush a fairly bold drawing is aimed at.

If you have made a mistake cleanse the brush with fresh water, and while it is still full of this pass it over the mistake. Then complete the erasure by rubbing. Do not rub too hard or the surface of the paper will be destroyed and refuse to take colour other than a misty blur or blot.

Clean blotting-paper applied to a mistake—first lightly brushed with water—will sometimes erase it.

Sketch in light tints, not dark.

In order to get a fine point, fill your brush with colour, wipe it on a cloth, or roll the tip round on a piece of blotting-paper.

To run a good deal of colour on your paper, charge your brush with paint and put it on with rapid touches.

For the darkest shadows, wait till your paper is drying and use the water sparingly.

Drawing with Charcoal

Charcoal is by far the most fascinating, as it is the most difficult medium, therefore it will be wise to keep this for our most advanced studies.

But we must bear in mind that no medium takes the place of charcoal. If we shirk its use and adhere obstinately to the 18

Introduction

pencil we shall lose the freedom that is essential for the development of our art.

You will require a small box of Vine charcoal and Michelet paper ; if you intend to use sheets of paper instead of sketchbooks—and this I strongly advise—you must have also a drawing-board on which to pin the paper, and an easel. (Only by standing do we get perfect freedom for the handling of our large drawings.)

Charcoal has several irritating qualities. It snaps easily and crumbles, and it rubs away despite spraying with fixative. Nevertheless there is no medium more fascinating and more satisfying. It is equally useful for delicate effects and for those of a bold and vigorous character.

Charcoal can be used at arm's length; it is usually held— for quick sketching of big subjects—at the end and not at the middle of the shaft like the chalk or lead pencil.

It requires very little sharpening and never a point. A flattened side answers the purpose.

Rub the stick on sanded paper or shave with a knife, shaving not toward the tip and bearing away, but holding the charcoal in the left hand and along the first finger. Pare the charcoal inwardly with the grain of the wood, for, as you probably know, charcoal is burnt wood.

The pith of bread (worked into small pellets) makes a better eraser for charcoal than rubber, though putty rubber is often used.

When fixing a charcoal study stand not too near the easel, but a pace or two away, so that the spray falls in a light, even shower over your drawing. When standing too near the liquid falls in blobs and blots the drawing.

CHAPTER I

How to Begin. Simple Subjects for Drawing and Painting

Do you like painting ? Does drawing interest you ? Have you a pencil, a box of chalks, or a paint-box ? Because, if you have even one of these things, you can open the door to such jolly times.

Do you remember Alice finding in Wonderland the little closed door, and how she longed to open the door and walk into the charming garden ? Well, there's a garden just as fascinating as the one seen by Alice, and the keys to it are your pencil and brush.

This garden, like Alice's, is full of wonderful surprises. You never know w^hat is lying in wait, what quaint, curious, and beautiful things are to be found. Would you like to go into it ? Then come with me. You have the keys in your hands.

But first I will ask you a question. Have you ever heard of the story of the shepherd-boy of Vespignano ?

Once upon a time there lived in Italy a little shepherd-boy who was so passionately fond of drawing that he would pick up a stick and draw with it on the dusty roads and sandy rocks.

You might ask why he used such rough tools ; it was all the material he could call his own. Paper and parchment were far beyond the reach of shepherd-boys. But Giotto, for that was his name, drew quite happily with his pointed stick upon the ground, and he had all the hillside from which to choose his subjects. He drew the flowers, the grass, and the pine-trees. Best of all, he liked to draw his sheep, and 20

How to Begin

these he drew with loving care. A great artist called Cimabue happened to pass one day when Giotto was absorbed in his drawing. His curiosity was awakened, and dismounting from his horse he drew near. To his unbounded surprise he saw, traced on the ground, a number of beautiful little sketches.

He began to talk with Giotto, and soon discovered that the boy's whole soul was in his simple art. And, being a wise and very generous man, he determined to do all that lay in his power to educate Giotto as an artist. In a very Uttle time the shepherd-boy left Vespignano for Florence, where he entered the great man's studio. Being extraordinarily gifted and more than usually industrious, he made rapid progress in his art. He soon outstripped his master, and in course of time was acclaimed the foremost artist of his day.

And that is the story of Giotto, who died ten years after Edward III came to the English throne.

Young people (and sometimes old people are not much wiser) are fond of excusing their laziness by saying, " I can't draw this—or I can't draw that. I haven't got the materials, or the pencil won't work." Which last excuse is about as reasonable as mounting a push-bicycle and expecting it to carry you up a hill without your moving your legs.

The shepherd-boy taught himself by drawing with a pointed stick on a smooth piece of ground. So lack of materials is no excuse for lack of effort.

One of my young readers may cry, " Draw ! Draw ! / draw ? Why, I cannot draw a straight line." As a matter of fact, a perfectly straight line is one of the most difficult things to draw. There are many artists who cannot easily draw a straight line. If you study Nature—and she is our safest guide—you will never see an absolutely straight line. If you do see one, you may be sure that the hand of man has helped to make it.

A very general excuse is that which pleads the impossibility of drawing two sides of an object alike. Have you ever seen two ' sides ' alike in Nature—a tree, a flower, or even

Drawing for Beginners

a single blade of grass, inch by inch and tint by tint, the same ? Look round and judge for yourself.

Only man makes things mathematically exact. He is forced to balance one side with the other side. The cup, the vase, the house, will not stand and support itself. Nature is bound by no such rules, and Nature is always an artist.

Would you like to know the most difficult thing of all to draw ? Without question, a perfect circle.

Strangely enough there was one artist whose fortune was made through the drawing of a circle. It was Giotto, the shepherd-lad whose story we have just been discussing. When his name was beginning to be known the Pope sent to learn more about him. He wished to employ the cleverest artist to be found in all Italy to paint pictures on the walls of the great church of St Peter at Rome.

And how do you think Giotto convinced the envoys of his fitness for the work ? He took a large sheet of paper, and, dipping his brush into red paint, he drew a circle with one sweep of his arm, perfect and exact.

" Take that to the Pope," he said.

And the Pope admitted that of all the paintings submitted by the artists not one equalled the perfection of Giotto's O ; whence we have the proverb, " As round as Giotto's O," signifying perfection.

We are not, unfortunately, all Giottos. Straight lines, symmetrical sides, perfect circles—perhaps when we are older we shall be able to attack these problems without flinching, but now, away with them and away with all excuses—let us begin.

Take a sheet of paper, or open your sketch-book ; pick up a pencil. Now what shall we draw ?

Some children bubble with odd fancies; men, horses, fairies, dogs come tripping to their minds ; but you and I are not so sure. We will choose something simple, something interesting.

What of a leaf, an ivy leaf ?—for that we can easily find whether we live in city or country. 22

How to Begin

It is a quaint shape when we come to observe it closely. Would you call it a long, square, or round shape ? I should say that it resembled a heart.

Then we will draw a heart-shape. Next we see a large vein running through the centre of the heart. It extends from the very tip of the leaf to the stout little stalk which eventually fastens itself on to the main branch.

Now we had better mark the chief points of our leaf, which are three in number. And also there are two or three a trifle smaller. These we also draw. And we note that the large central vein is met by two smaller veins, and that these, with two more, radiate from the stalk.

Turn the leaf and look at its back and see how wonderfully these veins converge to the stalk.

Put in some of the veins lightly and carefully, choosing the biggest and the most important.

Next we should note that the light comes from one side, and the side farthest from the light is in shadow. We might shade the edges of the leaf with our pencil and sharpen and shade the strongly curved stalk, and any other part that needs to be strengthened.

You may say that you live where there are no ivy leaves. Then take a maple leaf, a sycamore, or a chestnut; any leaf at hand. I am not laying down any hard-and-fast rules, but merely trying to help you with something that you want to do.

If you prefer it, draw a shell or a feather. I suggest these particular things because they are simple and easy to draw, and within the reach of most people.

A feather can be studied on the same lines as a leaf, presuming that it is a well-formed wing or tail feather—a not-too-fluffy affair. First observe its general shape. Elongated— oblong, is it not ? Then draw in an oblong shape. Next notice that it is broad at the bottom end, and that it inclines to a rounded point. We will shape off the side tips.

Next we trace the main stalk or stem from which the plume spreads. Observe the separating of the plume on one side,

Drawing for Beginners

the crisp firmness of the narrower vein, the fluffiness at the back of the thick stem, and the solid firmness of the stem itself.

We can work this with a pencil and trace the beautiful marking on the feather, or we can produce our paint-box and try to colour our drawing. It is an excellent plan to hide the model from sight, and see how much, or how little, has penetrated our brain.

Afterward try drawing some simple flowers : a snowdrop in a small vase ; a crocus— bulb, stem, and flower ; a daffodil with a few broad spear-like leaves.

And if we find it difficult to interpret shapes with our pencil, and our brain tires, and our fingers get weary, choose some very different and ' opposite' shapes.

The mere task of choosing requires a little stimulating reflection.

For instance, contrast a flat, squat-shaped, circular inkpot with a small, narrow upright tumbler; a big spoon w\th a broad-handled knife. Compare a lemon with a tangerine ; an egg with an apple ; a reel of cotton with a tube of water-colour paint; a matchbox with an ash-tray ; a tall slender vase and a dumpy bowl; a large breakfast-cup and a small cocoa-tin ; a flat, thin book and a sphere-shaped paper-weight.

Put some of these objects on a table, at a little distance from your desk, and sketch them two by two, and side by side.

You could draw some with your pencil, and some with your brush.

The lemon and the tangerine are excellent subjects for this test, because you have contrast of both shape and colour.

If you sketch them first with your brush, choose a tint of which they are both composed—say, a very pale yellow.

Draw first the lemon, the large, elongated, egg-shaped variety. Notice the characteristic knob, like a nose, at one end, and compare this with the round tangerine and its somewhat flattened top. You will find a further interest in comparing colours. How rich is the orange tinge beside the 24.

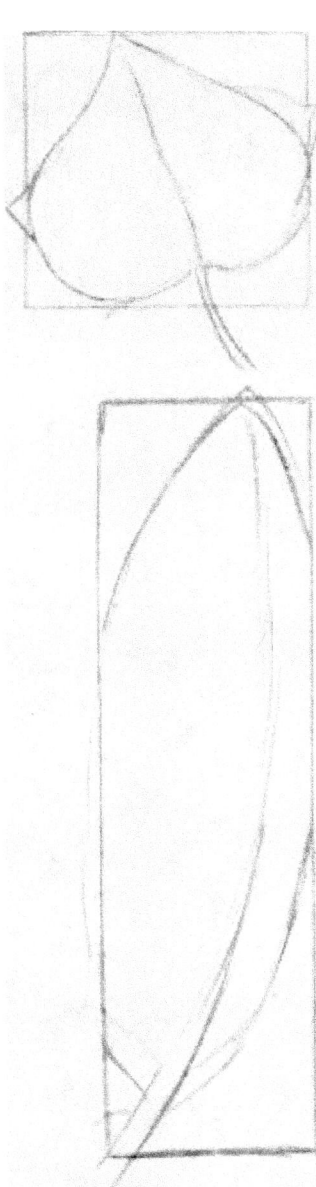

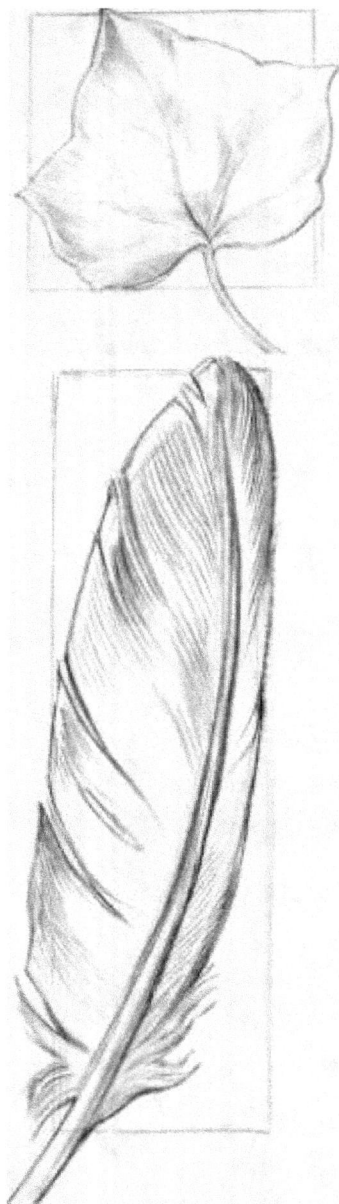

Fig. 3. Ivy Leaf and Feather

How to Begin

paler yellow! How deep the shadows of the tangerine appear when compared with those of the lighter-hued lemon ! For the lemon we must seek out our cool blues and pale golds ; for the tangerine, warm crimson, and even touches of bronze and brown.

If we wish to handle our pencils intelligently (to get from our pencil many varied touches), we should draw objects which are variously composed. In other words, made of more than one material. And here again we must don our thinking-cap.

We need not go very far. A few homely domestic articles would furnish us with some useful models.

Take a feather brush—that is, a brush composed of feathers, leather, and smooth polished wood ; hang this up at a level with your eye, feathers downward, and sketch it with your pencil.

Draw a long line to represent the handle, and indicate the rough fan-shape of the lower part. If the handle is grooved and turned, do not worry because you cannot get both sides exactly alike. First sketch the largest shapes and remember to keep the stick slender; next the three-cornered piece of leather which neatly hides and binds the ends of the feathers together ; lastly, the feathers themselves, spreading out in a loose, plumy fan.

Having sketched these shapes, darken the handle, which is polished and black. Leave the white paper to show through to provide the lights. Try to represent the polish of the surface by drawing with firm sharp touches.

The leather, being of a more pliable material and of a duller surface, needs a lighter treatment. If it has a dull tint, give it a shaded tone ; if it has folds, draw these folds in shadow.

Next the feathers.

A feather is one of the lightest of all substances. We say " light as a feather " when we wish to suggest something of the airiest description.

But although it is so unsubstantial, it is not feeble. It has a definite shape.

Drawing for Beginners

Each feather has a spine from which it spreads in a definite shape. Soft, yes, and dehcate, but with a curved spine and a broad tip. Look at those nearest to you . . . and draw their shapes dehcately. Hold your pencil lightly, give a gentle, feathery touch, and, as the feathers are bunched together, and some will be in shadow, put in the shadows lightly, but sharply. Then pause and look at your drawing.

Have you ' handled ' the drawing of the wood and the feathers differently ? Does the leather look more substantial than the feathers ?

The work is not easy, but practice will soon give a surer touch. You are playing a scale with your pencil as one plays a scale on a piano. Deep bass notes, then the middle strong notes, and lastly the soft delicate treble. We must try to make our pencil speak with a varied tongue.

Drawing different textures might include a kettle and a kettle-holder (shiny metal—rough cloth or velvet); a small piece of fur coiled near, or over, a hard cricket-ball; a cake of soap and a loofah. A woman's hat with a soft wide brim (not the pudding basin variety, which is most difficult for unpractised fingers), trimmed with a cluster of berries, or a twisted bow of ribbon, gives us several different textures.

We must hold the pencil delicately, loosely, and half-way up the shaft if we wish to convey the delicacy of fur and fine hairs. If we would show the richness of velvet, we must use our pencil with determination and shift our fingers for a shorter and firmer grip.

All this will come with practice. There is no need to worry yourself with harassing doubts. Do your best; no one can do more.

When we work alone, we are very apt to get weary and depressed with our difficulties.

We sit before our little models and look so often that we see less and less, instead of more and more.

It is very wise occasionally to cover up your model, or, at any rate, to turn your back upon it for a while.

This will often appear to increase your difficulties, but 26

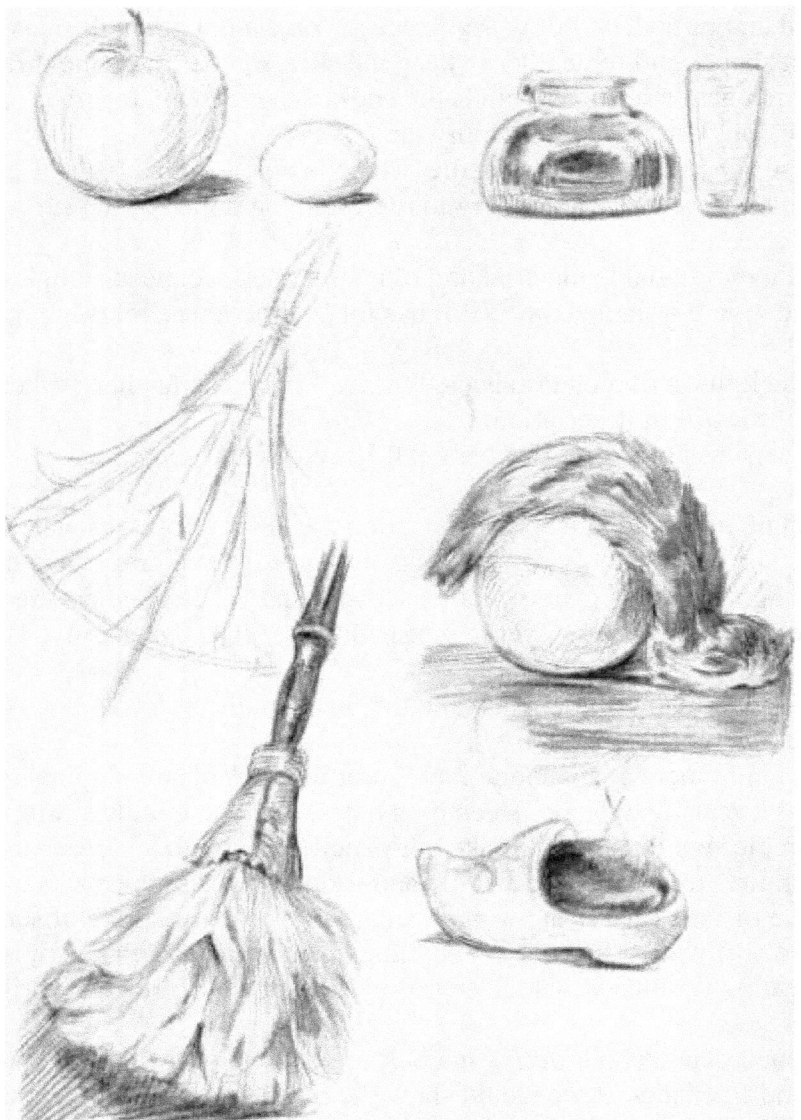

Fig. 4r. Models illustrating Varied Shapes and Textures

How to Begin

it will tend to quicken your observation, and this is worth any extra trouble or discouragement that may be entailed. There is a temptation to look continually at our models, and in consequence we look at them more often than is necessary. If, after looking at the model, we hide it from sight and then proceed with our drawing, obviously we must work from memory. The habit of working without models is soon developed, and it adds enormously to our powers of ' taking notice.'

CHAPTER II

Drawing our Toys

WHEN we are very small nothing seems too difficult for our pencil. If we wish to draw a tree, a horse, or an engine, we make no bones about the matter, we draw it. Possibly the drawings may look rather quaint in the eyes of other people, but they satisfy ourselves.

And behind these quaint early drawings lies, more often than not, a sound and practical line of reasoning.

You know, for instance, how fond is Baby John of drawing an engine in full steam.

" My fain," he will say, proudly pointing to a piece of paper covered with whirligigs of pencil.

He's right enough, I dare say. Did he not begin by drawing a queer bit of shed, some odd-looking wheels, and perhaps even a coconut thing with a few straight lines meant for the engine-driver's features ? And always he drew the shape of a funnel. And then . . . his fancy ran riot! Out of the funnel came smoke ! Lots and lots of smoke ! Wasn't the train the puff-puff of his infancy ? Pujf-piijf-'pujf came the smoke. It was glorious drawing ! Everything was covered in smoke.

He showed you his train, and, in all probability, you laughed, as I might have done in your place.

And yet he was doing what is a very difficult thing to do, he was drawing * out of his imagination,' or, as some people say, ' drawing out of his head.'

Once, and not a very long time ago, I was sitting alone and drawing in haste, when old Gary entered, curious and inquiring. She looked round the empty room, she looked at me, and she looked at my paper, on which several scenes were 28

Drawing our Toys

shaping, and then she said : " Ah ! I see you draw out of your fancy ! "

I loved Gary's expression " out of your fancy." Don't you think it far more expressive than ' drawing out of one's head ' or ' drawing from one's imagination ' ?

Few of us who are fond of drawing can resist, when we are young, drawing ' out of our fancy.'

Little girls fly to the enchanted regions of Fairy- and Flower-land, as surely as little boys turn to scenes of breathless and stirring adventure, ships at sea and ships in the air, soldiers. Red Indians, camp-fires, hunting, shooting, and games of thrilling interest.

Little girls push wide the enchanted gates of Fairyland. Flowers emitting tiny elves, gnomes dancing with toadstools held aloft, gorgeous ladies on prancing steeds or in flower-bedizened motor-cars, castle gates opening to the blast of a horn blown by a handsome prince.

And as we grow older we cease to draw our magical dreams —more's the pity 1 for there will be nothing as delightful in all the sparkling realms of art.

When we become more ' practical,' we get more matter-of-fact, and we lose, unfortunately, our early confidence.

Sometimes, see-sawing between the things of ' our fancy ' and the things that are simple facts, we get disheartened.

We are tempted then to throw away our pencils and paintboxes in disgust, to be discouraged by a smile, to be utterly disheartened by a laugh. And yet between the beautiful Land of Fancy and the strange approaching Land of Fact lies a simple bridge with a very familiar aspect, no more nor less than the companion of our babyhood—the toy-cupboard.

The nursery is full of inviting little models, models that we have handled for years and that are as patient as ever. Here I will let you into a secret. It is comparatively easy to draw the things with which we are familiar. The boy who has made a footstool will probably draw it far better than the boy who has never driven a nail. And it is an excellent

Drawing for Beginners

thing, when we draw an object, to take it up and examine it, whether it be leaf, feather, footstool, chair, or toys.

If we draw our toys now, toy girl, toy horse, toy tree, later we shall be able to draw real girl, real horse, and real tree ; confident because we have a little knowledge to help us on our way.

The toy tree is stiff and still, but has the look of a tree ; Mr Noah is straight and long, but Mr Noah is a man and he has sheep, cows, pigs, and birds ; though made of wood, these have a queer resemblance to their originals.

For a beginning let us take these little creatures and place them in procession along the table, the ark in front, and then, with our sketch-books on our knees (some stiff bit of board beneath it if it be a limp-covered book), sit on a low seat at the extreme right-hand side of our models, and with our eyes on a level with the table.

As in the preceding chapter we experimented with the different shapes of our models, so we will begin by noting that these little ark creatures vary in shape.

Having drawn them with pencil, we could then take up our paint-brush and paint them in gay colours, making a long narrow-shaped picture, a kind of frieze, or border.

What could be easier to draw than Mr Noah himself ? He is just a straight angular shape in several sections. The first and top section makes a queer little hat. The second—an oval shape—a face. The third section slopes outward from his wooden neck to provide his body and then, slightly indenting at the waist, continues in a straight robe to his feet, where we have the fourth section—wider than the others—the stand upon which he is balanced.

After we have finished with Mr Noah we might proceed to draw the animals. A sheep has a long-shaped body perched upon four straight little legs, a thick tail, and possibly two erectly pricked ears. The pig has a more drooping head, a thicker neck, shorter legs.

But I need not discuss the details of each one. The foregoing suggestions will enable you to apply the same principles to all. 30

Drawing our Toys

A toy tree might well bring up the rear of our procession. And a toy tree is a very simple affair, a thimble-shape on the end of a stick, very like a large T with elongated lines drooping on either side.

Looking at the tree as a whole mass we see that the branches extend more than half-way down the stem. Lightly we sketch the line of these branches. Then we look at the trunk of the tree. It is thick and solid for its height. Then thick and solid we will draw it. Next we come to its little green stand, like a sUce of the one which supports Mr Noah, and this stand is smaller than the circumference of the tree at the widest part.

Baby Tom's unbreakable Bunny is surely the simplest of all shapes—a flat base from which rises a rounded hill, steeper on one side than on the other. The steeper, more massive end corresponds with the crouching hind-legs (which we know to be the largest part of the rabbit and which help him to run so fleetly across the warren).

From the top of the head the ears lie flat along the body. Then we mark the small eye, the rounded soft nose, and the tiny forepaws. We look for folds of leg, paw, and ear, and we shade these with a light but firm touch. Bunny Rabbit is white and therefore must not be shaded too strongly. And if you wish to insist on his white coat, look for shadows cast by his rounded body on the ground or background.

The fish of painted celluloid is interesting and by no means difficult to draw, although at first glance we may be slightly puzzled where and how to begin.

A fish is long—one almost might term it domino-shape. Begin, then, as always, by sketching out this general shape.

This done, we trace from the wider and larger end of the fish the long sloping line to the branching tail. The forepart slopes steeply down from the ' shoulders ' and finishes with a rounded blunt nose. Next we notice that our fish—unlike a real fish—has a flattened underside upon which he rests on flat surfaces—and this we draw.

Drawing for Beginners

After this we proceed to sketch the gills, the curious breathing-apparatus of the fish, placed on either side of his head and behind his cheek.

Then we note the eye—circular in shape (not oblong like a human eye)—and the queer scoop of a mouth with the lower jaw jutting forward. We then sketch the tail, which is forked.

If we feel so disposed we can sketch a few of the fish's scales ; they overlap, beginning at the head and diminishing in size with the diminishing size of the tail-end of the body*

We may also build up a picture with a group of several fishes drawn from the single model.

Turn the fish round, so that the head comes nearest. This will not be so easy to draw, because here we are confronted with something that is not on a flat plane. But do not let this worry you. When we are sketching something ' coming toward us ' we draw first the part that is nearest, then the parts behind.

If you draw two or three or even four fishes you might add a swirl of water, and some reeds. Then you will have completed a little picture.

Observe real ponds and reeds at your next opportunity, and if a fish darts before your eyes you will see that his fins and tail agitate the water.

By observing and remembering—we cannot always have a pencil in our hand—we build up pictures in our minds.

Teddy Bear might next pose as a model.

He has a rounded head and a pointed snout. These we sketch very roughly—something like the shape of a pear.

He has a round, fat, pillow-shaped body, to which are attached his fat little thighs, the backward-sloping hind-legs, and his small but solid feet thrust sturdily forward. To the top of his head we must add his large, soft, round ears. The front part of his forehead curves in a decided kink, and his queer little snout soars upward. His nose is black and shiny, and the noses of bears are three-corner shape, wide at the top, curling round the nostrils and narrowing to the upper lip. The 32

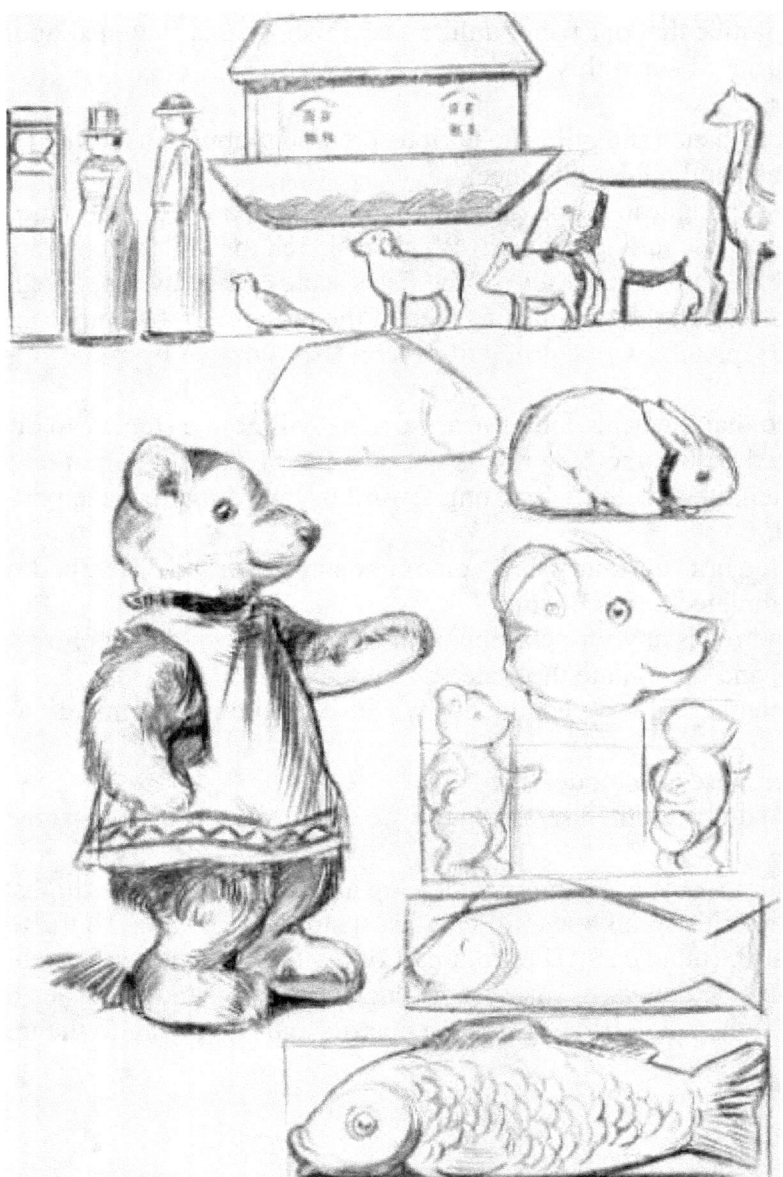

Fig. 5. Various Toys

Drawing our Toys

lower jaw of Teddy Bear is small and retreating, and his mouth curves upward in a pleased little smile.

His upper arms are very thick, and they scoop downward and outward and end in rounded paws. Teddy Bear might carry our study further. In all probability he will wear a coat or tunic. Then draw the little garment carefully. Draw the folds under the arms, and the belt round the waist, and the pattern about the edge of it.

Teddy Bear is different from the wooden creatures of the ark or the velveteen of Bunny Rabbit. He has a furry coat.

Try to indicate with several strokes of the pencil the furry shadows in his ears, behind his ears, in the bend of his arms and legs, and the shaggy little fringe of his paws and hind-legs.

Draw the furry lines lightly. His coat is of a soft substance. Draw some of the thick curls with their queer little twists, and the shadows on the curve of the ragged edges.

His eye is dark and bright. It has a shiny light, being of a shiny substance. Draw the dark shadow of the little eye with strong, dark touches, leaving the light untouched.

There, you see, we have the fur of the coat, the velvet of the dress, and the button of an eye. Three different substances requiring different handling of the pencil.

Dobbin, who has carried us so many miles round the nursery-floor that all his tail and most of his mane has sprinkled the highway of our fancy, Dobbin, after all is said and done, is a horse. He has four legs, a stout body, an arched neck, and a spirited eye and nostril.

See how smooth and round is his body, and how firmly the four legs are fastened to the corners, and how squarely the neck is placed ! His hoofs are stoutly fixed on the ground, the left fore-leg and the right hind-leg stepping forward.

First note the barrel shape of his body and draw that firmly, placing the legs at each corner and simply marking the angle from the top of the leg to the hoof. Then place the curved neck on the square shoulders and trace the long face. (The ' horse-faced individual,' a rude nickname we sometimes hear, suggests a man or woman with a very long face.) c 83

Drawing for Beginners

You may now place the saddle on Dobbin's back, because (we are now looking for more details) the triangular shape of the saddle throws a shadow and marks the curve of his flank.

Compare the various thicknesses of Dobbin's fore-legs. The width of the upper part, the firm square swelling of the knees, the narrowing of the fetlock, the curve and forward thrust of the fetlock, and neat little black hoofs. The hind-legs have a very decided and firm sweep backward.

The bridle is useful. The cheek-strap marks the thickest part of the horse's head, the frontal strap gives the width of the forehead, the long straight side-strap throws a shadow under the funny little painted eye and down the cheek.

It now only remains to draw his long thin face, and his rounded nostril, and his mouth open to receive the bit which has long since disappeared, and his two ears pricked intelligently forward. He has all the ' points ' of a good horse, has Dobbin !

And surely among all our scalped darlings there will be one fair lady to sit for her portrait. Primrose, who never closes her blue orbs, though she is rocked until her small mistress's arms ache with fatigue, and Dahlia, proud, snub-nosed, and long-bodied. Primrose has a real dolly face, rosy cheeks, big round staring eyes, arched eyebrows, and pouting lips. We might do worse than study Primrose. Her eyes are glassy and stuck in oblong sockets; beyond that they have no more than a general resemblance to human eyes. But Primrose has not such an ill-proportioned body as some of her little doll-sisters, though her legs are stiff, and her arms are absurdly small.

Sketch first her large head, then her long body, the angles of her plump legs, and her tiny arms. Roughly mark the position of nose and eyes, the shape of the bobbed locks cut squarely across the brow and at the level of the ear. Look at the length of the tunic, the skirt, and the socks, the edge of the sleeve folds under the arm. The feet being slightly upturned expose the tiniest slip of the sole of the shoes.

When you have the head on paper, then you can mark 84

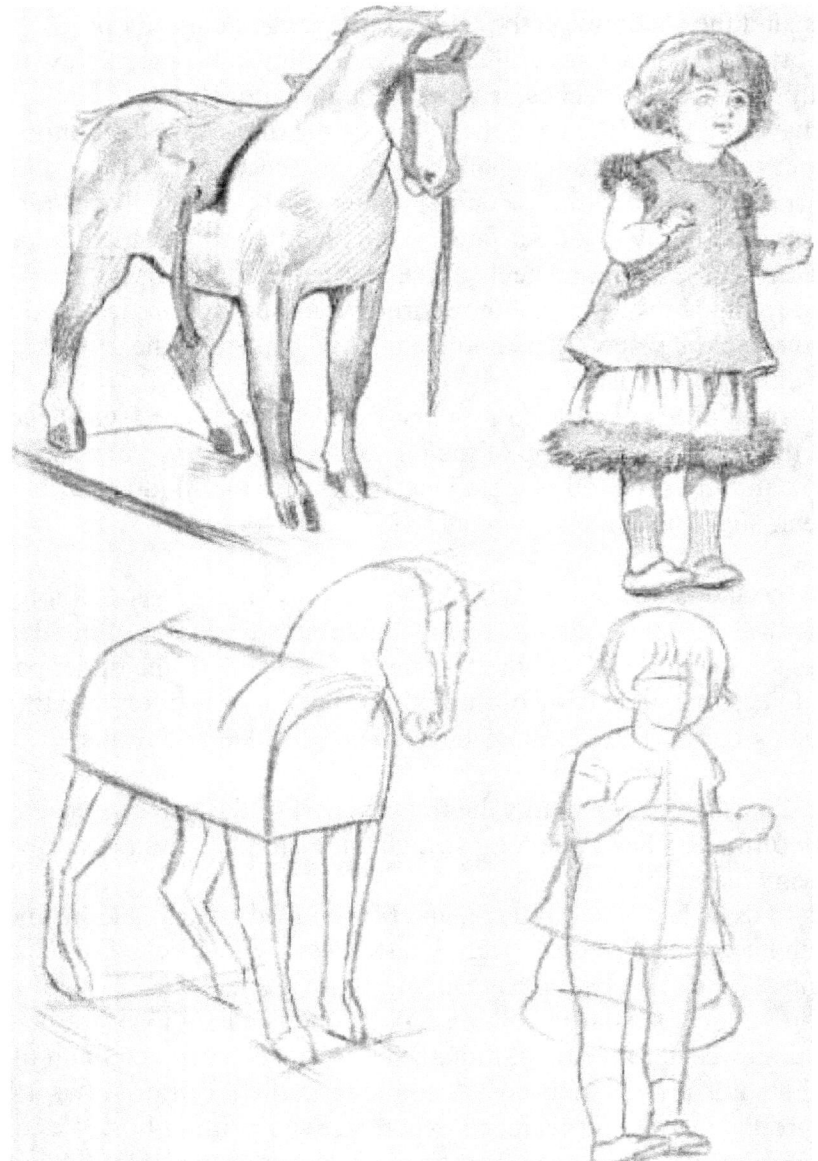

Fig. 6. Toy Horse and Doll

Drawing our Toys

the features; arched eyebrows, tiny nose, dimpled chin, and absurdly fat apple-dumpling cheeks.

Observe the large sockets of the staring eyes, the tiny pink lips.

Shade in the soft hair, and note that it clings to the shape of the head, and the ends are fluffy.

The velvet tunic sticks out at the hips, and the fur edging on the skirt just covers the knees.

Mark that the upper edge of the sock follows the curve of the fat legs, and notice also the curious dimpled fingers that seem proper to the little girl doll.

Don't trouble too much about detail. Draw the chief things and let the others slide. And having proceeded step by step from wooden toy to waxen doll, we might next consider certain little people of more importance—ourselves.

CHAPTER III

Drawing Ourselves and Others

WHEN we first try to draw each other it is best to choose fairly easy positions. Put your small brother into an exaggerated attitude—for example, rushing toward you with arms outspread, his chin in the air. You will very soon get tired "and discouraged ; worse still, so will he, and the probabilities are that his first posing will be his last.

So choose an easy position. Firstly for his sake, secondly for yours. It does not pay to be too selfish about these things, and posing, after all is said and done, is very monotonous work. Queer aches and pains develop in hands, knees, and feet. Extended arms holding banners or grasping trusty swords are apt to get heavy as lead. So I offer it to you as an invaluable principle, consider the feelings of your model.

By ' an easy pose' one that represents a simple position is meant. If we begin by trying to draw some one with body huddled together, legs crossed, neck twisted, and eyes gazing into ours, we shall soon be very confused.

Stand your brother upright, with his arms to his side ; or put your sister on a chair with her hands in her lap and her eyes looking before her ; or plump the baby down on a cushion on the floor and draw him sideways (he won't stay there, but that is a detail). Choose, in a word, easy positions.

It is a very encouraging reflection that all people who aspire to become artists are more or less in the same boat. We land on the same rocks, reefs, and shore, we battle with the same currents, tides, and storms. We should, therefore, be ready with a helping hand whenever it is required by others. 36

Drawing Ourselves and Others

" I will sit to you if you will sit to me," my brothers would say. As there were two brothers and one sister, all fond of drawing, we formed a Triple Alliance, and posed to each other in turn.

So we will begin with simple poses.

A hint here as to the size of our sketches may not come amiss. Do not draw on too small a scale. A sketch of a figure the height of your thumb will not teach you very much. Moreover, one is too apt to adopt a niggling, worried style of drawing. Take a good-sized sheet of paper and try to make your sketch as large as the length of your hand.

Shall we assume that Kathleen has kindly agreed to sit to us for fifteen minutes ? Let us place her on a stool on which she can sit upright and in a steady suffused light—not too near the window, the fire, the electric, gas, or lamp light, all of which tend to throw confusing lights and shadows. Then we give Kathleen a searching look—not too long—and we ask ourselves what shape does Kathleen, roughly speaking, present ? She forms a triangular shape. Yes. See the line of the back, the line of the upper leg, the line of the leg from the knee to the foot, and the upright supports of the stool.

Having seen, we record our impressions—lightly—for after all they are but first impressions, and we don't want to make harsh lines that can be erased only by much rubbing and spoiling of paper.

Next we consider the angles we have made and compare with Kathleen. We see that the angles are softened into curves, the forward thrust of the neck, the curve of the spine and upper part of the leg. We might note the position of the hands on the lap (they are not on the extreme edge of the knee), and we could look again at the head and indicate the roundness of the upper side, the comparatively flat oval of the face, and the hood-like shape of Kathleen's short mane.

Now we are searching for more detail. I know you are dying to give her a nose, eye, and mouth. Well, trace these details lightly and do not labour the eyelashes—we have something more important in hand.

Drawing for Beginners

Next we might note the arm. Turn up the sleeve if the elbow is hidden. Hinges or joints are very important, and the more we see of them the better we shall understand the working of the human frame. Kathleen has a thin but shapely little arm, the upper surface of which is gently rounded and the lower straighter and firmer because of the bones beneath. The thumb rises to a point, and the fingers fall outward more or less in the shape of a fan. The position of this hand is very simple. But ten to one, if the pose has been left to Kathleen's choice, she has clasped her fingers tightly together, for that is a very natural thing to do with an unoccupied pair of hands. And clasped hands are very difficult to draw. One invariably makes them far too large. It is not easy to fit four fingers and a thumb on that small thing called a palm until we have gained experience.

Having arrived at the arms and hands we continue with the lower limbs, tucking in the skirt (folds can be very misleading) to show the upper part of the thigh. The square angle resting upon the seat of the stool is sharply defined. The knee is more or less hidden, but ask Kathleen to touch the knees where they bend, or hold the skirt tightly across the knees, and mark it well in your mind, or on your paper, because from there we trace the lower part of the leg.

Now we follow the curve of the leg, noticing the flat surface of the front part compared with the calf. Your Kathleen may not have as much calf as my Kathleen. Girls have very often the thinnest of arms and legs, and it is a common mistake to give too much flesh. Next we draw the feet. The boat-shape of the foot seen in profile (or sideways) is broken up with the strap, which marks also the thickest part of the foot, the instep. From that curve it descends steeply to the root of the toes or the curve of the shoe proper. Stout, sensible shoes has Kathleen, and the sole and heel are easily traced, marked as they are with the shadows of the leather.

Lastly, note the most important shadows and folds ; also the hair, neckband, cuffs, or doubled-back sleeves—just so far as your interest carries you, but no further. 88

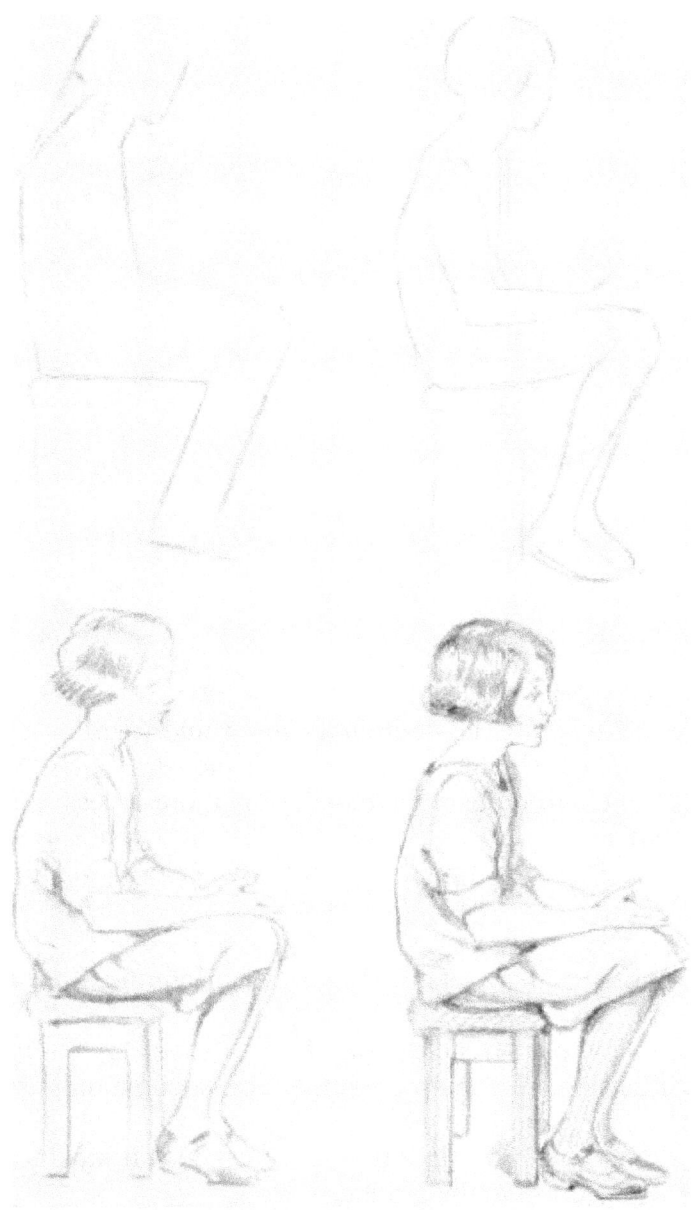

Fig. 7. KATHLEEN

Drawing Ourselves and Others

And so we have Kathleen down on paper. She deserves our thanks, and if she laughs, as she probably will, and exclaims, " Oh, how queer I look in your drawing ! " you can tell her that if she will only sit to us fairly often, we will

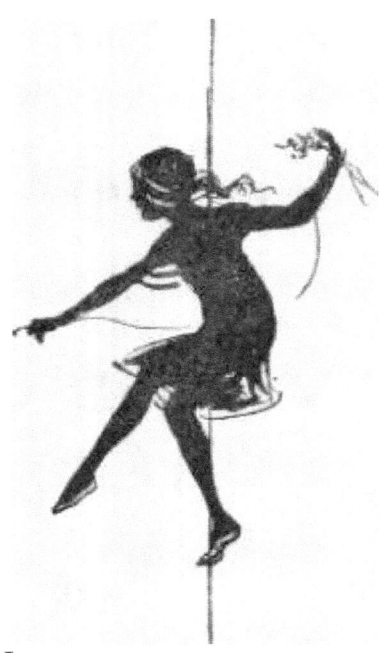

I

Fig. 8. The Balancinq of Moving Figurks

improve and hope some day to make her as nice-looking as she would wish.

Now what about Jack—do you think he would care to sit for his picture ?

Jack being a gentleman full of frolic will probably like to pose in more or less spirited action. Why not ? If he wishes to peer aft across the good kitchen chair with his back toward us, we shall probably find it is no more difficult to draw him thus than from a side view. His energy may be a spur to ours.

Drawing for Beginners

There is one fact about standing figures that you must always bear in mind. They must balance.

You will probably say with a smile you are quite certain of that without any reminder. But I am inclined to think that young artists are very unobservant, or else uncommonly careless, so often do we note a lack of balance in their pictures.

And you can see for yourself, artist or no artist, that if you throw yourself into an attitude, and lose your balance, you will come with a crash to the ground.

Your heel, or toe, or whatever happens to be your support, must come under the centre of your spinal column.

In Fig. 8 are shown a couple of silhouettes of figures in action to emphasize this principle. Suppose you were hopping on one leg, or dancing on your toe, or standing upright with your arms above your head, and Michael or Peter gave you a push, as brothers sometimes do, you would at once lose your balance—and the figure in your drawing will overbalance if you do not rightly plant him upon whatever is to support him.

Therefore, as soon as we have sketched in the angles of Jack draw a faint line down the centre from the back or half-centre of the neck, and this should reach the ball of the right foot. (Jack is depending on the chair with his left leg, and he could therefore lean backward or forward without losing his balance.)

First we glean a general idea of the big angles of the body, and the broad, sweeping line of the spine, the bending thigh and leg, and the standing leg and foot (in my sketch drawn on a smaller scale). Then we follow the angles, and find they break into large simple curves. We trace the great curve of the body, its backward thrust, the width of shoulders, and the comparatively narrow width across the hips, the thick curve of the thigh and its narrowing line to where the knee bends on the chair, the curve of the calf, and the flatter line of the knee to the foot where it bends downward in a great spoon-shaped curve. The right leg has far more delicate curves. The calf and upper thigh are drawn taut with the 40

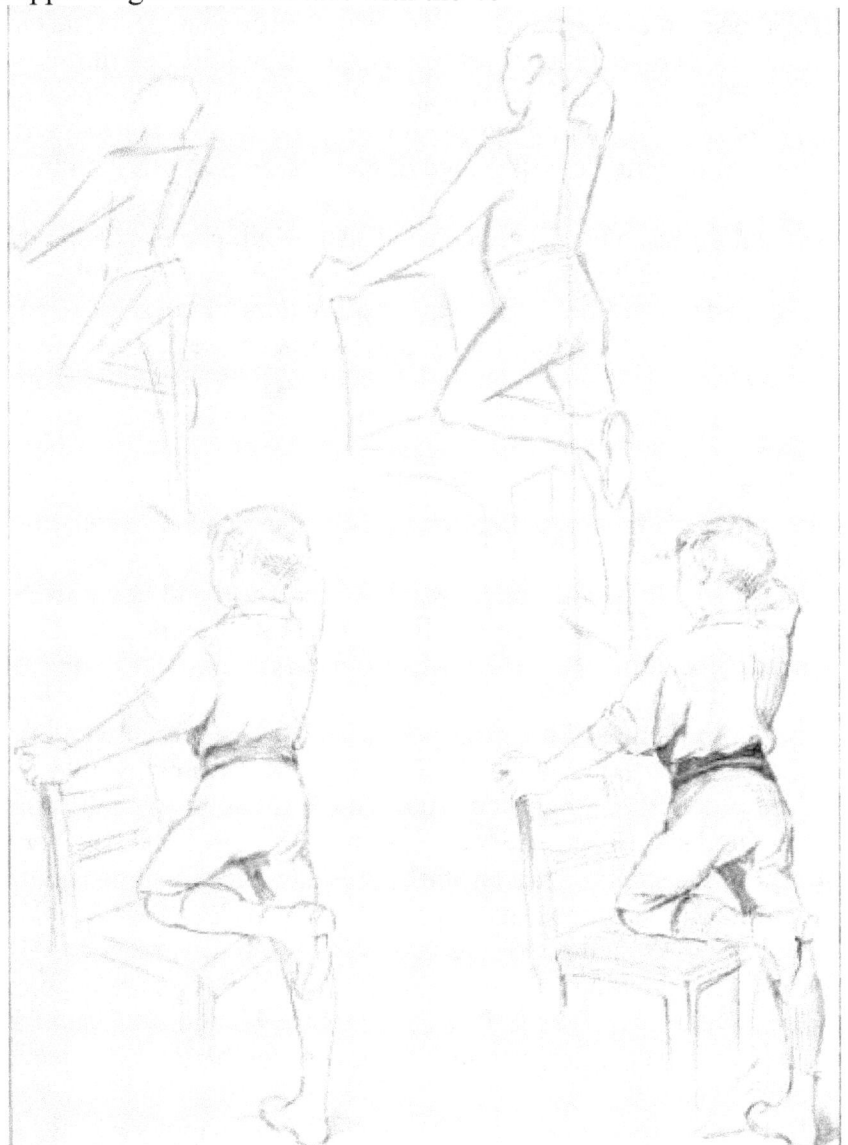

FijT. 9. Jack

Drawing Ourselves and Others

very upright position. (If you stand in this position you can feel the strain of the sinews at the back of the knee and the ankle.) The ankle tapers and the toe of the foot is turned outward, and thus we see both the back of the heel and the broad toe turned away in shape something like the bow of a boat.

Having noted the main forms and their relation to each other, we can next devote ourselves to detail. The line of the hair follows the upper part of the round bullet-shaped head.

The ear is valuable, coming as it does at the meeting of the jaw and skull, and we note the tiny niche where the neck rises above the collar.

Now we can mark down the big shadows—under the loose sleeve of the shirt, at the waistbelt, between the legs and the folds at the back of the knickerbockers, at the knee, and beneath the heels. We follow the grip of the hand on the chair, remembering that something solid and big flattens and pushes out the palm. The uplifted right arm is turned from us. We can see— and it is all that we can see—the small apex of the bending arm, the round edge of the elbow as it bends upward and outward, the folds on the inner part of the sleeve, and the tips of the fingers resting on the brow. After which you can carry on with anything that holds your interest. But keep your sketch a sketch. Do not worry after details. You will learn more at this stage from making sketches of quick poses and getting a knowledge of general proportions than by delving after detail.

Also you could reverse the positions of Kathleen and Jack. Kathleen might stand in the same pose as Jack, and Jack might sit on the stool.

And it is very amusing to dress brother and sister in their elders' clothes.

Give Kathleen a shawl and a handkerchief folded three-corner-wise and tied under her chin, put a basket at her feet, a closed umbrella in her hands, and we have an old market woman. Only remember that we bend with age, our head droops, our arms sag forward, and our toes very

Drawing for Beginners

probably would turn in a little after long years of weary plodding.

It is amusing to play with one's fancy, to bring out our colour-box and make a fresh drawing, tinting clothes, hair, and face.

Put the ' old lady' against a plain background, a wall, for instance, and begin by sketching the whole figure (as we sketched Kathleen as herself). That is, the simple angles, the big curves, then the smaller shapes of head, face, arms, hands, shawl, apron, feet; lastly, the details of hair, folds, features, fingers.

If you decide to colour your picture of the market woman, choose pleasing colours, / Kt^ Ny""^ tints that will blend pleasantly. //In rV"^ ^^ *^^^ French peasant woman would

wJl # y^Ts. i^g dressed probably in greys and blues, whereas a gipsy woman would have a highly coloured handkerchief and shawl. Jack might dress up as a shepherd The mISet'Woman (^^^h a long cloak or plaid across his shoulder, and a staff in his hand, and his knee on a rock) scanning the rough pasture ground for sheep that have strayed.

But beware !—draperies, cloaks, and plaids are very misleading.

We are inclined to ' lose ' the drawing of a leg, arm, or figure when we are trying to sketch draperies. The folds deceive the eye. The fall of a cloak may hide the position of a foot or an arm. If such is the case, then remove the drapery, make a note of the particular object about which you have doubts, and replace.

Should you prefer to leave the folds untouched because they are happily arranged, take a walk round your model and look at the hidden object from the opposite side. Never hesitate to survey the thing that you are drawing from a different angle. It is a common fault to worry over a detail, 42

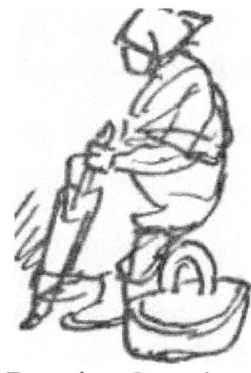

Drawing Ourselves and Others

to labour a difficult problem, when a glance in another position would make everything perfectly plain.

To return to the shepherd.

The colouring of the old shepherd's clothes should be more or less decided by his surroundings. One would not for choice give him a scarlet plaid and a Prussian blue kilt. These colours would soon fly in the mists of early dawn, the long days of rain and storm. A shepherd's clothes would probably share the tints of the hills and of the heather—mauve, green, brown, and fawn.

CHAPTER IV

Drawing Hands

HANDS are excellent things on which to practise drawing. Firstly, because they are difficult; secondly, because having two we can always spare one and draw that. And we can draw hands early and late. We shall never draw hands too often nor study them too much. It is often said that we can judge an artist's work by the drawing of the hands. If the hands are good the rest of the work is good, and if bad, then so is the rest.

It is not wise to make hard-and-fast rules; still, there is a good deal of truth in the saying, as we shall very soon discover.

When first drawing hands we must apply the same broad rules—of simplicity. We must choose simple positions.

For instance, that hand with finger pointing, with which we are so painfully famihar; that ugly, ill-drawn hand— " This way to the Menagerie," " This way to the Performing Bears," " This way to the Cricket Pavilion," " This way to the best Teashop in the Town." " This way," we might add, " to our first drawing of a Hand."

Having the offer of our left hand, we can begin without delay. Let us sit squarely at a table, resting our left elbow on a book and pointing the index finger straight in front of us.

Observe the whole shape carefully; block in the strong square angles and proceed from the beginning of the wrist to the upper knuckle—then along the forefinger to the more or less square block of the inner finger, and on to the sweeping curve of the thumb.

Now open your hand, spreading out your fingers. As you 44

Drawing Hands

move each finger up the knuckles loosen and dimple the skin ; as you clench them once more together the knuckles curve into clean sharp forms. Each finger is based in a good strong knuckle, remember that. Young artists are too fond of crowding knuckles together, and if hands grew as their drawings indicate they would have a poor chance of gripping an oar, a handle-bar, or even the useful knife and fork.

Having noted that the biggest mass is composed of the doubled fist, and that the angles of thumb and forefinger bear away from each other, we see that the line of the wrist forms yet another angle.

Of course it is quite probable that your hand may not resemble mine, but the general principles hold good. My thumb is large, my fingers are long; yours probably will be shorter and the thumb more slender.

Look at the sweeping line as it proceeds from the back of the wrist to the knuckles, and notice the swelling curve of the thumb beneath and the manner in which it bends back. We will now give our attention to the forefinger. How straight and determined it is, pointing and almost speaking its command, how thick it is at the root, and how it tapers to the tip !

We now begin to search for more details. We draw the finger more carefully, marking the wrinkles on the upper part, and the corresponding curves on the lower; then we notice the way in which the loose flesh folds in springy curves, joining thumb to forefinger in a useful hinge.

We mark the clean sweep of the thumb and the wrinkles on the back-curving knuckle, also the shape of the nail, a square-cut, important-looking nail, curving on the outer edge and following the curve of the thumb-tip. Then back we trace the thumb and note the wrinkles on the largest swelling curve; back to the wrist we go until we meet its firm tendons.

From thence we might jump to the knuckles once more, noting the deeply cleft wrinkles in the bend. We should

Drawing for Beginners

then be ready to draw in the dark shadow of the doubled fingers, the upper nail (like a portion of a tiny pink shell), and the square shadowing of the thumbnail.

Before we leave the drawings of our own left hand there are other poses to consider.

For instance, your own left hand holding a small object such as a coin, a flower-stem, or a reel of cotton. The latter, being a light object, you would hold lightly between your first finger and your thumb, supported by the second and third fingers.

Sketch first the upright shape of the hand and wrist, then the first finger and the knuckle from which it springs, the upright thumb, and the angle of the reel of cotton.

Here, by the by, let me say once more that you need not feel bound to pose your left hand in exactly this position. If you should prefer another pose, with the palm more I exposed (or less), by all means adopt yours in preference 1 to mine. These hints may then be used as a general ." guide. My positions are chosen because they present simple problems.

And now let us return to the hand with the reel of cotton.

Having roughly sketched the forefinger, the thumb, and the general proportions of the wrist and hand, we should then pay a little more attention to the hand itself, the back of which lies like a flat upright line breaking into small indications of the second or third knuckle. The first knuckle is slightly indented, and the root of the first finger descends in a firm swelling curve to the folded muscle of the thumb.

The thumb presses inward against the reel, and, marking the angle of its nail, we sketch the firm long line of the knuckle down the swelling curve to the root of the thumb, behind which we have the lower swelling curve of the palm.

The first finger and the shape of it must be carefully noted. My fingers, though long, are plump, and yours may present sharp . bone and knuckle. I trust that they may, for bony substances are easier to draw. Their shape is clean and 46

Drawing Hands

definite, their angles more acute and therefore more quickly noted.

We note here the tip of this first finger and the apex coming at the front of the nail. Next we draw the folds of each finger-joint.

From the second knuckle we can trace the second finger, hidden behind the first finger, but seen in a tiny space between the reel and first finger, and the tip of it obtrudes on the far side of the reel.

The third finger rises from the third knuckle, and is seen in the space between the first finger and thumb, and again beyond the thumb, behind which we know it supports the reel.

The little finger merely waves a graceful tip, like the clown in the circus, doing nothing in particular. This hand, though simple, can be carried to almost any length of study. Note the shadows of the thumb, the shadows of the knuckles, of the first finger-tip, and those cast by the reel. The reel itself, being of black silky thread, is (in my study) the darkest tone of all.

The left hand holding a fan suggests another variation— this time with the palm broadside on, and the finger-tips coming forward.

First note the pear shape of the pointed fingers, bent fingers, and flattened palm, meeting at a slender wrist.

Observe the angle of the object that is held correctly, because from that position the fingers curl.

The fan is a fairly stout object composed of thin slats folded together, and so nicely adjusted that the touch of the tip of a finger displaces them.

The thumb holds and supports the fan in a firm upright position. The thumb rises from a long swelling base, flatly on one side—despite the faint indication of the bones—and in two long swelling curves on the others, meeting in a firmly rounded tip.

Beyond, and curled round the fan, we have the first fi].;;er ; then the second, third, and fourth fingers tightly grasping the

Drawing for Beginners

end of the fan. These we block in as one mass, marking the angles of the outer joints, the inner joints, and the finger-tips; the palm flattens and bulges to the wrist.

Then we again revert to the thumb and the finer details, the pointed finger and the shadows, the first, second, third, and little finger (we have ^.Iready sketched this in mass and therefore shall have no great difficulty with details), the knuckles bending inward, and the tips of the fingers closely holding the fan. Mark all the darkest shadows. Under the

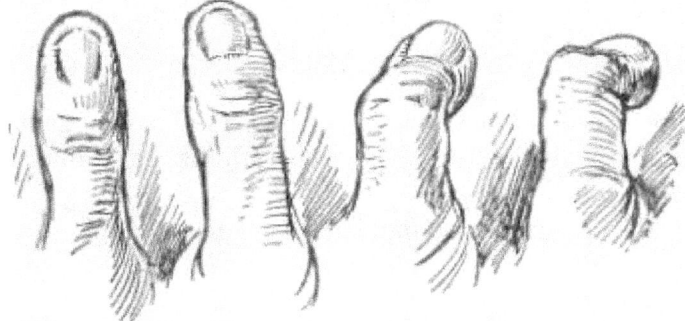

Fig. 13. Thumbs Upright and Foreshortened

first finger is the curve of the thumb, and under the fan (the lower part of the palm indented by the ring of the fan) the sharp firm shadows between the fingers.

More poses for the left hand might include :

Left hand beckoning, or palm extended and back presented ; hand clenched ; hand lying flat on the table palm downward, or palm uppermost. Both are rather difficult studies.

Rest your elbow on the table, clench your fingers, and extend your thumb. Draw only the thumb.

Turn your hand toward yourself with the palm uncovered and draw your thumb—bent.

You should become well acquainted with all your various fingers by drawing each one separately—and many times.

Suzanne Lenglen, the great tennis-player, said that it took her six months to learn a certain stroke. It will take us 48

Drawing Hands

certainly longer to learn how to draw all the fingers of our left hand.

Little children are very clever at painting and drawing gloves. Sometimes I have pinned a shabby old leather and fur gauntlet to a board, and the painting has been surprisingly good. And yet had I suggested the drawing of a hand, a wail of despair would have gone up. A glove is a step toward the drawing of a hand.

Have you drawn a hand, gloved ?

If not, I advise a trial. Take for choice a glove of a firm substance, leather instead of wool, and thick leather in preference to thin; if it has a gauntlet of fur, so much the better.

Ask some kind friend to put his gloved hand on the top of a stick or an umbrella, and make a careful study of it. It will be simpler than the hand unclothed. The palm will be more of a mass, the seams will give the direction of the fingers, the wrinkles of the leather will give—more or less—the base of the thumb, the knuckles, and the wrist.

Having made a study of the gloved hand, ask your friend to remove his glove and resume the position with the bare hand.

If you can make the two drawings on the same sheet of paper you will find that your previous effort has helped you considerably to draw the ungloved hand.

Tight gloves distort and contract the hands, loose gloves vdisguise the shape. Do not let this worry you. Try to draw what you see— as you see it.

Another time you might persuade some one to hold up a hand, palm toward you and fingers together. (See No. I, Fig. 16.)

Do not begin with sprawled fingers spreading apart, it is bewildering for a start.

Block all the fingers together and draw an imaginary line from the tip of the thumb to the fingers to check your proportions. Close up your own thumb and note that it reaches to the first joint of your forefinger. Thumbs, because of the deceptive nature of a curve, are often deprived of strength, length, and muscle. Note the large surfaces of muscle, the D 49

Drawing/or Beginners

almost square shape of the palm. Once you have the larger proportions of fingers and thumbs well fixed in your mind it will not be difficult to observe each finger, each knuckle, each finger-tip separately.

The rather listless fingers (No. II, Fig. 16) can be indicated on the same lines ; the fingers, though they are separated, can

be first blocked in together.

When drawing a hand holding a ball be sure that the hand does hold the ball. I would emphasize the point that often, very often, young artists draw a hand holding a ball, or a pen, or a hockey-stick, and so absorbed do they become in drawing the fingers that they neglect the object the fingers are clasping, with the result that it reappears in a distorted form.

And the excuse offered generally is: "I had to draw it in such and such a way or the fingers would not have come right." When drawing a hand grasping Fig. 15. Deaw the Object that ^n object draw first the pen, or IS HELD FIRST, THEN THE whatcvcr thc objcct may be, and Fingers round it n. . i o t •. i i •

fit the fingers round it, rubbing out

later the part which is hidden. If the thing held is straight or round, obviously it must be drawn straight or round.

Have you seen an X-ray photograph of a hand, or held your fingers up to a bright light and seen through the film of pink flesh the dim shape of the bones ? Muscles, tendons, veins, flesh, and dimples attract our attention. The bones we are inclined to neglect.

Indeed, it is curious how fond we are of looking for things that matter not at all.

For instance, how often do we see a hand pleasantly but feebly drawn ! We wonder vaguely what can be wrong. Ten 50

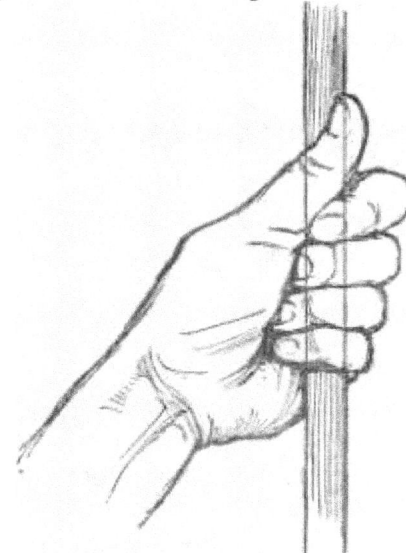

Drawing Hands

chances to one the artist has paid too much attention to minor things. He has tried so hard to give the nails the right shape ; but what attention has been paid to the knuckles, to the base of the fingers, and firm shapes between each joint, to the joints themselves, all of which are a great deal more important ?

The ring on the finger, the watch on the wrist, is eagerly depicted, for it is ' jolly interesting.' So it is. But if the metal is beautifully and intelligently drawn, and the finger, or the wrist, looks feeble and patchy, what then? And the wrist is often neglected. It is the link between the arm and the hand, as the ankle is the link between the leg and the foot, and both shapes are fascinating studies for the artist.

We must try to ' get at' the framework. Once we have the bony structure in our minds we shall find the outside shapes less baffling.

Not that I would advise you to begin by drawing the skeleton.

c^ i J • c 1 Fig. 17. Bones of Hand

htart drawmg freely.

Only, when you feel yourself becoming confused, give a thought to the bones ; they are a wholesome check. Seek out shapes. Don't be satisfied with pretty curves and dimples, cushioned palms and tallow-candle fingers. Move the fingers to and fro. Twist and turn the wrist. Never be afraid of losing a position. You will gain something of far more value than that which you may lose.

The bones of the hand are small but fairly easy to understand. They have no cup and ball or rotary movements like those of shoulder and forearm ; neither are they shrouded in huge muscles like those of the ribs and back. Moreover, they are plainly seen in the hands of the very old, crisscrossed with big blue veins.

51

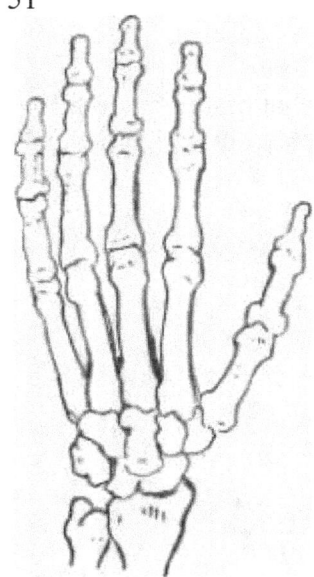

CHAPTER V

Drawing Feet

IF we all walked about in sandals instead of boots and shoes, the human foot would be much less difficult to draw.

If centuries of cramping leather, of high heels and pointed toes, had not spoilt the shape of modern feet, we should be more interested in drawing the ' human foot divine.'

Artists often declare that a pretty foot is the rarest of all rare things.

But all start in life fairly well equipped in that respect, and therefore we may consider ourselves fortunate if we have the opportunity of drawing Jack's bare foot or Baby's queer little curling toes.

And this presents an idea. Feet—that is, bare feet—often being impossible to ^procure as models, why should we not begin by drawing shoes and boots ?

Baby's ' bootikin,' absurd little shape though it is, gives a rough idea of the foot, as Baby's small fingerless glove presents a rough impression of the shape of a hand.

There is plenty to observe in a shoe or a boot, and it is rather a fascinating study if we choose one with a highly polished surface. Then, again, a bedroom-slipper of quilted satin and fur is a joy to paint.

Examine the bootikin. Do we not get a crude shape of a foot ? Stuff it with paper and perch it on a table before you. Make a sketch of it, and then sketch Baby's foot in the same position, and on the same broad outline as the bootikin, treating it first as two simple angles—the sloping angle of the leg, and the forward thrust of the small plump foot. The baby's ankle is so cushioned with fat that it is difficult to 53

Drawing Feet

discover the bone, but that we must try to find, because from the ankle-bone we get the triangular shape of the heel and the flat tread of the sole. The fold of fat above the ankle

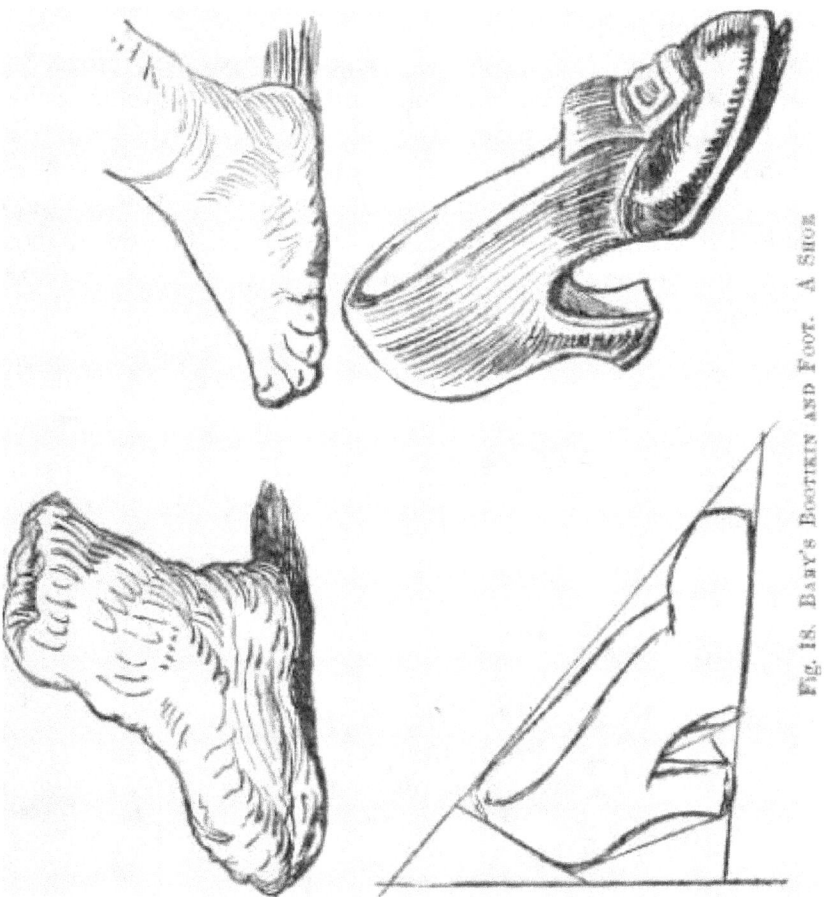

Fig. 18. Baby's Bootikin and Foot.   A Shoe

marks the deepest part of the foot and the highest line of the instep. This line descends steeply to the root of the toes, and expands in the bold curves of the five toes.

Now borrow your mother's shoe. Place that before you and on a level with your eye. (If you begin by trying to draw the shoe very much beneath you, or, for the matter of

Drawing for Beginners

that, very much above you, you will have a more complicated problem.)

Try first to draw it in a simple position—a side view.

At fi.rst sight one is apt to think a high-heeled shoe a rather complicated shape, but if you try to analyse it as a rough block, it is no more nor less than a wedge. The high heel gives the greatest depth, the toe gives the narrowing point, the tread of the foot—heel and sole of the shoe—a flat line. Having marked this simple triangular shape we note the large oval opening, the stumpy and rounded toe, the beautiful ' slick ' curve of the heel. Of course we know that no part of the foot enters the high heel, which is merely compressed leather or wood ; and we should, therefore, trace the foot within the shoe, in our thoughts if not with our pencil.

Then perhaps we shall catch Jack in a specially charitable frame of mind, ready to sit bare-footed.

Quick ! let us get pencil and paper, and plant Jack on a stool with his foot resting on the floor, and to give more action—and consequently more interest—to our study we will raise his heel by propping it up on a fairly thick book.

Next we sit down on a low seat or cushion on the floor, as near as possible to the level of Jack's foot.

Again we are all for simplicity. A profile of Jack's foot, presenting an angle with the ankle and leg, would be an interesting study.

Having roughly drawn the triangular shape of the bending foot, we next proceed to note important facts. The mass of the heel, the shape of the ankle, the broad fine sweeping line of the instep (Jack has a particularly well-shaped instep), and the ball of the foot—the springy cushion upon which the tread of the foot presses.

Afterward observe the masses of light and shade, and see how the light picks out the strong tendons about the ankle. I find it helpful to shade as if I were chiselling out shapes —a method that may not appeal to you. So long as you shade intelligently, not beginning a shadow and leaving it off without reason, but using the shadow to emphasize a 54

,/
f-—^"If^^*^

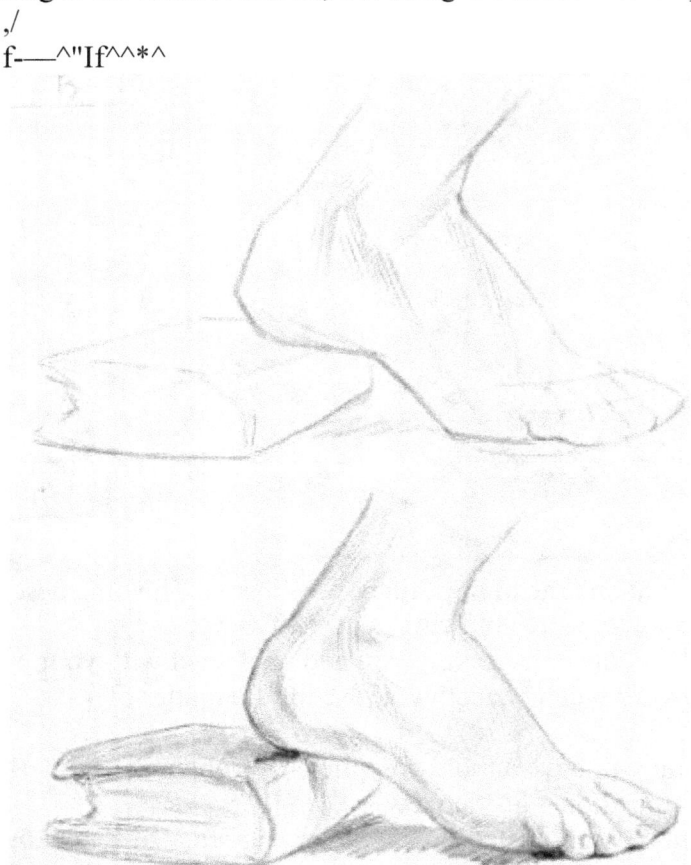

Fig. 19. Jack's Foot
Drawing Feet

shape, a swelling, a curve, a bone, or a tendon, that is all I ask.

Another time we might try a ' full-face ' or three-quarter view of a foot. And as this presents us with the problem of foreshortening, let me advise you to begin by drawing the foot in shoe and stocking; afterward draw the foot in the same position without the shoe and stocking, for the very same reason that we first drew the hand gloved, and later ungloved. The covering simplifies matters. Instead of the angle of the toes and toe-nails we have the broad sweep of leather covering it all in a three-cornered form.

You may prefer to draw the foot with the heel on the ground. I have chosen to represent the heel lifted. For one reason it gives action and life to the position, and for another presents a more acute and more interesting angle.

We have the leg representing one angle, and the foot yet another angle, and the apex of this angle lies in the ankle, which we know to be the end of two bones. The ankles are the ends of the leg-bones, the wrists are the ends of the arm-bones.

When we are very small we usually draw the feet as two little spoon-shaped objects, something like a couple of feeble golf-clubs, which is not so very wrong in effect.

Therefore, when we draw a foot, no matter what the position may be, the two simple angles of foot and leg are most important. Once they are settled we can devote ourselves to noting the tread of the foot and the heel, the curve under the foot, and the curve of the toes.

Margery has not a very big ankle ; the outside bone is higher and clearly defined ; the inner one is barely seen. Partly by observing the folds of the stocking, and partly by deduction (for we know the ankle-bones are opposite each other), and also because of a shallow depression, we mark the position of the bones. That, you see, is a valuable fact. Ankle-bones settled, we next mark the curve of the heel, which is slightly exaggerated by the thickness of leather ; then we note the curve of the foot as it treads on the ground,

Drawing for Beginners

and compare the two sides of the foot, one a long sweeping line, the other shorter (shorter because of the fullness of the rising instep), meeting at the toe with an abrupt and slightly indenting curve.

The sharp shadow under the toe lifts the foot from the ground, and a shadow defines the top of the instep. The curve of the strap of the shoe provides another shadow, and also emphasizes the depth of the foot from instep to arch. Margery's stocking, being of lighter material than the shoe, adds to the variety of the surface of our drawing. As the folds in a stocking indicate the position of the ankle, so will the bend of the leather in a boot or shoe mark the tread of the foot and the bending joints of the toes.

A highly polished leather is easier to draw than a soft dull glace or suede, for it accentuates light and shade. The bright light on the toe, the half-moon of light on the side of the foot, the dull disc of light that indicates the ankle, are of great value ; they show the position of the bones. Keep these bright; do not dim their surfaces.

Having now drawn Margery's foot in shoe and stocking, perhaps we shall persuade Margery to pose in the same position without her shoes and stockings, as if she were on her way to paddle in the sea.

Now you see the bones more easily, and having marked the two large and simple angles of leg and foot, as in the previous drawing, we continue with the rest of the foot. The heel looks a trifle smaller; the toes, being unhampered with leather, spread, and the big toe asserts itself. Block first the toes as a large shape, noting their tips and roots, and working from the tendons (seen between the ankles) and the arching muscles of the upper part of the instep, and then divide and sketch the toes and their various angles.

The drawing of the foot clothed has, I am sure, helped you with the drawing of the naked foot.

The sandal worn by the Romans, with its half-covering of the toes, and its straps and ribbons across the instep, and its thick sole—and one can roughly contrive a sandal with 56

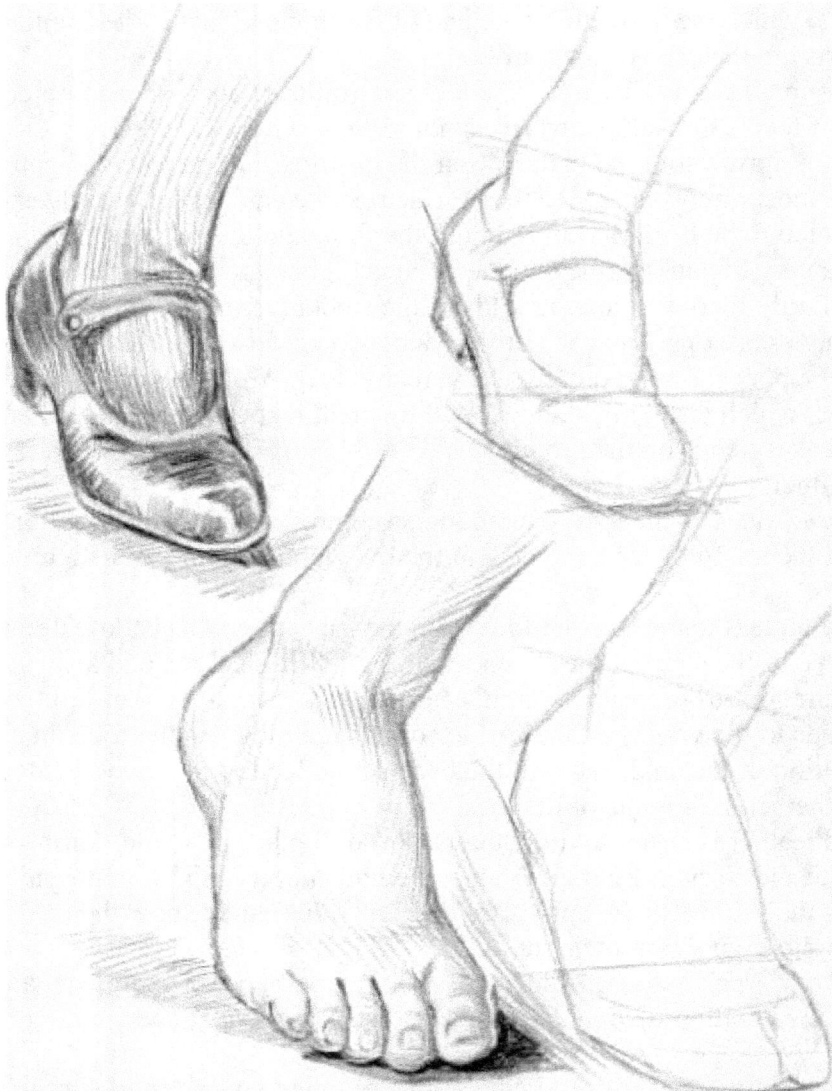

Fig. 20. Margery's Foot

Drawing Feet

the monkeys, the tree-as we use our thumbs,

cardboard and ribbons at home—makes a most interesting subject to draw.

Sandals, by the interweaving of their straps, draw our attention to the variety of shapes of the toes, which we too often overlook. The big toe is an important member of the foot; indeed, of the whole body. When the foot is raised it is the big toe that spreads and separates from the other toes, and helps to balance the foot. The big toe is as characteristic as the thumb. (Indeed, climbing animals, use the big toe to grasp and hold the branches.) It is usually square-tipped, thick, and muscular. The next toe is slender and long, the second and third toes graduate, and the little toe is curved or doubled up, and is almost more negligible in size and appearance than the little finger.

It is interesting to learn that by the use of the feet and the manipulation of the toes, artists, or, at all events, craftsmen, have been helped in their work. A famous craftsman of Cairo, who works in wood and produces beautiful lattices for windows and doorways, uses his left foot as a third hand ; because of his skill in the use of this foot he is known to the city as ' the three-handed man.'

When the foot is seen from the back the heel is naturally the most prominent feature. Also the ankles are more easily observed.

Having marked the angles of the leg and foot, we should next notice the straight tendon that runs down between the ankles and spreads into the firm swelling apex of the heel. On either side of the foot the ankles are clearly seen. Note the shapes well, and note also the height of the upper part

57

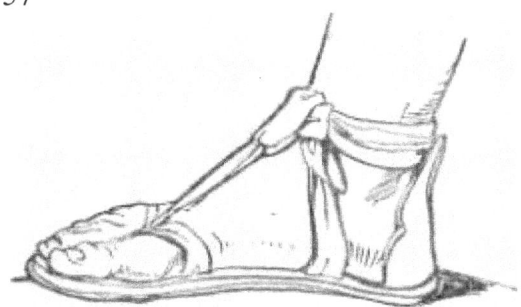

Fig. 21. The Sandalled Foot
Drawing for Beginners

of the foot (this is always the widest section), and its sharp descent to the toes. Seen from the rear these toes present a bhmted and rather flattened curve. Trace the flat under-surface of the foot, the tread and balance first, afterward the curves of the heel, and the space between the instep and the ground, remembering, always, the foot within the shoe.

The sole of the foot is a flattened surface on the outside edge. This you can see for yourself in the two sketches which show both the inside and the outside of the foot. Moreover, if you take off your shoe, you can pass your finger under the inner side of the foot, but on the outer edge there is no space at all.

Walking, kicking, dancing, stamping, swimming—here we have an immense variety of poses. Dancing, the foot rises at a steep angle, the heel clear of the ground, the ball of the foot and the toes resting lightly. (I do not refer to ballet-dancing, which is more or less of a gymnastic feat; the shoes are heavily padded at the toes, and on these pads the ballet-girl rests.)

Stamping, the foot comes down with an all-over flat action, heel and toe held level. Kicking, the foot thrusts out, toes upraised. The kicking position shows us the sole of the foot, and the sole is a curious shape—one that we should not neglect. Should we draw one of our brothers sitting by the fire leaning back in a chair, it is highly probable that he will cross his legs and put up his feet to warm. Shorn of heel and thick leather soles, the sole of a foot is a flat elongated shape. The human foot has the padded soft flesh beneath the tread, with wrinkles on the inner side, and a small firm smooth heel, something like the outline of an elongated pear.

The shape of the modern shoe worn by the small child gives us, as it claims to do, the natural shape of the sole.

Turn it over and observe it well.

The general shape of the five toes resembles the general shape of the four fingers. When you doff your shoe and stocking look at your toes. Then put up your hand and observe the back and tips of the fingers. Fan-shaped—are they not ? So are your toes. 58

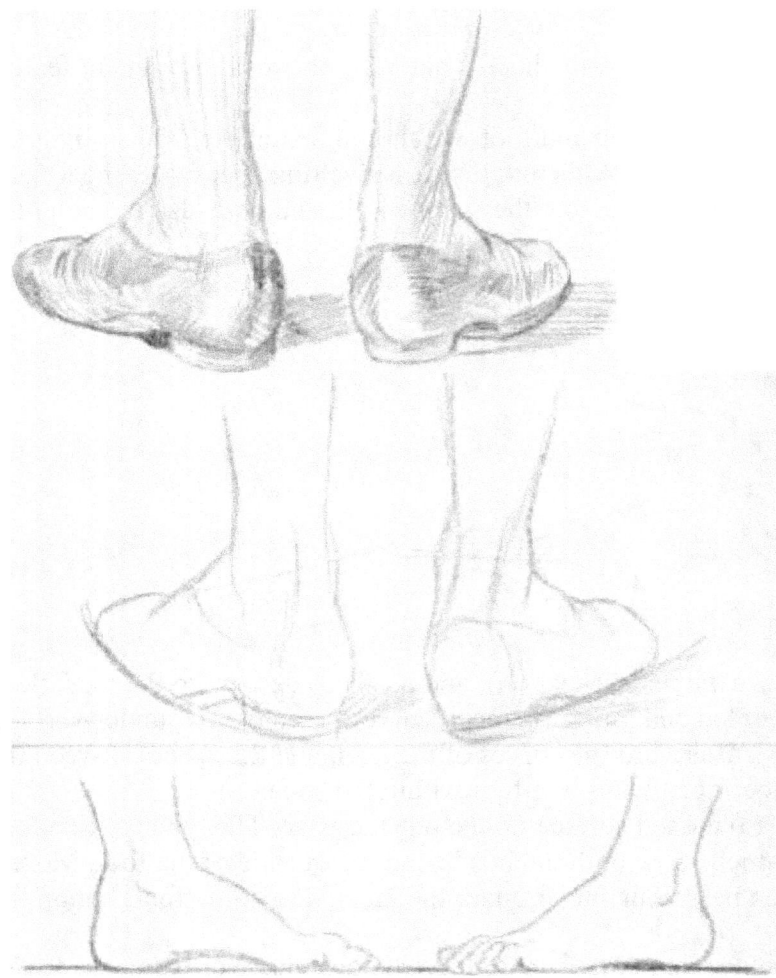

Fig. 22. Back and Side View of Feet

Drawing Feet

There is as much character in the foot as in the hand. The tall, slim, long-limbed person has invariably a long slim hand, and a slim and narrow foot. The plump short girl or boy-has the plump hand and foot. The long-fingered hand usually goes with the long thin toes.

Fashion inflicts queer shapes on the foot. At one time it insists that all our shoes shall be narrow and peaked, another time squat and round-toed ; then heels must be worn like stilts, or shaved down to the thinnest substance.

In China we all know what a fetish was once made of the

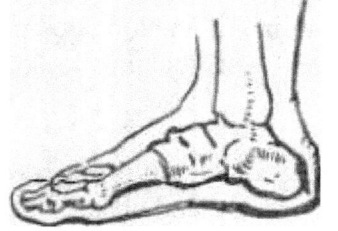

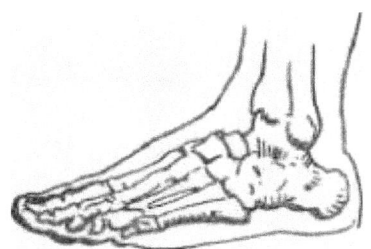

Fig. 23. The Inside and Outside of a Foot

tiny foot. When swaddled and compressed, the poor little foot has no chance at all. And there was a time in English history when the toes of the shoes were so long that they had to be buckled back to the knees.

All of which indicates the absolute necessity of knowing the shape of the foot. Fashion may deceive the many, but the artist must know that it only tries to disguise the true form.

If we want to see the foot unspoiled then we must go to the countries where fashion and manners have not affected it, where generation after generation has walked the earth on the bare foot, or with only the slight protection of a sandalled sole. Then we see how finely it supports the body, what a thing of strength and beauty it can be !—firm heel, arched instep, springing muscles of the sole imprinting the ground with its firm tread I

CHAPTER VI

Drawing Head^ Face^ Features^ and Hair

I REMEMBER, years ago, poring over an old-fashioned drawing-book which contained—among many other things —diagrams that reduced head, face, and features to the very simplest of problems.

The author began by comparing the head to an oval or egg-shaped substance.

Full face presented a simple oval.

Sideways (or profile) presented a deeper oval, with the forepart flatter than the back, which thickened a little at the base.

On this egg-shaped form were traced curving lines, following, of course, the curves of the surface, one central line, and three transverse lines. The central line marked the centre of the brow, the angle and tip of the nose, and ran through the upper and lower lips to the point of the chin.

The cross, or transverse, lines marked the angle of the brow above the eyes, then the angle of the nostrils, and lastly the angle of the mouth.

When the head tilted and sank forward the lines of the face curved downward.

When the head was thrown up and backward the lines of the features curved in a like manner.

Seen in profile (or sideways) the line of the brow, carried to the back of the head with the line of the nostril, gave the position of the ear.

This is a valuable little key to the quick placing of the features. In a word, it helps with the perspective of features. 60

Head^ Face^ Features^ Hair

The unpractised artist is very prone to devote too much space to the face and too little to the head.

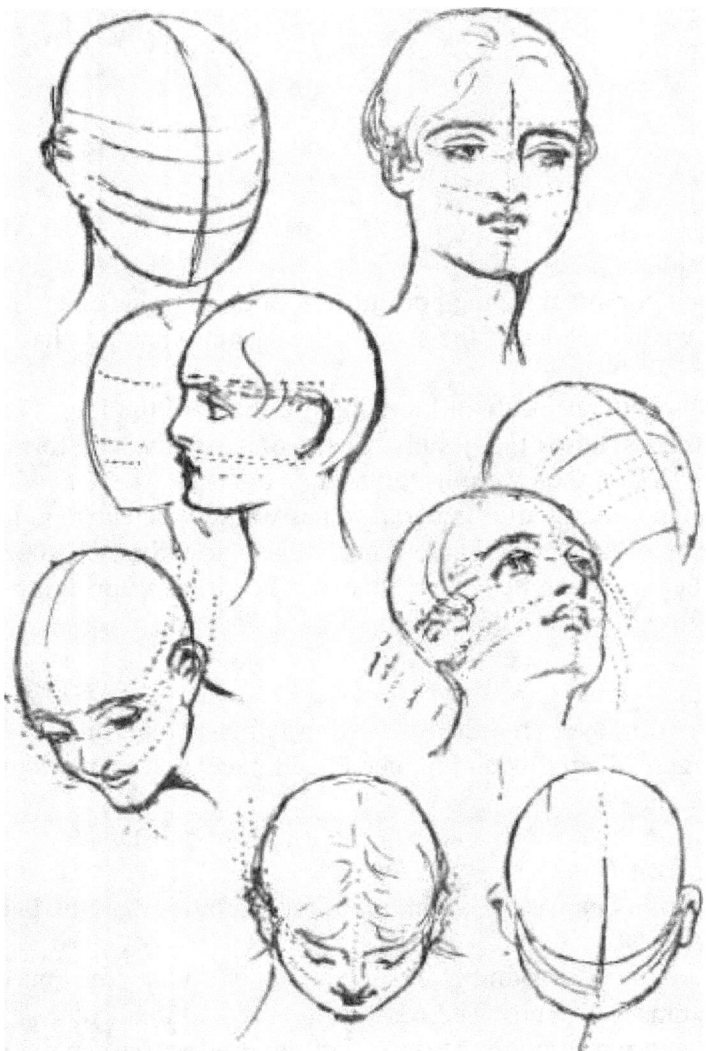

Fig. 24. The Head and Face

We all know that babies have abnormally large heads • that children's heads are large in comparison with their

Drawing for Beginners

bodies ; that only the adult's head and body balance in nice proportion—that is, the head is neither too large nor too small for the body.

But the face never occupies the entire space of the head, as young artists often seem to imagine that it does.

Look at the size of the crown of the head, at the back and the sides thereof, and do not spread the forehead right up to the crest of the head.

Note also the beautiful balance of the head on the neck, the neck on the shoulders.

The indenting curve at the base of the skull is not level with the jaw—but see !—it is a little below the level of the ear and on a line with the nostril.

The neck is full of interesting drawing.

There is the full curve of the throat,

and the shorter and stronger

l3 ^ S <2 ^ curve from the base of the back

^ ^ of the skull to the nape of the

neck and the spine. The large

bones of the vertebrae, which Fig. 25. The Head and Neck ^g ^^^ fg^j ^j^j^ ^j^^ t^p^ ^f

our fingers, resemble, as the French word chainon has it, the links of a chain.

Two large muscles (mastoid) often attract our attention when the head is twisted aside. Extending from behind the ear to the forepart of the collar-bone, they are always more strongly developed in a boy than in a girl, and in a man than in a woman. These you can feel at the root of the neck and the forepart of the throat by twisting your head right and left; and they form a cup-like depression when your head is straight.

The neck, you will notice, is so strengthened with muscle and bone that it rises like a small pillar from a very solid base.

A girl's neck is slender, a boy's equally thin, but more muscular. A woman's neck is full of entrancing curves ; a 62

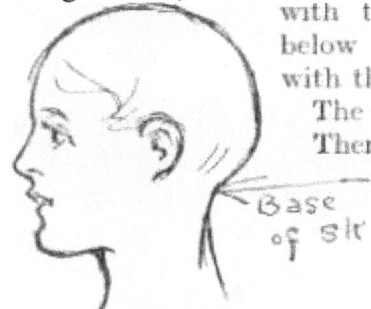

with t

below

with tl

The

Thei

Base of sit

Head^ Face^ Features^ Hair

man's neck very strong, very muscular, and consequently rather thick.

As with all other parts of the human body, necks exist in every variety—short necks, long necks, thick, thin, muscular, strong, feeble, and fat; but, and the fact is worth noting, the base of the neck where it joins the body is always its thickest part.

With this slight introduction to the general proportion and shape of the head, we can next turn our attention to the face and the features.

One hears many curious remarks from young artists ; for instance : "I simply love drawing people, but I can never draw a face." This is by no means an uncommon experience. Another equally frank statement is often heard : " Faces ! 'Rather ! They are simply topping ! But / can't draw hands and things ! "

And there we are !

A curious world it would be if ygung artists were confronted with embodiments of their own drawings ! Imagine the shock of meeting a gentleman in plus fours with no face but a turniplike smudge, or a lovely languishing lady with exquisite shingled head and nothing more substantial than a few slight lines indicating a body—and those quite wrong !

Believe me, it does not do to run away with such ideas. We may say things so often that in time they seem to weave a spell.

A young and most promising artist-friend of mine drew faces admirably, and refused to draw anything else. She would not draw a hand or a foot. And in time it really seemed as if she could not—which of course was absurd. Anyhow, to this day she draws exquisite faces, and the rest of her drawings would shame the veriest beginner. She is an artist—spoilt.

If we take our subjects one by one, and make our progress step by step, we may be slow, but in due time we shall' arrive.'

And as an excellent aid to our own home studies let us provide ourselves with a hand-glass or small mirror. This

Drawing for Beginners

is an invaluable help, indeed, a necessity, for the studying and drawing of our own features.

And at the outset I would utter a word of warning about the drawing of a face.

It is surprising that young artists often draw the eyes and mouth as if they were mere patterns stuck on the face, a method that is evidently copied from fashion and poster artists, who are very fond of this effective but mask-like effect. The eyes in their pictures are heavily outlined, the lips are thickly painted with purple crimson tints. It is a wrong point of view, and a very harmful one, as you will soon discover.

Look at the eye, your eye, anyone's eye. What a luminous, expressive feature it is, composed of most subtle and exquisite parts!

Look at the iris, the ring of colour, the velvety depths of the pupil, the shining white surface of the ' sclerotic tissue ' surrounding the eyeball, and the soft pink inner corners. Remember the ball of the eye is a large object covered by lids which reveal only part of the whole. Look at the curve of the lid and its graceful fringe.

But lashes, though dark and sweeping, are not as important as pupil and lid. Do not draw the lower lid in a thick hard outline. You will produce at once a mask, not a face. If, for theatrical purposes, you rub a stick of darkening stuff beneath your eyes, you then see your eye forced into a slitlike shape, but only then. The eye is the most expressive feature. Laugh, and your eye must laugh. I have seen people smile with their lips when the eyes were not smiling, and what a futile smile it was !

To picture the lips as two thick slabs of colour is just as great a crime.

Your mouth may be full and dimpled, it may be small and thin, it may be wide and of no very definite shape. But it is not, it can never be, a moulded pattern stuck like a postage-stamp on your face.

Draw down your mouth, pout, smile, laugh—and note the 64

Head^ Face^ Features^ Hair

teeth revealed. " Roses filled with snow," sang the Elizabethan poet of his lady's pretty lips.

Let us take up the hand-glass in our left hand and a pencil in our right, and examine our features.

An eye is an oblong shape set in an oval cavity. We see it in primitive drawings as a round black dot to which is added a pointed lozenge-shaped frame.

The iris, being the coloured part of the eye, will probably first attract our attention. That, we notice, is a circular shape, covered above and below by the upper lid and the lower lid. Draw the circular shape boldly. We will assume that the upper lid is firmly and clearly seen, not hidden by the brow. Having observed it closely and recorded our impressions we pass to the lower lid, which should be drawn lightly, for it is a tender delicate form.

Next we examine the inner corner of the eye (nearest the nose), where are the soft pink tear-ducts, which we touch in lightly with the pencil.

The outer corner of the eye forms a sharper angle, with the upper lid curving downward to meet the flesh of the lower lid and its corresponding upward curve.

Having sketched the shape of the eye as a whole, we might next return for a closer observation of the iris.

Is there anything in nature more lovely than the iris of the human eye ? The liquid tint of blue, grey, or brown is like the luminous colouring of a strange flower. And it is colour. Therefore, it is a shade deeper, many shades deeper, than the opaque whiteness of the eyeball. Then shade it with your pencil.

Within the iris we have yet another shape, the little black pupil of the eye through which the light passes. This is of velvety richness, but before shading carefully note the shape of the bright light on the pupil, and ' leave ' this light, working the shadow round it.

Suppose we ignore this light, and shade it in with the pupil; at once the eye looks lifeless.

Having done all this, we might add a few of the long lashes E 65

Drawing for Beginners

—not all. We should no more draw every leaf on a tree than draw every lash of the eye. We choose the most important.

Finally, we take a general survey, deepen shadows, add a few details, and then notice that the eyebrows have been neglected.

We should compare the eyebrows with the shape of the eye.

The hairs of the eyebrow are usually thicker at the base —that is, nearest the nose—than at the outer edge. They begin full and thick and incline from the nose outward, framing the eye in a wide curve.

Eyebrows there are of every variety. You may see every day eyebrows thick, thin, bushy, soft, fine, and coarse; eyebrows dark, and eyebrows so fair that they can hardly be detected except in a very bright light; eyebrows traced as delicately as if they were made of a single hair, and shaggy, overhanging eyebrows from under which the eyes gleam like little pools. Note the eyebrows and draw them carefully.

It would seem foolish, having made a close study of one eye, not to draw both eyes with equal care.

We might this time choose to draw our eyes from another angle. And as we are drawing a pair of eyes, we have twice as much to bear in mind. First, we should roughly trace the position of the two eyes. Sketch the position of the brow, and the angle of the two eyes, and the size of the eye and eyelids.

It is useful to remember as a general rule that the space between two eyes is the length of an eye. Then, having sketched the position, general angle, shape of eye and eye-socket, it would be wise to note the position of the iris and pupil.

These we know must agree. Unless we are very careful to sketch the iris of both eyes looking in the same direction, we shall certainly give our drawing a most horrible squint.

If the iris lies in the outer corner of the near eye, it must lie in the inner corner of the far eye. (If you wish to sketch a cross-eyed person, then you place both irises near the nose.) 66

Head^ Face^ Features^ Hair

Lightly trace the iris and the pupil, and the shape and position of the light on the pupil.

Next we note the shape of the upper lid of the near eye (and its long curve), the deepest and the narrowest part; the shape of the inner and blunt end of the eye, the sharper curved angle of the outer part of the eye. We look at the far eye, and this curves slightly away from us on the curve of the cheek. The eyeball nears the blunt end, and exposes a large space of white.

Lid, pupil, iris, eyelash, eyebrow, all follow in their turn ; add such shadows as you wish, and you must certainly not forget the shadow of the nose and the forehead. The eye lies in a socket. In old people this is very noticeable. The shadow of the brow falls on the socket and gives a very sharp and bold outline for drawing.

Drawing eyes from the mirror has certain limitations, so let us ask some one to ' sit' for us with an eye in profile.

Bear in mind an important point. The eyeball is covered by the lid. Then obviously the lid must project beyond the eyeball. Young artists often draw the eyelid and the eyeball as if they are exactly on the same level. But anything that covers must be larger than the object covered.

You would not, for instance, draw a tea-cosy smaller, or even the same size as a teapot, for you know very well it would not cover the pot. You would not draw a hat exactly the same size as the bare skull. It must be larger. Then why draw an eyelid (^hat covers the eyeball) the same size as the eye ?

Also you must allow for the thickness of the lid. If you turn your head upward, and look down at your reflection in the glass, the thickness of the lid will be very apparent. You will notice the inner edge resting against the eyeball, and the outer edge fringed with the lashes. This can be seen even more plainly if you open your eyes wide, as if in astonishment or surprise.

The open lid is not so frequently seen as the small lid and sunken eye, which fact worries the unpractised artist not a

Drawing for Beginners

little. The eyelid of course is there, but the brow swells forward and conceals part of the lid.

When you draw eyes of this description sketch the ball of the eye, and the lid, and then sketch the brow.

Eyes, of course, there are in infinite variety. Some are heavily lidded, some are large and round, some are lashed with long silken hair. There are the small ' piggy ' or half-closed eyes, the eyes that pierce with sharp keen glances. There are the dreamy eyes, the laughing, twinkling eyes, and the sharp, suspicious eyes.

There is nothing easy about the drawing of an eye. It will always demand the closest care and attention.

Even when we are drawing the eye of a sleeping person, when the lids cover the eyeball, there is the exquisite meeting of the lids, the mingling of the lashes, and the shadows cast by the lashes on the cheek. We must not forget, by the way, to indicate the roundness of the eyeball beneath the lids.

A nose presents more difficulties to the young student than any other feature ; more especially the drawing of a nose in full view—when we see as much of the left nostril as the right. And the reason of this difficulty is one of perspective. We are confronted with something which fills our mind with perplexity, something of which we shall often hear, namely, ' foreshortening.'

Yet a nose is not such a very alarming shape. Certainly not as difficult to draw as a hand pointing straight out of the picture. It is merely two small cavities placed at an equal distance from each other, winged in flesh and protected by a round tip and bridged to the face by bone and gristle.

When you draw the nose full face draw the shadow of the bridge, and the shadow under the tip of the nose, and the shadow beneath the nose, boldly. Think, if you will, of the keel of a ship, of the corner of a box. Don't be fearful of making the nose ugly. Rather a big, well-shaped nose than one—as we see so often in our drawings—timid, feeble, and of little account. 68

Head^ Face^ Features^ Hair

Your nose will in all probability be smaller than the first example selected. It is a bold nose. It has a firm bridge, a rounded and full tip, curved nostrils.

Examine your own nose in a glass, and try to sketch it as I have indicated in the first example. Begin by drawing an upright line, then trace down each side of this line the bridge of the nose, with the shadows—I hope you are sitting with the light coming from one side—cast by it. Notice the round tip, and on each side the two little curved nostrils, and round each nostril the wing of flesh. These will probably be only slightly defined, for these lines deepen with age. Beneath the tip of the nose a shadow will fall, and also on the very tip will be a fainter but decided little shadow. The shape of this shadow on the tip of your nose is very important.

If your nose is slightly tip-tilted, then this shadow will be sharp and incline in a three-cornered shape upward.

If your nose is Roman, then this shadow will dip down in a firm half-moon shape.

Now incline your head away at a slight angle, and observe your nose.

Again you will notice the long straight line of the bridge, and the firm tip, and from the tip you get the decided triangular shape of the under part of the nose, with the two nostrils inclining toward the centre. The near nostril is more clearly seen than the far nostril. It is round and full and narrows toward the tip, and the wing of it curves in a very decided line.

If you close your mouth and draw in a deep breath through your nose you will notice that your nostrils will quiver and expand, and if you draw your upper lip down over your teeth, your nostrils will elongate. These observations help us to understand the muscles and movement of the nose.

The nostril of the far side is slightly hidden by the point of the nose, and presents a three-cornered form, the nostril inclining toward the tip, the wing of the nostril correspondingly shaped.

Again we notice the shadows on the tip of the nose, the

Drawing for Beginners

shadow on the bridge, the shadow of the indented lip where it falls in a dimple above the upper lip.

The line that extends from the nostril to the corner of the lip may also attract your notice ; this is the curve which deepens when we are moved to expressions of mirth or grief.

Throw up your head.

Your nose rises boldly like a small peak on your face, the nostrils wide at the base, narrow to a point; the wing of each enclosed nostril is also long and narrow.

Persuade your sister to bend her head downward.

The nose rises from the broad brow pointing downward and outward, hiding the upper lip and possibly part of the mouth and chin. In this position we get the tip of the nose very well defined. If our model be a child, the width of the delicate nostrils is very apparent.

The nose seen in profile, with the head flung aside, is sharply defined ; the bridge slender, end slightly tilted, nostril curved, and the wing of the nostril well marked.

Now, we know that a nose has two sides, two nostrils ; we know also that there is another eye, another eyebrow on the far side of the face. We must never draw a profile as if it were a flat surface (as we are sometimes inclined to do), but suggest by the curve of the eyebrow, the eye, nose, and mouth, the side of the face that we are not drawing.

For the head itself is a ball-shaped object, as we must never in any circumstances forget.

We should take every opportunity of studying noses in reproductions of pictures. The Old Masters never scamped difficult problems of drawing; and you may also gain a certain amount of knowledge by examining the photographs in the daily papers. Once embarked on this fascinating study of features, you will glean helpful ideas from all sorts of unexpected sources.

Always try to simplify your objects ; and accept a wrinkle from the Old Masters, who usually posed their models in half-lights—namely, with the light coming from one side only. 70

Head^ Face^ Features^ Hair

A nose seen between two lights is more difficult to draw than a nose seen in one light—and that from above.

And there is such an infinite variety of noses ! You can amuse yourself by noticing the different characteristics : snub, aquiline, peaky, pointed, inquisitive. Artists declare that a pretty nose is seldom seen, but a pretty mouth, I think, is almost as rare.

Only once do I remember to have seen the ideal mouth, the Cupid's bow, with the pouting, rather full under lip, and the upper lip rising into two small dimpled curves. But how many times do we see long lips—the mouth that shuts with a thin, ugly, straight line, the loosely drawn under lip, the pursed-up, discontented mouth ?

Hold up your glass and study your own mouth.

The mouth is sometimes depicted as a mere slit in the face ; curved upward it represents mirth, curved downward grief or distress.

Try first sketching your lips closed. Draw a single line across your paper as a guide, and finding the thickest part of the lips in the middle, sketch the flattened pyramid shape of the upper lip and the lower lip with one long curve.

Next you will notice that the upper lip is composed of two slightly indented curves. The under lip probably curves slightly in the centre.

Next we look for the shadows. The upper lip, protruding slightly, casts a shadow, as does the lower lip in a lesser degree. Observe wrinkles or folds, the shape of the corners, and the soft indication above the upper lip and beneath the nose.

Then, for a second example, we might smile at our own reflection and draw the parted lips, revealing the teeth within. Here we have the curved line. Draw the upper lip and lower lip first, and then the arc of teeth within, remembering that the lips hide the greater part, and, therefore, not making these few teeth too many, too big, or too prominent.

The corners of the lips will, no doubt, throw a deep shadow, and the lips curving round the teeth will also be thrown into shadow ; shadows there will be on, and under, the lip. The

Drawing for Beginners

curve of the cheek will help to accentuate the smile, and the groove running downward from the nose to the mouth expands over the teeth.

When drawing the mouth in profile we must of necessity ask some kind person to pose.

Try first drawing the mouth closed, then open.

Closed, the mouth is a curious little triangle. We at once notice that the upper lip extends slightly beyond the under lip ; we notice, too, the depth of the upper lip and the more sharply decided line as compared with the rounded under lip. We must look for shadows, and mark the opening of the mouth, and anything that will help to explain the corners of the mouth, for these are exceedingly expressive, and change with baffling quickness.

Now look in your glass once more.

Throw up your head, and your mouth follows the curve of your face, forming a semicircle. You see under the under lip, do you not ? And the upper lip rises in a very distinct and acute curve.

Now ask your friend to bend the head downward.

Do we not get the position reversed ? The curve of the lips is now thrown down, the centre points downward, the corners curl upward.

And this we offer as a really sound piece of advice. When you wish to study faces do not draw a stolidly staring, bored countenance, but ask the friend who is ' sitting' to scowl, or smile, to look pleased, or disgusted. It is infinitely easier to study features in motion than when set firm as if moulded in wax.

Our little friends Mr Sad and Mr Glad, whom we are so fond of tracing on the margin of our books, have a good deal to commend their honest countenances. They have the lines of laughing and crying faces crudely expressed. With chin upraised and eyes twinkling, cheeks pushed up in dimpling curves, and nostrils and lips curled upward—behold Mr Glad 1

And, when we cry, do not our lips curve down in unutterable woe, dragging our cheeks in straight lines from our 72

Head^ Face^ Features^ Hair

nostrils, puckering our eyes into sad half-moons—like Mr Sad in very truth ?

While you are studying the features, choose some interesting subject to enliven model and artist alike. Though you may not complete your original intention, make a beginning on, say, the subject of a small child sniffing up a slightly disagreeable scent from a small bottle. Such a conception may provoke such hilarious amusement that your drawing will bubble with laughter.

Art students often begin their studies by painting the head of an old man or old woman. And the reason is that it is far easier to draw age than youth, for the features become more marked with age and therefore more distinct. Compare, for instance, the nose of the old man and the nose of the infant; the tiny button of a baby's nose, as against the big bold bridge, the heavily marked nostril. As the saying goes, one can hardly ' miss' the drawing of an old man's nose.

Compare the mouth of a young girl, full and pouting, parted over the white teeth, and the old man's, grim, straight, and lined; and the wide clear gaze of the boy with the heavily lidded eye of age. Even the ear of the old is loose in shape and wrinkled about the lobe.

Which brings us to those very important organs—the ears. There is something peculiarly interesting in the drawing of an ear. There is the soft texture, the delicacy of its curves, and the contrasting shapes of the large upper part and the slender lobe. It is a feature of which the amateur too often falls foul. For some inexplicable reason the ear in a weak drawing is often its worst feature. Invariably it is given a queer little waist at the central part.

73

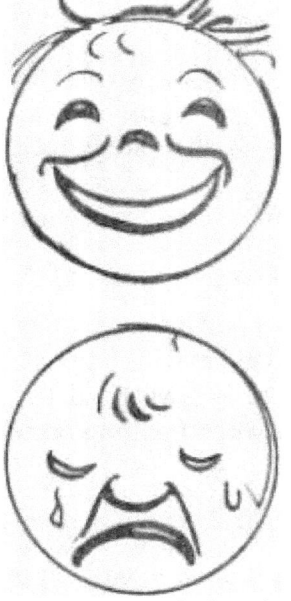

Fig. 29. Me Glad and Me Sad

Drawing for Beginners

Where several young artists are gathered together they can easily draw each other's ears in turn. For, with all the goodwill in the world, we cannot study this feature alone and with a hand-glass.

The ear is an oblong, the upper part of which is wide, while the lower part contracts toward the lobe. It bears a slight resemblance to a huge interrogation mark. The ear is composed of so many exquisite curves that it presents a somewhat baffling subject to the pencil of timid young artists.

Look at the ear as one mass and do not at first trouble yourselves with its manifold hollows and curves. Sketch very lightly the oblong shape. By slicing the corners of the upper part, and carving a considerable portion from the lower part, you have the angles of the ear.

Then look at the large and beautiful curve of the outer rim and the flattened upper space which creeps from behind the fold nearest the cheek and swells into a smooth surface dipping down toward the lobe ; the orifice itself is a dark and mysterious little cavern tucked beneath the coral-pink projections nearest the cheek.

Having marked and sketched the biggest shapes, we should turn our attention to the folds. The ears of young people are usually of a simple pattern. In the example given, there is only one large fold curving round the upper rim. There is also the deep curve or dimple of the inner part, and this we can shade, following the shape with our pencil and exaggerating rather than losing the indentations ; within the outer rim we have a deeper shadow, while the orifice gives us our darkest tone. We might also suggest the shadows behind and under the ear.

The ear that you are trying to sketch may not resemble the ear in this example, but of course it is ' up to you ' to draw yours as faithfully as possible. The ear you are sketching may be wider, it may have a more flattened appearance, the lobe may not be pointed.

It is difficult to suggest any rules to help in the drawing of an ear. The main thing to bear in mind is the use of the ear. 74

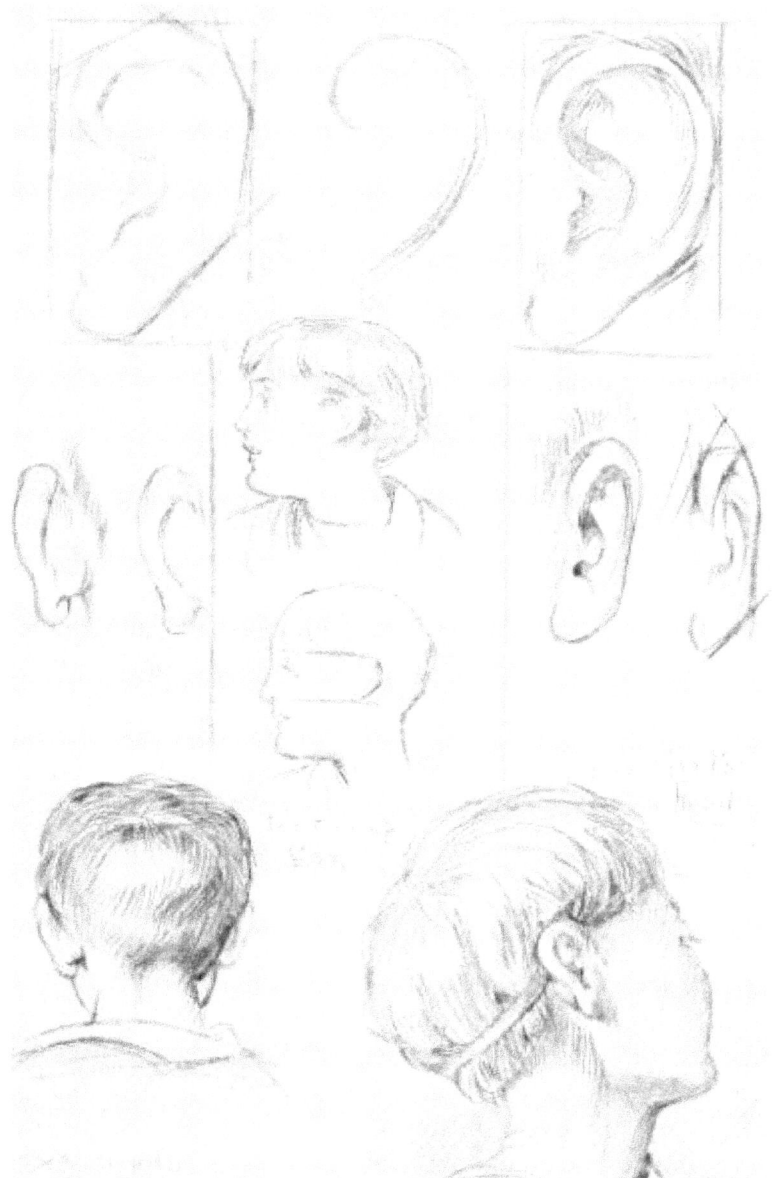

Fig. 30. Ears

Head^ Face^ Features^ Hair

As an organ of hearing it rarely lies as flat against the head as some young artists depict it.

Seen from the front, it lies apparently very close to the scalp, but from the back the ear presents a very different appearance. When it is the ear of a small boy with his hair cropped smooth, it will often project in a very singular fashion.

The ear rises from the head, a flat trumpet-shaped opening to catch sounds. The projecting cup extends and rolls over in a large fold or curve, hiding the upper part from view, and revealing only a tiny portion of the lobe. The position of the ear, the way in which it is moulded on the rounded receding curve of the skull and the cheek, and just above the juncture of the jaw, can be plainly seen. Open and shut the mouth and feel the motion with your finger-tip under the lobe of the ear.

Seen from the front, and almost full view, we have an elongated shape. The upper part, though flattened and receding with the receding side of the head, still presents the fullest curve, and the lobe is as a drooping or pendent shape.

Mark the large folds first, and then the inner curves, and the shadows beneath and within the ear. One fold tucks behind the other fold, resembling, so it often seems, the petals of a pink rose.

Present these folds simply; mark the shadows crisply— that is, with quick, bright touches of the pencil. In the foreshortened position a man's cheek swelling forward will hide a portion of the ear with whiskers and with beard.

If you should happen to be one of a group of young artists who have taken the opportunity of alternately sketching and sitting, you will find that it is helpful, interesting, and perhaps surprising, to lay your sketches side by side at the end of a sitting and compare the various shapes of the various ears.

Some ears lie flat on the head, others stick out. Some ears have long lobes ; in others the lobe is small and pointed ; others again have no lobe at all. There is little chance of being bored with a too-uniform pattern.

Drawing for Beginners

Hair is a fascinating theme for the artist, whether it be the bobbed and shingled hair of the modern girl, the floating locks of the mermaid, the small boy's cropped poll, or the silvery ringlets of old age.

Hair is a strangely deceptive substance. It expresses, though it veils, the form from which it springs. It may lie thick as a cloak, or as lightly as the fluff of a feather ; it can be coiled as massively as gleaming metal, or crimped with strange outstanding puffs and bushes ; it may be clipped short as a beard or trained in wisps of whiskers. There is no end to the tricks played by (and upon) the hairs of our head.

Small wonder that we find hair a difficult, baffling subject!

Says Mary plaintively :

" My hair "—she is of course speaking of a drawing—" looks like a wig."

" And mine like a doormat," adds Madge, even more plaintively.

The reason why the hair in our drawings resembles wigs and doormats is that when drawing the substance of the hair itself we forget the shape beneath the hair. Also, that hair has very peculiar qualities of its own. Every coil, every cluster of curls, every curl, has its own shape, its own light and shade. It has a beginning and an ending. Hair doesn't rise stiff and stark from the face and head like a new brush, but in soft down, in short, silky hairs merging into long locks. False hair and false beards look false because they do not grow gradually as hair grows from the skin.

Note the way in which the hair springs from the scalp, the thickness of the roots, the silky tendrils of the temples, the soft down at the nape of the neck. When we are young our hair springs thick and long. When we approach old age the hairs thin, not suddenly, but gradually. And the reason that shingled hair has an artificial appearance when seen from the back lies in the fact that the barbers shave the smooth fine hairs on the nape of the neck.

Look at Rosemary's little curls. The hair clasps the little 76

Head^ Face^ Features^ Hair

head with the daintiest web of silk. Note the curve of each curl, the wave, the kink, and the final upward fluffy thrust. Diana's bobbed hair, though stiff and prim, has strong light and shadows. If we shade it as one mass, it will naturally look mat-like. But Diana's dark hair covers the shape of the crown, and the light strikes on the curve of the head and reveals its shape.

Take a single lock of hair, and mark its shape as if it were a single object, instead of a mass of fine hairs falling together. Draw first the general shape. Trailing as it does, without touching or clinging to the shoulder, we observe its curious snake-like appearance. Then lightly draw that shape.

Next we notice a twist in the lock. Draw the twist; within the twist a shadow is cast by the thick over-hanging mass; draw that shadow. Another shadow we observe beneath the lower curve; indicate that also, likewise the several broad shadows which will probably appear above the thickest mass. That being done, we sit back and look at our drawing critically. Too solid, we say, and not sufficiently hairy.

Hair, unless very wet or thickly saturated with oil, has a wayward disposition.

Within the lock you will probably note a parting of several hairs, extending from the upper part to the lower kink or curl. Then note some of these separate hairs, and indicate with the lightest possible touch.

Diana's bobbed hair, stiff and prim, has valuable lights and shadows.

First sketch the shape of Diana's head, next look for the parting from which the dark masses of hair arise and fall about the ears, brow, and neck. Draw the line of the parting, the dividing-line of the hair.

On one side you will notice a very sharp little shadow defining the crown of the head ; sketch this lightly. From the crown the hair springs and catches the light. Cropped firm and square, the shadows beneath the lower edges must of necessity be also firm and angular. Across the light spaces

Drawing for Beginners

you will probably detect hairs. Draw some of these hairs. They will ' break ' the light and give a hairy appearance to what might otherwise appear rather like metal or woven silk.

Hair that is frizzy, and grows golliwog-fashion from the scalp, must be drawn with the lightest touch. Hair smooth and silken, and parted and worn close to the head, can be drawn with more firmness. But there is no general rule to be followed with safety. Hair is so diverse in tint and texture that only by constant practice can we ' make good ' with our pencils.

When drawing hair we should keep a light but not a feeble touch. Draw with delicacy and look for stray hairs to break the firm masses.

Babette's thick plait offers another variation. Ask her to turn her head aside and sketch the back of the head and hair, the parting, the smooth hair covering the crown and then dividing and twisting into a silky plait. If the drawing of the plait gives you trouble, practise with some twisted skeins of coloured wool, or silk ; only recollect that in this case the material will be of equal thickness, whereas the plait of hair graduates from thick strong roots to wispy tail.

The movements of the body, the action of wind and weather, all affect the hair of the head.

Indeed, the little details of floating hair and flying beard are invaluable when we sketch figures in motion.

Young artists will draw people dashing through space, flying down or upstairs, chasing balls, bowling hoops, with their hair as neat and smooth as if they were calm and motionless, whereas ruffled hair will give the effect of movement. In this age of tight and narrow garments, when flowing robes and cloaks and long veils are seldom seen, hair is an asset we dare not neglect.

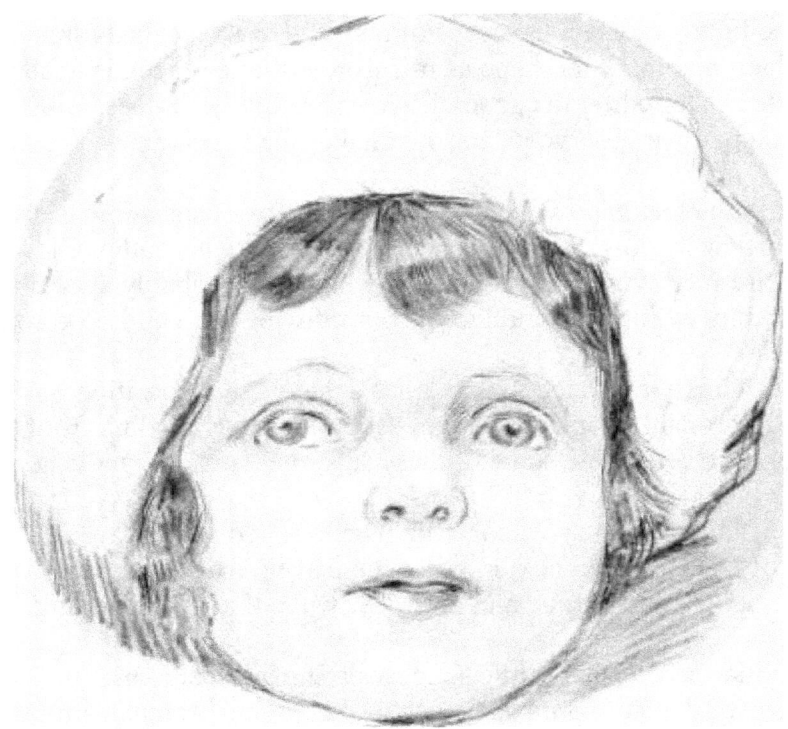

Fig. 32. Baby's Head

CHAPTER VII

Drawing People in Right Proportions

WHEN first we draw human beings we are very much inchned to draw the child and the man in the same proportions. Indeed, it is a mistake we invariably commit.

We draw a tall man with long legs and swinging arms, and we draw at his side a little man with short striding legs and swinging arms. We label the tall man ' father,' and the little man ' son.'

But they are not a man and a child, they are merely a man and a smaller man. Sometimes we have an uncomfortable feeling that our children do not look very childish, and we complain in discouragement: " I canH make my little boy look like a boy ! "

It would seem perfectly logical to draw children as little people, and yet, if we pause to reflect, is it really so ?

As a kitten is different from a cat, a chick from a hen, so must a child be different from a man.

Have you ever remarked to yourself the huge size of Baby's head in comparison with his body ?

Though the head is large, the features are almost negligible, the tiny neck is a mere roll of fat. Baby has a large round eye, a flat wide nostril, a button of a nose, and a half-open, flower-like mouth. (See Fig. 32.)

The months and the years slowly pass, Baby's features form, his head develops, his body grows, his limbs extend.

Compare the photographs of Pamela at one year and Pamela at twelve years ; and look well at Pamela when she trips beside her aunt.

If we draw Martin and his father sitting side by side on a

Drawing for Beginners

bench watching a football-match, in all probability we should draw a big man, and at his side a little man less than half his size. Martin may inherit the square shape of his father's shoulders, but they will be less than half in bulk. The thick, strong, muscular neck of Martin's father is very different from Martin's thin weedy little one. The head of the man is well shaped and firmly balanced, but the boy's will probably look very large, a trifle bumpy and big behind the ears. The ears of Martin's father lie flat against his close-cropped hair, whereas Martin's stick out from his thin jaws and neck like little handles on a big vase. Martin's legs are thin and lacking in calf, his feet consequently appear rather too large for his height; but his father's legs are finely shaped, muscular, and well proportioned.

Now having considered these few points, would you still feel inclined to draw Martin and his father with the same proportions ?

There are a few accepted rules that are useful to remember, though we must never blindly follow any rules, for we know the human figure is capable of every variety of form. Still, as a check to an observation that cannot always be correct, as a trifling guide when perplexing moments beset us, these facts are worth noting.

A grown man of good proportion, when standing erect, usually measures seven and a half heads high. Remember, however, that this is the proportion of a perfectly formed man. A very, very tall man would not have an elongated body, but longer legs. The bodies of most men are the same length. A man when standing with his arms to his sides will rest the tips of his fingers a little more than half-way between his hips and knees.

A figure when sitting roughly represents three lines of a fairly equal length, measuring from the nape of the neck to the seat, from the seat to the knee, from the knee to the foot.

An elbow usually rests in the hollow below the waist, as you can prove for yourself by clapping your arms to your side.

A hand measures the same length as the face. Put the 80

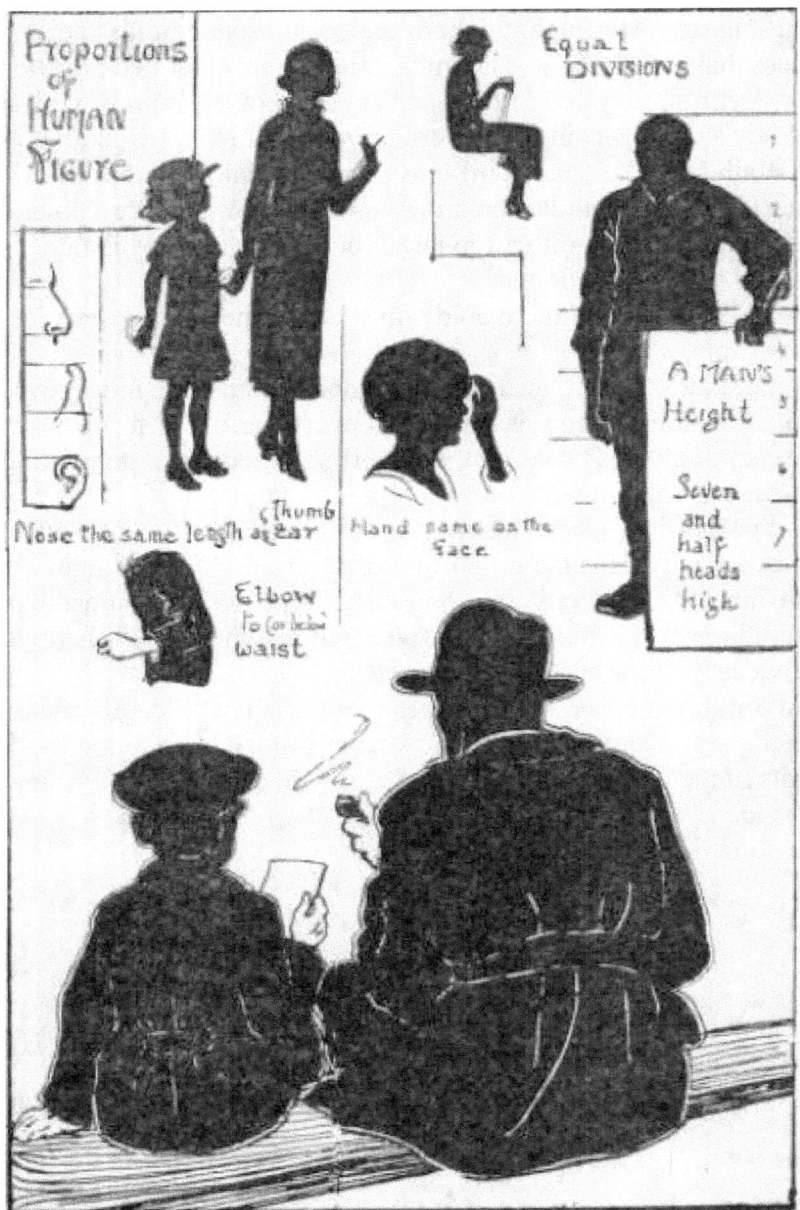

Fig. 33. Pkopoetions of the Human Figure

Drawing for Beginners

palm of your hand against your chin and spread your fingers upward.

A nose is the same length as a thumb. The ear the same length as a nose.

And, having gleaned these few ordinarily accepted rules, you will probably find your next model will have arms too long, legs too short, and a nose disagreeing most profoundly with the length of the thumb. Nature is a law unto itself, and I bring these few suggestions to you with some misgivings.

If your eye insists that your model measures but five heads high, accept that as a fact. Very few human beings are correctly proportioned.

n

CHAPTER VIII

Drawing Inanimate Things

HOUSES, hats, motor-cars, chairs, beds, and boats— all these and many other inanimate things are fruitful of much worry for the young and inexperienced artist.

"Why is it," we ask ourselves, "that the hat of the man in my drawing does not look as if it would fit on his head ? How can I make it right ? "

And the reply comes, " Measure—measure the size of the hat against the size of the man's head."

It may be that the hat is held in the man's hand, or that it rests against his chair, in which case measure the size of the hat with your pencil and put the measurement against the man's head. In all probability you have committed the very usual mistake of making the hat too small for the head.

Hats are not as easy to draw as some young artists seem to believe. The depth and width of the hat can be the most deceiving and perplexing problem.

Personally I never hesitate to measure hats most carefully against the heads of the owners.

Tall hats are more than usually difficult, and consequently more often than not wrongly depicted. The term ' tall' is, to begin with, a misnomer. In the old days of rough high beavers and curled brims the words ' tall' or ' high ' were quite appropriate. But nowadays it is not so, as you can prove for yourself by placing a tall hat against another object, and checking its height; for instance, against the leg of a dining-room chair. You will find that the hat barely reaches the first rail of the front leg. Which brings under our consideration ordinary chairs, queer enough looking

m

Drawing for Beginners

affairs in our early drawings, represented with very small (and always unpadded) seats, perched on long, crooked, and stilt-like legs.

The seat of a chair is a little lower than an adult's knee. How uncomfortable it would be were it otherwise ! And the back of the chair (I refer to the ordinary dining-room chair) lies half-way between the knee and the hip, and level with the outstretched hand of a grown person of average height. Ask your mother, father, or big brother to stand for a second by a chair and check these proportions for yourself. The height of a dining-room table is higher, but only a little higher than the height of a seated man's elbow. An inexperienced artist is inclined to draw the table far too high. And a table either too high or too low would complicate matters pretty considerably for the diner.

A chair is an interesting subject to draw. Even the roughest and most primitive has good lines and a certain grace. First sketch the skeleton shape, the seat and the four legs, as you would a box, by drawing lines from point to point. This will enable you to get a clear idea of the perspective. Then compare the curves of the back legs with those of the front, carry the curve from the legs up to the back, and add the arms.

Chairs there are of every description, lounge-chairs, and chairs fashioned out of all kinds of materials. When chairs are given for tests in drawing examinations they are usually the simple wooden or Windsor chairs, and if you should feel inspired to try your hand in this direction, add something of an outside interest, a velvet or silk cushion, a fur stole or a woollen scarf; or, better still, persuade Pussy to lie curled upon the seat. Then you will have several kinds of textures. Couches, settees, and sofas are often under-represented in our sketches. They are really very large objects, and made to hold a grown person when lying full length.

Beds, too, are commonly shorn of half their width and length. A bed, even a small one,

occupies a good deal of space. If we err over the length and width, we are on the other 64
I ke 5ea h of achaiv IS a
Sn adulb's /rnee.

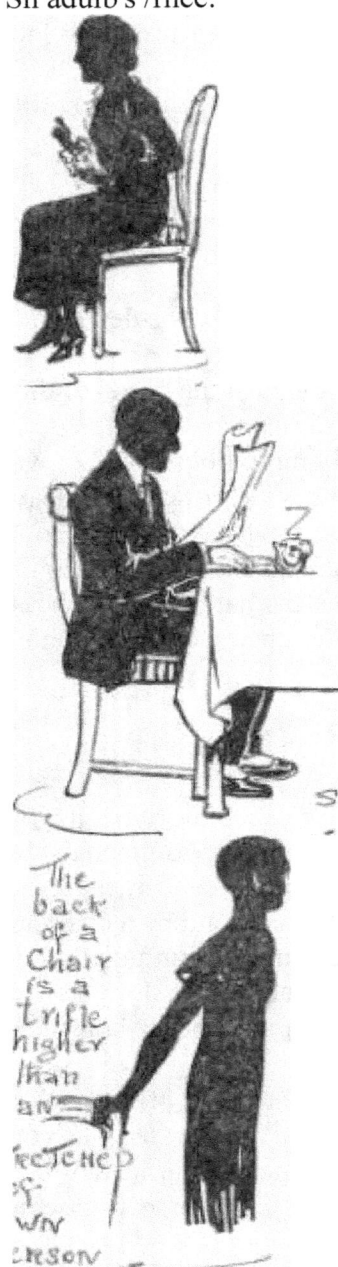

a littlo ttian elLo.w
uohcru
A Kat
IS a iattlc. larger tKau ttio head.

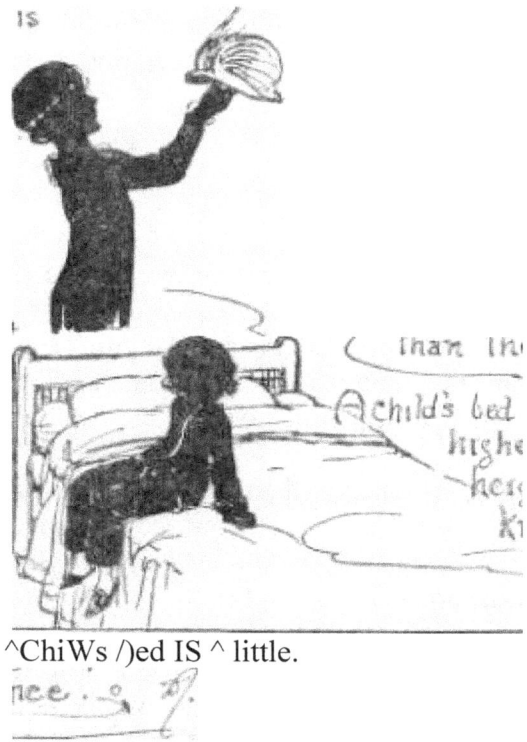

than the

A child's bed
highe
her
K

^ChiWs /)ed IS ^ little.

Fig. 34. The Peoportions of Chairs, Tables, Hats, Beds

Drawing for Beginners

hand very prone to draw beds a great deal too high from the ground. The old-fashioned four-poster with its curtains and plumes belongs to a bygone age. The bed of to-day is usually low and lightly framed. Would it not be extremely awkward if it were higher ? We should certainly require a ladder to climb into the beds depicted in the drawings of many young artists.

When drawing tables, couches, or beds make a point of first drawing the framework, the long seats of the sofas, the legs, and then the backs and the arms. Tables fall naturally into simple forms with the top first decided, and then the angle of the legs. Suggest the length, width, and height of the bed, adding afterward minor details of sheets, blankets, pillows, and counterpane.

Boats we rarely draw large enough to hold the crew, let alone the passengers ; motor-cars are usually depicted far too small for their owners.

Heads, faces, and shoulders emerge happily enough from the tops of cars, carriages, and boats, but it is often in the nature of a conundrum to find accommodation for the unfortunate bodies and legs. Therefore, always draw these hidden limbs, for even if you make mistakes with shapes and proportions, the mere fact of sketching bodies and legs will serve to remind you that a certain space is required ; and they can be erased as you proceed with your drawings.

Another difficulty that besets us is the matter of spacing the floors of the houses, the windows, and doorways. Tenants are often seen strolling about their front lawns, and the houses in the background have windows so closely presented that nothing larger than a well-proportioned mouse could possibly move in the rooms. Yet a room, even a small room, is a considerable height. Your father does not knock his head against the ceiling. He stands erect, and there is ample space above his head. Try to remember that the gentleman and lady require rooms large enough to use. This matter of drawing inanimate things in proportion is chiefly a matter of common sense. Leave sufficient space between 86

Drawing Inanimate Things

each window so that the floors are not crammed closely together and the windows are drawn fairly evenly. Reflect how uncomfortable it would be to live behind windows sprinkled haphazard about the front of the house !

If we apply a good deal of common sense, and compare the size and shape of one thing with another, we shall find the difficulties of drawing inanimate things gradually fading away.

CHAPTER IX

Drawing our Pets and other Animals

FIDGETY-PHIL-WHO-WOULDN'T-SIT-STILL has a very serious rival in our feathered and four-footed friends.

We can reason with Fidgety Phil, but no power on earth can prevail if Timmy the cat, or Spot the terrier, wishes to alter his pose. It will signify nothing that we are in the middle of a masterpiece ; and the fact that we and our models are well acquainted will not, by any means, ease the situation ; the reverse will probably be the case.

My dog Prince always sat on my sketch-book when he spied on the face of his mistress a certain expression which conveyed to his mind that a sketch of himself was about to begin, instead of a sensible walk on the hills.

Dogs, cats, horses, and birds, especially birds, no sooner spy a pencil and a piece of paper than up go their heads, away go hoofs, wings, paws, or tails.

In the first place, when we wish to draw our pets we must invest in a very large—we might almost say an inexhaustible —store of patience ; in the second place, if we are wise we shall sketch our models when they are at rest; in the third, we must use a large sheet of paper. For our model will most assuredly move, and if we are properly equipped with paper, we can make a fresh start without any erasing or smudging.

We must also be thankful for small mercies. We must sketch an ear if we can't see a head, a fraction of a paw if the body is hidden, a comb or beak if that is all that meets the eye.

We must, in short, " take the current when it serves, or lose our venture." 88

Our Pets and other Animals

With a large sheet of paper and one or two pencils ready pointed, steal near to Mufti (the cat, Fig. 36), sleepily coiled on a couch, and begin.

By crouching beside Mufti we shall have a fairly close observation. Preferably choose a position a little below rather than a little above. It is usually better to look up to your model than down.

Possibly we may sigh at the difficult and baffling shape presented by Mufti.

First, however, make a rough note of the curious, almost circular shape, and then seek for any definite ' bits.'

Can we detect any of the big bone shapes, any projection of the spine, neck, or shoulder ? Yes; having traced the half-circle of the back we note that the far shoulder pushes up and presents an angle (softened, of course, by the fur), from which angle the loose skin slopes in a gradual curve to the head.

Notice, too, that the large pointed ears lie opposite each other, and a line drawn from ear to ear will give the tilt of the head. Between the ears, a curved line following the forehead downward will strike the centre of the face between the closed eyes, and extended downward and outward will pass over the projection of the nose, the muzzle, and the mouth.

Next we might pay attention to the width of the broad back and flanks.

The spine can be traced by the light which strikes on the fur, the tail being, as we know, an extension of the spine.

The curious square mass of the doubled-up thigh and the leg beneath is fairly apparent. 89

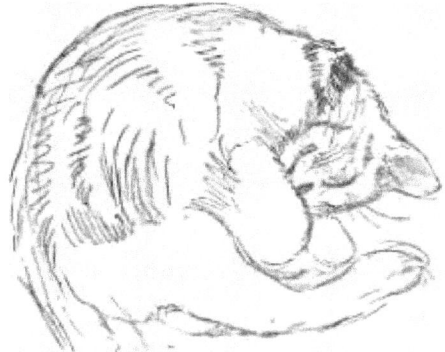

Fig. 35. Flttffy

Drawing for Beginners

Look for the opposite thigh and mark any projection, for that will give you the angle of both flanks.

Sketch the lower part of the face, jot down the position of the right leg upon which rests the head, and get the angle of the hind-leg tucked up and meeting the chin.

Next look for more detail. The shape of the ears, the angle of the eyes, the position of the tiny pink nose—once those three things are settled we can study the marking on the fur. And here I must strike a note of warning. The marking is very misleading, as are the great lumps of loose fur, and the fluffy, silky down.

First get your facts, and here the word ' facts ' means the big bone shapes—the shape of the skull, the shape of the body, the legs, and the tail.

Then we shall know we are clothing a frame of reasonable form.

Having arrived at tuis stage, then comes the chance to note the way in which the fur follows these big bone shapes. First draw the direction of the fur as it curves over bone and muscle—then the marks, stripes, dots, and so forth, the smooth silky down that covers the ears, the soft fluffiness undeif the limbs and about the muzzle, and the thick protective length of the fur on the back.

The marking on the fine fur will be more delicate than the markings on the thigh and back. Use your pencil with a light firm touch.

By way of a final observation, see if any valuable shadows have been omitted where the firm body presses on the ground, possibly beneath the tail, or under the chin and paw.

A short-coated pussy with black fur is easier to draw than a striped and tabby cat. The fur being short and unmarked will not conceal and confuse the structure to the same extent; moreover, the light will strike on the glossy coat and define the big bony shapes more sharply, the flanks, thigh, shoulder, head, and paws.

Whether we sketch Pussy asleep or awake, reclining on a wall, or playing with a leaf, we cannot fail to notice his invari-90

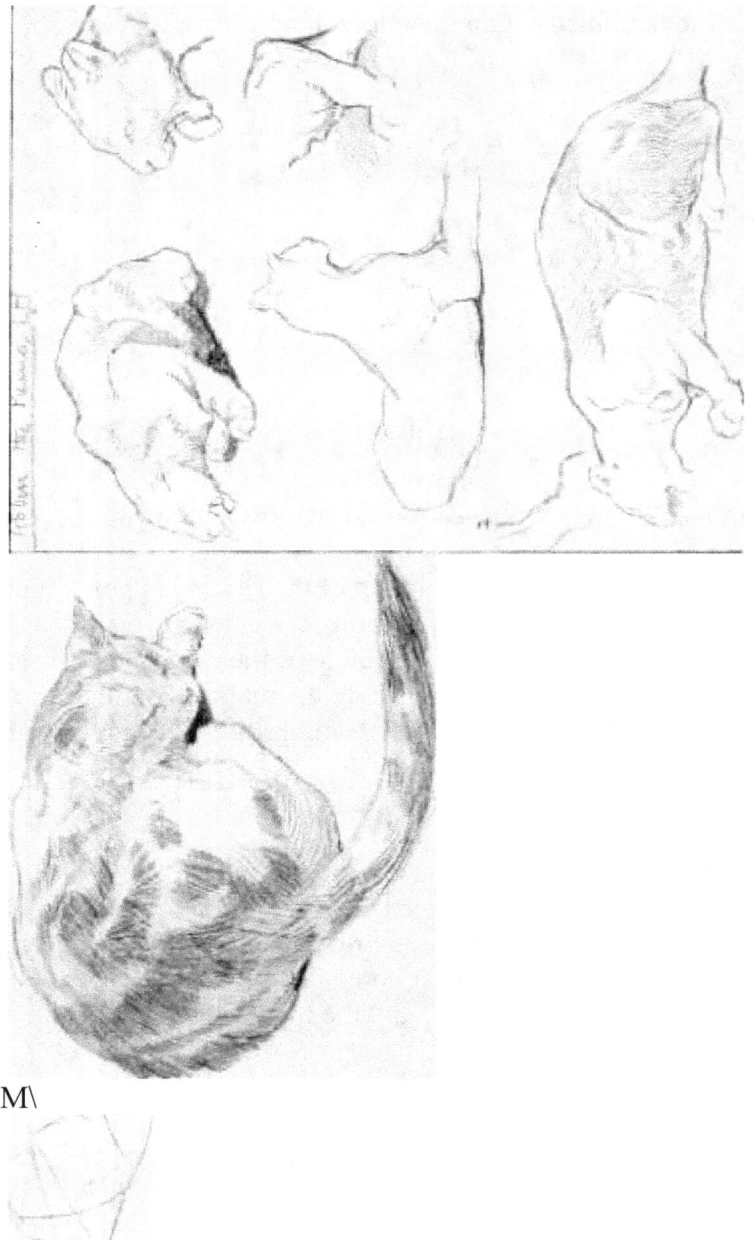

M\

Our Pets and other Animals

able grace. Never do you see an awkward or ungainly movement. Which fact alone should be an invaluable training for our pencil. From the tip of Pussy's whiskers to the tip of his tail, mark the long flowing line of the graceful limbs, the exquisite curves.

The large open eye, the large upright ear, these are very

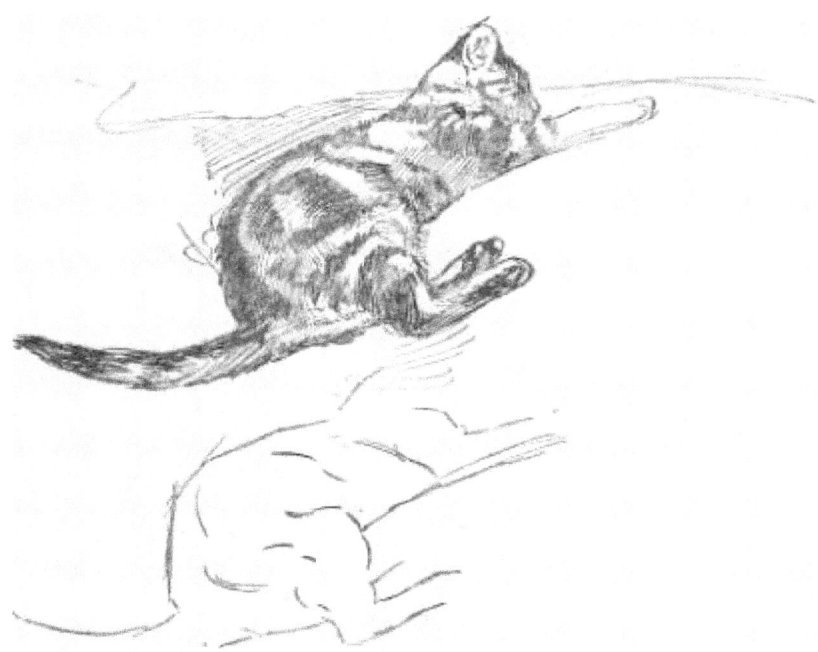

Fig. 37. TiMMY

characteristic of the cat tribe. Mark the width of the cheeks, the short blunted nose, the receding under-jaw. Note also the stretch of the cat's mouth when open ; the muzzle pulls up and reveals the gape at the back of the mouth, and the upper and lower jaw square one with the other. The tiger, the puma, and all the cat tribe share these peculiar characteristics.

Robin the puma (sketched in the London Zoo, to which he was presented by a friend of ours, having outgrown his

Drawing for Beginners

pethood) is a distant relative of Mufti's, and for all I know to the contrary may be as familiar to you as Mufti.

Make a few comparisons between the household pet and the ' American lion.' Robin is of course many sizes larger, and of a stronger and more powerful breed. His limbs are thick, long, and sinewy, his head small compared with the muscular neck, his ears rounded. Note the great pawt and note also the large extension of the jaw when R^bin is yawning.

It is curious to reflect that for one study of a bird we shall see fifty of a cat, and more curious when we consider that with birds we have usually a fairly close association. It is true that birds are difficult studies. They are the most elusive models, and it is impossible to glean more than quick, snap-shot impressions and rough notes, and in that we probably fin^ the real reason for neglect. Birds are not easy, but they are inlensely interesting. With all their wealth of beauty in form and colour, they are a rich harvest for the pencil and the brush.

Who, for instance, could be more attractive than the perky little robin with his brown coat and scarlet waistcoat, his sleek, neat plumage, the cock of his bright eye, and the flick of his pointed tail ? A most characteristic little gentleman ! Search your memory, and try to sketch him out of your head, and preferably with your brush.

Make a bold dash at catching his likeness. Mark the long slope of his back, the clean, sharp swelling curve from the bill downward, the intersecting lines of the tail and wing, the short bill curved above, flattened beneath, the eye close to the bill, the slender strength of the tiny legs, the perfect balance on the long talons.

By contrast, too, we learn much, and drive observation deeper.

Compare the singing canary, his slim golden body and dainty limbs, with the raucous-tongued parrot, his powerful beak, thick talons, and muscular thighs. Contrast the skylark, the exquisite lightness and buoyancy of his movement 92

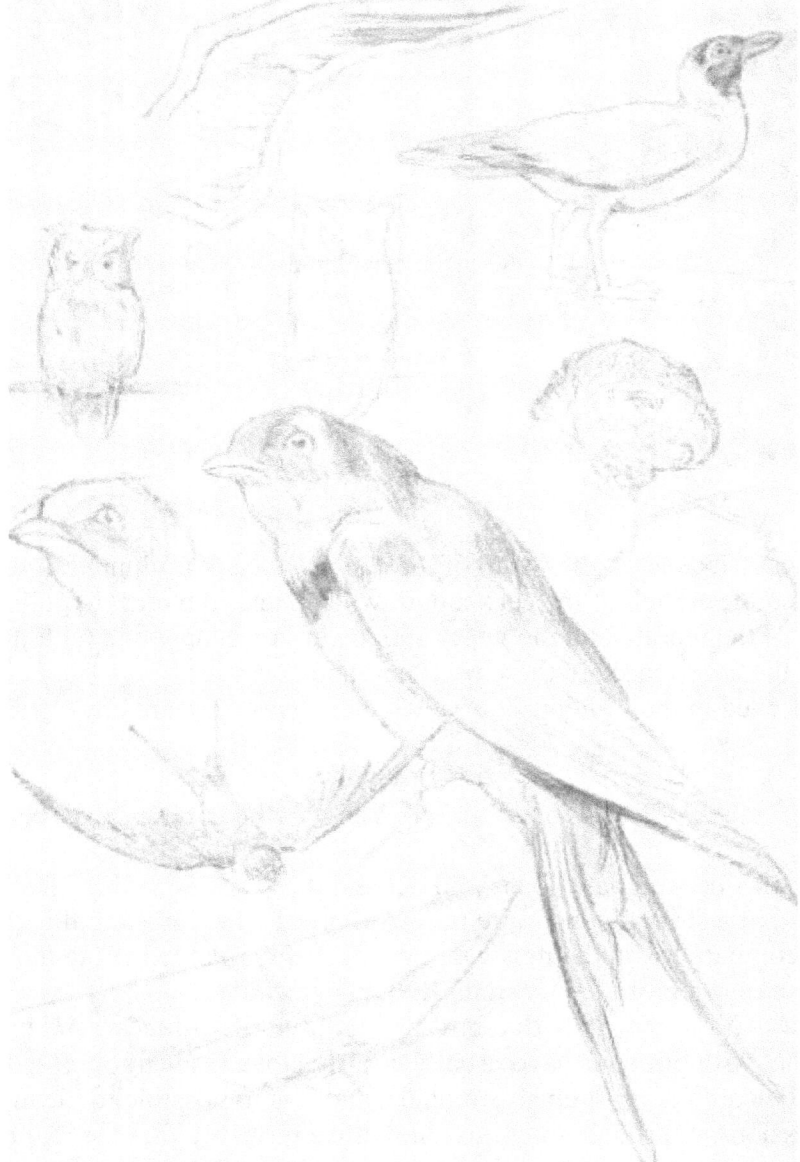

Fig. 38. Birds at Rest and in Flight
Our Pets and other Animals

and form, with that clumsy, soft, noiseless bird of the night —the owl. An owl is a good introduction to the study of birds ; he has one invaluable asset—tracked to his lair by day, he can be observed quite closely. His is a simple and comparatively easy-to-observe shape, as he sits huddled on his perch, blinking his eyes, a quaint compact oblong form, from which depends a soft blunted tail; with shoulders humped up to his neck, head large and square, and talons well tucked under the soft breast feathers.

Mark the large hood-like shape of the head, the curious mask effect of the face from which the tiny beak emerges, and the eyes, large, round, and heavily lidded, and encircled by rays of softest feathers. Mark the rich dark shadows of the eye, beak, and talon with a firm touch. Because—and this is an important fact when we are drawing birds—it is by insistence upon such shadows, the soft depth of the eye, and the strong curve of the beak, and the lines of the tail and the wings, that we obtain our effects.

When drawing birds try to keep your touch crisp, firm, and light. Birds suggest delicacy more than strength. The bird on the wing has something of the buoyancy of the air through which he flies.

Consider the bony framework of the bird. The small head and pointed beak with which it cleaves the air, the long neck (having twice the number of bones of a human being's), the oblong boat-shape of the breast-bone, ribs, and back, the length of the legs, back curved, and, above all, the large armor wing-bones somewhat resembling the zigzag shape of the last letter of the alphabet—a large Z.

When sketching birds take a broad observation. Embrace the whole shape in a glance, and sketch that shape. Sketch the slimness of its body; if it is a bird such as the swallow, perching and at rest, sketch the balance of its legs and feet, the angle of its head ; notice the way in which the wings fold across its back and the tail depends. Then mark the position of the eye with regard to the beak, the shape of the beak itself, the short curve of the upper bill compared with

Drawing for Beginners

the lower. Look swiftly from the beak to the eye, from the eye to the beak. Notice the shape of the head. Mark all these positions lightly before settling down to the careful drawing of each particular feature.

When we draw the head of a girl or a boy we draw first the cranium, then the face, and lastly the features. We check one thing with another, as we have discussed very fully in an early chapter. We must apply the same methods when we are drawing our pets, animals or bipeds.

Compare (and of course with the pencil) the beaks of birds : the beak of the seagull with that of the swallow, or with that of the parrot. In the last-mentioned bird the beak seems to predominate and form the greater part of the skull. Sketch the curious square shape of the parrot's upper and lower beak, together with the wrinkled skin, and the sharp cunning little eye.

Birds' feet and legs exhibit astonishing variations of form. What, for instance, could be more dissimilar than a stork's leg and an owl's, the duck's web and the swallow's claw, the eagle's talon and the sparrow's ? We are very much inclined to be careless about the drawing of birds' feet. How often do we see the leg drawn in one long line, from which fork three long strokes (purporting to be the claws), and the talon behind the leg, corresponding to the heel of a human being, forgotten—or, if not quite forgotten, almost negligible ?

Note, also, that when the bird with the taloned feet moves along a flattened surface, the feet rest on pads, and the projection of the long talons pushes the feet in curves from the ground.

It is true that the webbed foot of the wading bird lies flat on the surface of the ground, but never the foot with the talons and claws.

Note the fluffiness of the feathers on the thigh of the birds, then the thick muscular skin of the leg itself (wrinkled often on the forepart). Try to sketch the joint, the spread of each toe, the curved talon and the pointed nail, with strength. 94

Our Pets and other Animals

Do not be fearful of exaggerating muscle. Mark the grip of the talon and the clutching strength of the tiny claw with equal decision.

The wing of a bird is sometimes likened to the arm, wrist, and thumb of the human arm. The joint of the leg, which has the appearance of the human knee (bent backward), resembles the ankle of the human being, for the knee-joint of a bird is higher and hidden by the plumage.

No doubt you have often remarked that the neck of the bird resembles the letter S. This is especially noticeable in the swan when proudly ' floating double' with his neck carried in beautiful curves ; the stork and the ibis elongate their necks—the S is more drawn out, while in the case of the flamingo, cassowary, emu, and ostrich the neck more closely resembles an interrogation mark.

But we must not linger too long over details. We must return to a more general survey, and we have not yet touched on the most attractive aspect of the subject—birds in flight. Here, indeed, is a fascinating subject for our pencils.

How entrancing are the impetuous rush of the tiny body, the fluttering spread of the buoyant wings ! Yet no sooner do we whip out a pencil than the bird is gone beyond recall.

Think of the wonderful non-resisting shape of the body that slips through the air as a fish glides through water, the rudder-like shape of the transparent tail, and the tremendous span of the spread wings ! How often do we draw wings that would be of no real use to our birds ! The length of the wing outspread is prodigious in comparison with the size of the body.

Observe the seagull with wings folded to its side, and the way in which the wings are incorporated with the slender length of the body. Then look closely at a wing extended, note the clean-cut delicacy of the pointed quills, the vigorous muscle, and the strength of the shoulder.

When we draw the bird in flight we should first sketch the angle of the body, then the angle of the wings.

Drawing for Beginners

Make a rough cross indicating these angles, then, having marked the tilt and swing of the bird, define the shape of the body, the wings, and the tail.

Whatever the position of the bird on the wing may be, whether swooping toward you or flying away, whether the wing be upraised, or down curving, you must aim ^rst at getting the angles of body and wings.

Have you ever seen a kestrel fall like a plummet from the sky, and marked the forward thrust of the head as it hangs suspended ? Have you noticed the seagull whirling and circling, dipping first one wing and then the other in the fringe of the foam ? If so, you will understand how necessary it is to grasp the bird's position at a first glance.

Take up a place of observation in an open field, pencil in hand, and make jottings of your little feathered friends. An exasperating task I know ! But your patience will be rewarded if you can sketch the fluff of two little folded wings, the tiny coiled-up claw, the perk of a glossy head, the saucy round eye peering through the leaves, minute but invaluable fragments.

We need not go far afield ; the ordinary poultry-yard will afford plenty of interesting study.

For choice I should pitch on a young cockerel to sketch. Of all restless creatures I would give him the palm. But wait until he sinks into a dusty corner and his jewel-gold eye is closed. The shapely body and the wondrous complexity of head, beak, comb, and wattles are something at which to marvel; it is only by the closest observation, by utilizing the various suggestions we have already made, that we shall feel we are ready to cope with the problems they present.

First sketch your sparrows, robins, owls, swallows, and tiny feathered friends, later try the more difficult subject— and for all these sketches you might well take with you your brush and water-colour box. Sketch with your brush, instead of with your pencil, for a bird without colour is most strange and unnatural. 96

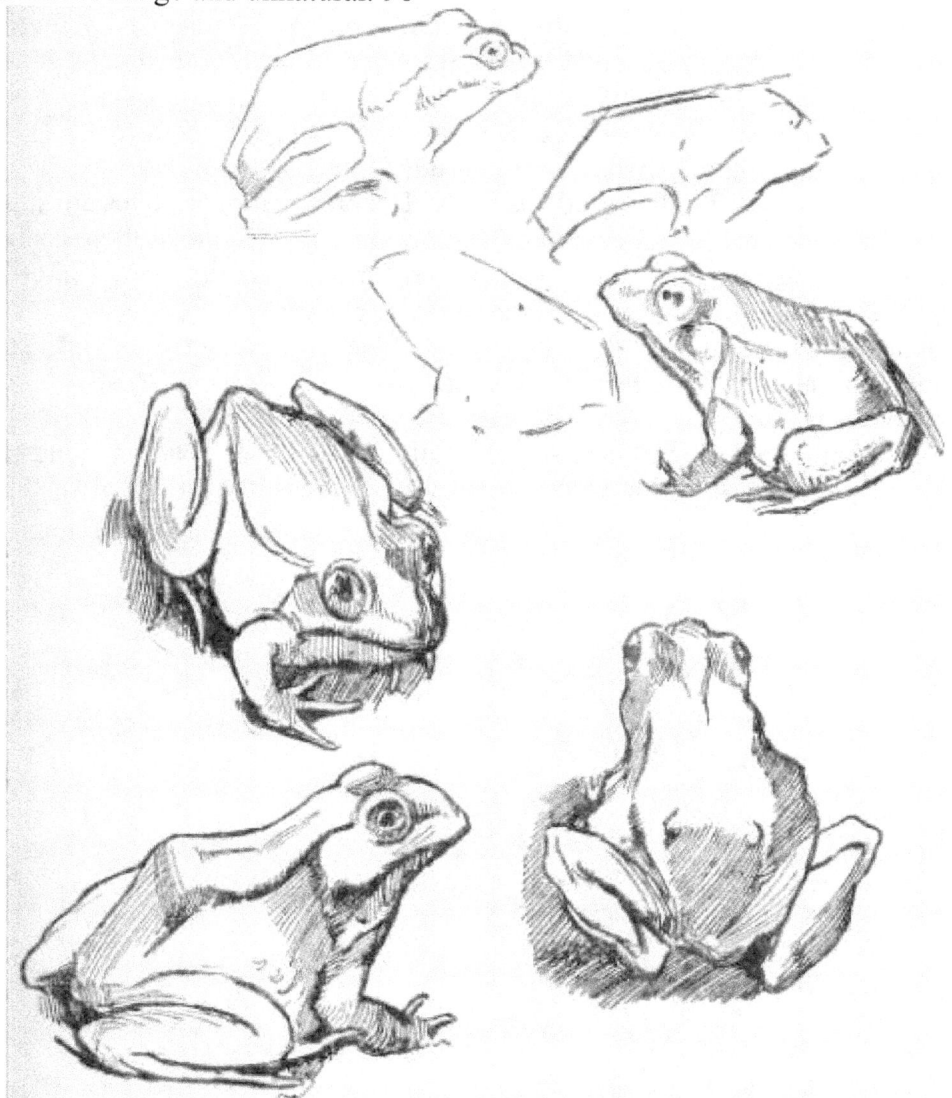

Fig 39. The Frog
Drawing for Beginners

From birds on the wing we might pass to the reptiles on the ground, and those homely little gentlemen the toad and frog are not to be despised.

When drawing these small people you must get close to their level. Try to pose them on a bank or raised surface.

There is something so solidly square about the shape of a toad that it is not surprising that it lends its name to many curiously shaped rocks.

The European frog, shown in Fig. 39, of glistening eye and shining back, is more elegant in shape than brother toad; his toes are slimmer, his nose more pointed.

Mark the upward tilt of the back, the slant to the top of the head and nose, and the long sweeping lines of the curiously shaped hind-legs. Note the forward and outward thrust of the strong little elbow, and the bandy-legged straddle of the front limbs.

Of all things a frog's mouth is the most curious. Look at the gape and the length of it, and the muscles which extend from beyond the grin to the eye-cavity, and down again to the tiniest dot of a nostril piercing the blunt nose.

And if you should wish to portray the frog in action, you will be surprised at the enormous stretch of his hind-legs, one second folded in a close curve over the long-taloned feet and the next opening in a large sprawling S shape.

From the frog at the foot of the tree we might pass to the sprightly squirrel on the branch above, cracking nuts and distributing shells over the heads of the passers-by.

Squirrels are almost as difficult to study as birds. The only stationary ones are stuffed and in museums, and no matter how beautiful and natural stuffed things may look, there is always present the fixed glassy appearance that we invariably exaggerate when drawing. Therefore draw in museums only when debarred from drawing straight from Nature.

When you are drawing a squirrel do not let yourself be diverted by the magnificence of his tail from more important things. (Is he not called Sciurus —' Shadow-tail' ?) 98

Our Pets and other Animals

Begin by sketching the definite shapes—the small mouse-shaped head, the long curved back, the small but strong hind-legs with which he shins up the trees like a flash of

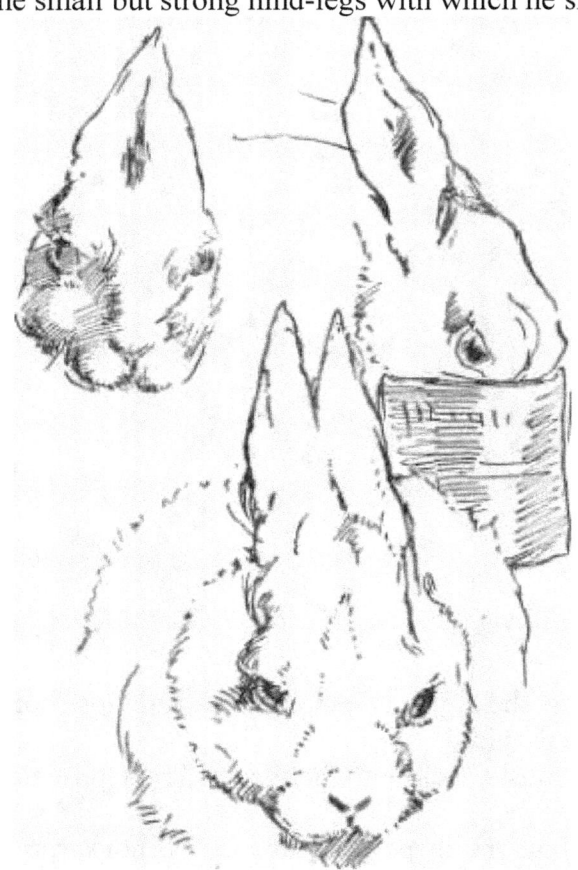

Fig. 40. Rabbits

lightning; his eye—the dark, bright piercing eye, set diamond-shaped in his head; the small pointed nose; the rounded curves of whiskers; the shapely ever-moving ears. Note also the dainty feet and paws, the delicate strength of the claws and talons.

The squirrel, together with the mouse and rabbit, form <^ 3 S 0 I fe 99

Drawing for Beginners

part of that large family known as rodents. The word ' rodent' means ' gnawing.' This is helpful to remember when we are drawing these animals, for it explains at once the characteristic shape of the teeth, mouth, and head.

When we sketch mice or rats the long, narrow, pointed muzzle and long, narrow, overhanging teeth are very noticeable; once we have marked these, and added the long sloping f^^rehead, the small under-jaw, the wide upstanding rounded ear and bright dark eye, we have the main characteristics.

Squirrels and rabbits have shorter snouts and more blunted muzzles, but the teeth are long and pointed ; this we must carefully note in our drawings.

Rabbits are endearing but difficult models, for they seldom stay long in one position and are easily startled by a sudden noise. Nevertheless, if you sit by the hutch and keep very still, pencil and paper in hand, Master Bunny will eventually creep from his straw.

Then note the three-cornered shape of his head, with the long ears closely placed on the very apex, and the beautiful, wide-open eye with its long lashes. The nose, always twitching, is blunt and short and pink, the nostril very small but of a very decided shape, and the muzzle rounded and full. The hind-legs are of an extraordinary size, but gathered together in a hunched position as Bunny sits in a hutch nibbling morsels of food they are not so noticeable ; the spine rises from the head in a long steep curve from the neck to the top of the thighs.

There is nothing more soft and fluffy than the tail of a rabbit—' Cotton-tail,' as he is called in America. So soft is it that we must indicate it with the most delicate touches, noticing the way in which the hairs grow from the root of the tail and spread outward and upward like the down of a powder-puff.

By drawing our small friends, rabbits, squirrels, frogs, birds, and cats, we shall be aided in attempting, presently, the more ambitious creatures, dogs, cows, bulls, and horses. 100

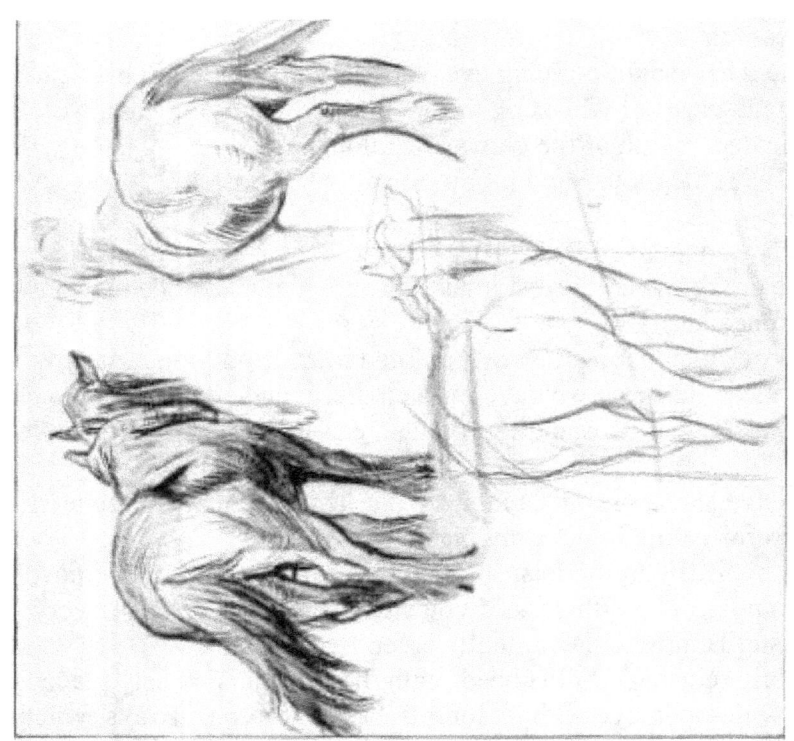

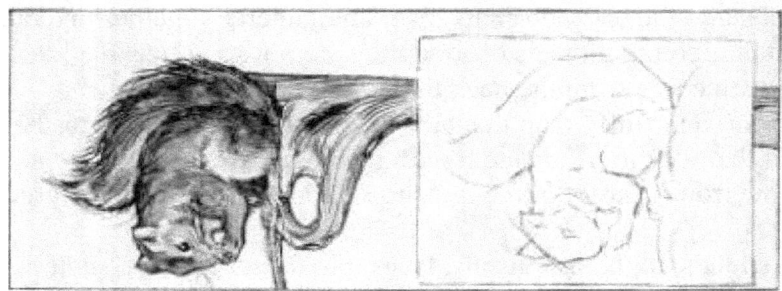

Our Pets and other Animals

Horses are of all animals the most difficult to draw. To their exquisite proportions, the wonderful delicacy of their slender limbs, the spirited grace of their beautiful bodies, we feel, despairingly, that only a Rosa Bonheur, a Lucy Kemp-Welch, or an A. J. Munnings can do justice.

Let us study first the heavier breeds, the big dray-horses with their kindly frank faces, their great fetlocks, their splendid massive bodies. These will give fascinating subjects which need not overwhelm us.

If you have no opportunities of sketching the cart-horse in the farm-yard, you may possibly make a rapid sketch from a window, or track your subject down in a side-lane, as I have done in this drawing.

The positions of my two cart-horses are foreshortened. The long bodies are hidden by the hind-legs, and the finished sketch is nothing more nor less than a square, from the upper part of which extends the neck and crest of the head.

As I have said before, when drawing things foreshortened, sketch the nearest shapes first, and the receding shapes later. If we mark the angle of the flank, the angle of the large bones of the back of the knee, the shaggy fetlocks, we shall perceive that the fore-legs—having the length of body between—are shorter than the hind-legs. The body, too, dwindles.

Drawing the horse approaching toward us or as seen sideways, we must run the eye from one point to another.

Look at the angles of the limbs, the ' slew ' of the haunches ; glance from knee-cap to knee-cap ; from the massive deep chests to the beautifully rounded hindquarters. Note how the curves and muscles of the arched neck compare with the muscles and curves of the thigh, and the silky thick flow of the mane with the long wavy ripples of the tail and the shaggy clustering of hair round the fetlocks.

Try to make separate studies of the separate parts of the body, head, and legs. When you are sketching the head in profile remark the great length of it (the skull of a horse is an amazing size, almost as long as the body of a human being), then mark the greatest depth from the eyebrow to the outline

Drawing for Beginners

of the bones of the cheek, trace the long nose, the rounded nostril, and the curve of the soft mouth, the lips, and the swelling curves beneath the under lip, then reproduce the softer portions, until you reach the cheekbone again. Mark the position of the beautifully shaped ears, and drop a line from the ear-socket to the socket of the eye, checking this position with that of the brow and cheek. Get the angle of the eye, the lid, the shape of the beautiful eye itself; then give attention to the nostril, which we are apt to inflate too much in our drawings. Notice the softness of the muzzle and the shape of the nostril, and the way in which the forepart tucks behind the sides.

Having sketched the main features, you can revel in the drawing of the different textures, the luminosity of the eyes, the soft delicacy of ear, nostril, mouth, and muzzle, the muscles and veins seen beneath the skin, the forelock, and the rippling waves of the mane.

Take a full brush of colour and, wiping it to a point, try to sketch a pony galloping, a horse rearing over a fence, or cantering across a grassy meadow. You can do much interesting work by your remembrance of horses in action. Obviously you cannot draw a horse in action from anything but close observation wedded to memory.

Study, too, pictures of horses. Look well at photographs in the newspapers, and copy those with the brush, remembering always the one great handicap of the camera, that the near things are distorted and made to appear too large. (This fact you have doubtless proved often for yourself when photographed with your feet crossed and pointing at the camera, giving the astounding impression that you have the proportions of a well-nourished giant.)

And behold ! we have travelled all this way with but a passing glimpse at our most favoured pet—the dog ! The study of dogs is a whole world in itself, from the tiny shivering black toy terrier to the magnificent English mastiff.

Sketches of dogs are inclined to be scrappy, as indeed are all the sketches of our active little friends. But first we 102

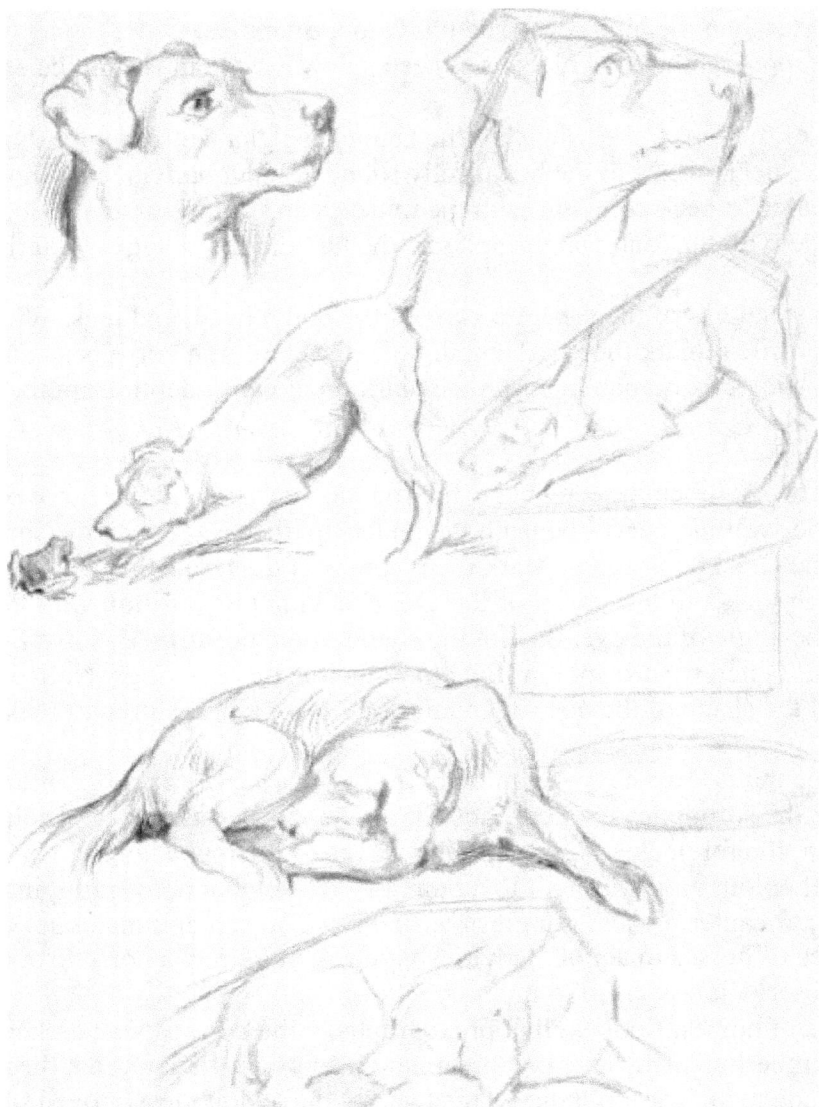

Fis. 42. Dogs

Our Pets and other Animals

must decide in our minds the chief characteristics of our models.

What with the distorted short legs and long body of the dachshund, the length and grace of the deerhound, the stocky sturdy build of the wire-haired terrier, the prodigious muscle and width of the bulldog's body, we have ample variety.

We must bear in mind the general build of the dog. If not, we are apt to give the Cairn legs as long as the pug, the schipperke ears as starkly pointed as those of the Alsatian wolfhound. It is easier, of course, to draw the breeds that have short and silky hair than those that are clothed in long plumes of fur, for then we can see the shape of their limbs, the symmetry of their bodies. A bull-terrier is easier to draw than a sky-terrier, a greyhound easier than a borzoi.

Here we have the head of Benjamin (an old English terrier) with ear cocked and eye alert.

Observe first the long barrel shape of the head, then the blunt muzzle and the rounded nostril. Having marked the position and angle of the head, we can next note the breadth and slope of the round forehead, the angle of the eye, the position of the far eye (indicated and accentuated by an eyelash), and the curve of the muzzle.

The mouth is partially hidden by the soft white hair (and there is nothing softer in Nature than the mouth of an animal). Look carefully at the receding—slightly receding—nose and jaw. The protruding under-jaw gives at once the suggestion of the bulldog strain. The massive, protuberant under-jaw is characteristic of that breed.

Ben has a full eloquent eye. The overhanging triangular flap of the ear lends a sharp and useful accent to the rounded shape behind the eye, and behind that we can perceive the full lobe and root of the ear.

Sambo (Fig. 42), mystified by a frog, is yapping away in a crouching but vigorous position—in which you may be sure he did not remain very long; hence the absence of the other

Drawing for Beginners

two legs. (But this is the way I wish you to tackle your doggie friends. Dash at any position, even if it is fleeting.)

Sambo's body is somewhat contracted, and so is his neck. Roughly, he represents a triangular shape, as shown. The big muscles have fair play ; the thin flank of the hind-leg and the shoulder-bone of the fore-leg are very noticeable. Also the shadows behind the upper part of the front leg and back leg force the rounded shape of the ribs.

Next comes beautiful Bracken (so named because of her glorious golden-brown and red coat). Her back is curved and her fore-legs coiled ; on these rest her muzzle, now, alas ! growing grey. The position suggests a perfect curve—out of which trails the long tail and left leg. Aim first at sketching the large coil of the big body, then the flat angle of the hind-leg, and the fullness of the trunk. The extended leg pushes up the position of the left shoulder-blade ; also we can see the inner line of the neck. Between these two shapes trace the curve of the neck itself and the triangular shape of the head, and the soft flat line of the chest against the ground.

We should now examine the curious curve of the hind-leg and the way in which the muscles and sinews draw back, also the shape of the bone as it touches on the ground, and the great paw as it comes forward and lies limply at rest.

How different is Bracken's ear from Ben's—long, soft, pendulous ! And the brow is more benevolent and more deeply indented between the soft brown eyes.

A word of warning about muscular creatures at rest. When muscles are lax and sinews free from strain we are inclined (in our drawings) to forget them altogether, and a finely built dog sleeping will look, if we are not careful, far too limp and flabby a creature. We must always remember the muscles ; note and draw them carefully, they will keep our drawings up to pitch.

Dogs leaping and jumping, dogs running—the jog-trot of the terrier, and the easy gallop of the deerhound—here are interesting subjects for your pencil and brush. 104

Our Pets and other Animals

We might take up a brush fairly full of paint and sketch a little fresco of dogs in action. I say advisedly ' brush.' We can't stipple with a full brush. We must make up our minds, and draw, without hesitation, the thin or plump body, the long or thick legs, the short or pointed nose, the flowing or stunted tail. The fresco may not be very true to Nature, but it will certainly teach us a good deal.

CHAPTER X

Colour^ and how to Find it

COLOUR is the most deceptive thing under the sun. No two people see colour in exactly the same way, no two people reproduce—or paint—colour with exactly the same blending of tints.

If a colour-group is placed before several young artists with paint-boxes in their hands, we shall not find—providing, of course, that they are not copying each other—the artists choosing the same tints wherewith to paint the same objects. In all probability every painting would be quite different. Which proves that colour appeals to all of us in varied degrees.

Painting is not a mere matching of tints, or placing one tint against another tint.

We might begin our picture with a conscientious desire to match every colour exactly and yet produce something horribly wrong. Because we began with a wrong idea in our head. We started from an entirely false basis.

We must not begin by asking ourselves, " Is that an orange, blue, or green tint ? " but, " What is the colour that pervades and envelops the whole ? "

Have you ever walked in the meadows or down a street in a city and remarked to yourself how different everything looked when last you were there ?

Perhaps it was then a brilliantly sunny day, and on the day on which you made the remark the same street was dripping and shining from recent rain-storms. It would indeed be different. Then the sun filled every chink and shadow with golden warmth. It played on the fronts of the houses, it sparkled on the window-frames, it picked out the red flush of the bricks, it spied the orange peel in the gutter, 106

Colour^ and how to Find it

the jewels of a lady walking along the street. It was a gay scene, beneath sunny blue skies dashed with warm clouds. And the charm of the country scene would be even more intensified by the brilliancy of the clear air and bright sun, which emphasizes the lichen on the cottage-roof and walls, the yellow in the old flagstones, the gleaming of the ricks, the rich shadows flung by the soft green foliage of the tall trees.

Then—the next time !

Heavy rains swept the streets or drenched the meadows, clouds hung dark and threatening, pavements gleamed coldly, the muddy lanes were glittering, heavy foliage dripping, thick soft mists arising, all was wet, grey, and cold. There were dull shadows where the people walked the streets, the tops of the houses were shrouded in murky fog, and in the country lanes the cows moved between the heavy hedges wrapped in a moist cold air.

Do you realize that there must always be one general hue that envelops, and blends, and harmonizes ?

Have not you sometimes said of a painting, " I don't know what is the matter with that picture . . . but I don't like it " ? You have a very definite reason, but you cannot put it in words. You don't like it, and if you lived to be a hundred you feel you would never like it more or hate it less. In other words, you feel there is something that jars upon you. If we tried to analyse your feelings about that picture, we should probably discover that a crash of discords upon the piano bore a strong resemblance to the jarring colours of the picture.

The man who painted the picture did not try to discover the general colour that ran through his picture, and blend it harmoniously together; but, like a simultaneous crash of all the notes on the piano, he banged every tint thick and fast upon his canvas.

On certain islands in the South Seas the native mothers fill hollowed-out trunks of trees with water and in this water boldly place their infants, and the babies swim.

Drawing for Beginners

From this example some people argue that all babies will swim as naturally as they will later walk and talk.

On that particular point I am not prepared to give an opinion, but this I do know, for it has been often proved : if we put a box of chalks into the hands of a small child of four or five, the child will as often as not use the colours rightly and naturally. I have seen paintings by tiny children as good as any done by practised artists. Give the child a string of beads, a coloured ball, a bunch of cherries, or a twisted morsel of coloured thread, and Baby will chalk these colours with astonishing ease. The shape may be funny, but the colour will be pure, fresh, and sweet. Which proves that the sense of colour is a natural sense.

It is a very stimulating thought that we are born with this delightful gift, which only needs a natural development.

As we grow older, and more diffident of ourselves, we seek out rules and hamper ourselves with stupid regulations. But if we merely ask ourselves a few simple guiding questions, such as, " What is the general colour of the thing that I wish to paint ? " and keep our mind focused on that one thing, our troubles will melt away.

Each colour depends to a great extent on its surroundings.

There's Timmy, the tabby cat, for instance. What colour would you call his coat and eyes ? "A buff fur striped with sharp black lines, and yellow eyes," you would most probably reply.

But look at Timmy lying on the summer grass. His buff and white fur reflects the green of the grass ; his glossy black stripes fade in the sun like old silver, and deepen in shadow like the rich dark colour of the tree-bark; his eyes, most curious of all, empty into round pools of colourless light. Thinking of Timmy's colouring suggests another subject on which we have not time to dwell—the protective nature of colour. It also reminds us that colour is influenced by other surrounding colours.

" What is colour ? " cries the young artist.

We say that black is black and white is white, that snow is 108

Colour^ and how to Find it

white, the clean Hnen handkerchief is white, the ermine fur that you wear round your neck is white. Drop your handkerchief upon the snow, lay your ermine on its unbroken surface, the one will look murky and grey and the other yellow.

Black is just black, you say. But is it ? Objects are black because they come in contrast with other colours.

Search about for black things in the room. You will see that there are as many shades in black as there are in other tints, according to the light in which the black object is placed, and also according to the colours with which it is surrounded.

Look at the black coat of a man in a subdued light, when, for instance, he is sitting in a room ; and look at the same black coat when the man is walking out in the streets under the blue sky.

The black coat under a subdued quiet light is deep and rich and warm, but in the open air the light strikes on the shoulders, the arms, and the skirts of the coat, and if a cold blue light is reflected from the sky, then the black coat will reflect that colour and tint. Obviously, being a dark material, it will absorb ; but light and shade there must be, and the black will mingle with the general colouring of the street.

' A sense of colour' in the mind of an artist is simply the faculty of choosing tints.

One artist may revel in exquisite golds, reds, and blues ; another may prefer silvery greys and blues, warm fawn, and dull reds. But it is not true to say that the latter has not as much sense of colour as the former. His choice of tints is different. He sees Nature in more subdued hues. That is all. His theme of colouring is quieter, more subtle.

If your taste inclines to more delicate shades, do not be discouraged because by that choice you are told you haven't much sense of colour. That you know in your heart of hearts is not true. The beauty of twilight, or the delicacy of a misty landscape, or the sombreness of the grey old woman in her dark frock have fully as much ' colour' as

the gorgeous sunset, or the meadows rioting with gold and crimson blossoms.

It is worse than useless to plaster your picture with brilliant reds, yellows, and blues because you think by so doing you display a fine sense of colour.

It is perfectly true that we must use the colours as fully as we feel justified. But we must feel justified.

The great colourists of old used their crimsons, and golds, and blues, and purples lavishly, they revelled in rich silks and brocades, in brilliant skies ; in short, in the dazzling mixture of many tints. Out of these gay scenes of streets, piazzas, palaces, and market-squares floated the brilliant colours, blended and made harmonious by the dazzling light of the sun.

Nature always harmonizes, and blends tints unerringly.

When we with our miserable little colour-boxes would paint crude tints. Nature takes us by the hand and shows where we go wrong.

Imagine a subject composed of nothing but clashing colours. Could anything, we ask ourselves, right that wrong ?

Once I saw a girl standing in a field not far outside the city of Madrid. She wore a purple handkerchief on her head, a crimson and purple skirt looped over her petticoat. She had in her arms a huge sheath of blue cornflowers and she stood knee-deep in scarlet poppies. Not one red agreed with another red, the purples were vivid, and the blue was crude. Yet the whole scene was pleasing because it was bathed in a brilliantly clear air. The purity of the atmosphere made all the crude tints harmonize.

Painting does not mean placing all the paints upon a sheet of paper. That any foolish person can do.

But painting is selecting the right tints, and playing our tunes with those tints harmoniously.

Suppose we take a simple object, a small Flanders poppy, scarlet hued, with folded petals of silk, and look at that with a view to painting it.

Then we will ask ourselves, " What is the colour that flows 110

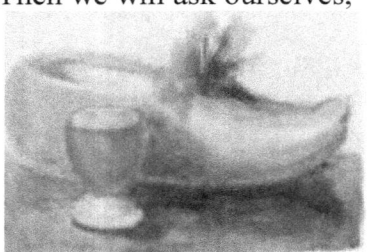

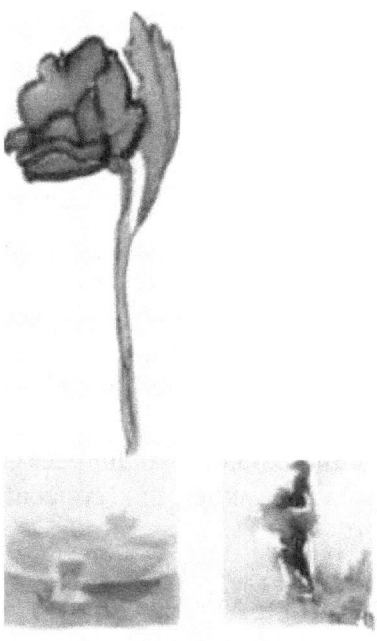

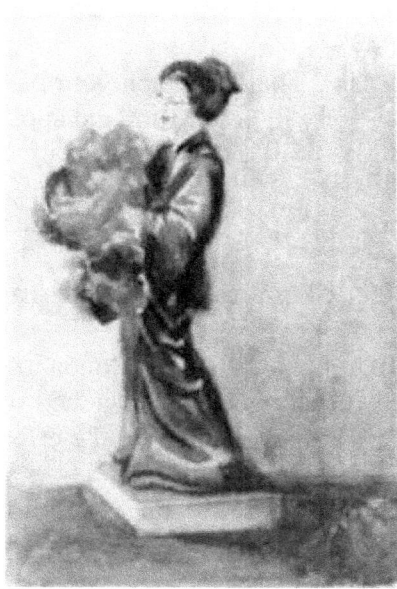

IT sHul'LIi Xo|- KK PAINTED, \'7bb) Two CiiUlin; SCHEMES,
AND Fllisl' iMl'llKSSKtXs (iF linTlI

Colour^ and how to Find it

through the poppy-blossom, stem, and leaf ? " The poppy is composed of red and green tints, and yellow there is in both red and green. Therefore, if we wish to paint the poppy, and we are of course drawing with the brush and with colour, we could safely decide to sketch it in a pale yellow tint.

On painting the scarlet petal the yellow will melt and become one with the red, and again on painting the stem and leaf the green will absorb the yellow.

If we had not taken the precaution to ask ourselves that question and had simply sketched the poppy in any tint, say Prussian blue, then the result would have been a dirty cold blue creeping into the purity of the scarlet and destroying the vivid glow.

Or, if we had waited for the blue to dry before applying the red, we should not have improved matters. Our poppy would have had a harsh blue outline, and who ever saw a poppy so decorated, except on a china plate or on an old tin mug ?

Possibly you might argue that the subject is a simple one for the brush, that the problem will be very different when more complicated subjects are attempted.

Gather together several colour-groups and test the problem of colour for yourself—a stick of asparagus, a leaf of rhubarb, apples on a dull painted platter, a sprig of honesty, or a spray of Ted or yellow (single) chrysanthemums in a copper-coloured vase, a coloured straw hat decorated with a prettily shaded scarf, a Japanese lantern, lighted, and a few objects placed around it. And, having settled upon one of these subjects, ask yourself the same question : " What is the general colour of the subject ? " Is it cold ? Is it warm ? Does a yellow tinge prevail, or a cool grey-blue ? Has it a flush of red, or is it suffused with pale pearly tints ?

When you are painting groups it is just as well to place them before a plain background, a wall-space, or an angle formed of two plain boards of wood joined together, thus concentrating light and shade and preventing your attention

Drawing for Beginners

from being distracted by movement in the background. Backgrounds should be plainly tinted. Some neutral tint (neutral meaning ' neither ' in the sense that it belongs to no very definite colour), fawn, buff, or grey. Then your colour-group will have every chance of asserting itself.

When using water-colour always work from light to dark. That is, sketch your painting with a light colour. If you sketch it with a dark tint, then that tint will either run, and spoil your delicate tints, or else it will outline the edges with a harsh dark tint like the edges of clouds in a stormy sky.

Also avoid ' body colour'—or flake white. White paint is thick and opaque. Once white paint enters our painting, there it must continue. We cannot make dabs of white paint without a patchy effect. White gives a different texture, and, being thick, takes away all clearness and sparkle, all richness and depth.

A common fault into which young artists often fall is to paint the white clouds in a landscape with white paint. But the delicate colouring of the clouds should be sketched with the faintest tint (the prevailing tint of the landscape), and the white paper left to give the effect of the white clouds.

Never be afraid of using pure colour. To enrich or deepen shadows, to sharpen high lights, to lend sparkle or brightness, place the pure tint straight on the paper without mixing or putting it first on the palette.

To soften and blend your tints take a full brush and flood the water on the paper and let the colours mingle on the paper.

Should you have an unpleasingly harsh effect, do not tinker at your painting. Let it dry. When it is quite hard and bone-dry take a brushful of clear water and pass it over your drawing, and work on the drawing when it is moist.

Small children find it amusing and instructive to map out discs or squares and fill these spaces with colours. By blending, mixing, and playing with a few tints you realize the immense variations that can be obtained by judicious handling. 112

Colour^ and how to Find it

A few petals plucked from a brilliantly coloured flower (a geranium, say) will give one's colour-box a great stimulus. Try to paint the petal; paint a number of petals, and notice their dazzling tints.

For purity, depth, richness of tint, the breast feathers of a brilliantly coloured bird (parrot, macaw, or parakeet) are perhaps unrivalled. Lay one down on a small sheet of white paper—an envelope—and try to paint the shape and tint. Try also to mix the tint and lay it on the paper with the burst of freshness that is the chief charm of the feather. Fill your brush generously full, and apply it quickly, lightly but firmly. When it is drying define (or draw) with a few sharp shadows and strokes the tiny stem, the fluff about the stem, the broad vane.

Leaves, too, lend a delightful variety, leaves with their gorgeous autumn raiment. Small children revel in painting their varied tints and shapes. Nature is very lavish with her bright colours and she uses the widest range of tints.

Again I must insist, at the risk of appearing wearisome— bear always in mind the general colour of the object. Which rule applies with equal force to a lemon or a landscape.

Of course you will make mistakes. We all do that. You may begin your drawing as a cold scheme of colour when it should be warm, or vice versa. It is quite possible that you may veer round and find yourself finishing in direct opposition to your starting-point; in which case your picture will be far from successful.

If you are painting from Nature and out of doors, you may be betrayed by Nature herself, for the weather has a habit of changing suddenly and so complicating matters.

But provided you do make up your mind and nothing prevents you from persevering in your choice, you will have accomplished something pleasing because you will have achieved a pure harmony in colour.

CHAPTER XI

Measuring and Perspective

THERE is no general way of doing things," says a great writer on art. " No recipe can be given for doing as much as the drawing of a bunch of grapes."

If there are no known recipes for drawing things successfully, there are, nevertheless, several methods by which the young artist is helped out of difficulties and started on the right path.

The application of a few rules of perspective, the use of plumb and parallel lines, the measurement and comparison of one part of a drawing with another part—all these things contribute toward the training of the eye and the quickening of the brain.

Provided that you honestly desire advice, there is nothing to be ascertained but the direction in which that advice should be followed.

In short, what do you wish to know ? What is the special difficulty that perplexes your mind ? Does your drawing look out of proportion ? Is it too bulky for its height, too short, too thin, or too tall ?

Then we will measure one part against another part.

Perhaps it seems to you that the object or objects in your drawing are falling forward or inclining backward.

Then we will apply a plumb-line.

If you have embarked on an ambitious subject such as the drawing of a house, or a street, and you cannot ' make it look right'—" It won't go back," or (equally possible) " It won't come forward "—then we must delve into the mysteries of perspective and apply common sense and plain argument.

Perspective is sometimes called the grammar of art because 114

Measuring and Perspective

it assists us to draw correctly, as the grammar of a language helps us to speak and write correctly.

In the first place let us consider proportions.

If you are sitting at your work, lean back in your chair and face the object that you are drawing, and hold a pencil or ruler

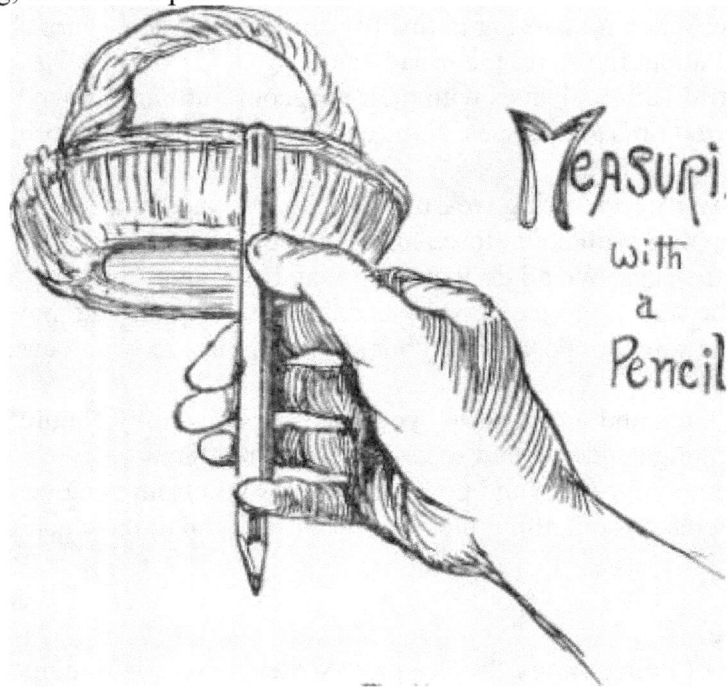

Measuri.
with
a
Pencil

loitfr *
Pencil
Fig. 44

up at arm's length and level with your eyes. Close one eye and measure from one end of the ruler, or pencil, to the thumb, then swing the hand—still at arm's length—and compare the measurement with another portion of the same object.

Look at your drawing.

Compare the same proportions in your drawing. The proportions must agree.

Let us presume that you are drawing a simple subject such as a small basket and you are in doubt as to whether the depth of your drawing of the basket is too great for its width,

Drawing for Beginners

Hold your pencil at arm's length and mark the depth with your thumb. Swivel your wrist, keeping your thumb in the same position on the pei;icil, and place it in mid-air on the outside edge of the basket, measuring the width and counting : " once," then shifting, " twice," again shifting, " thrice " (probably not quite three times).

Drop your arm and look at your drawing.

Measure the depth of the basket itself with your finger and thumb on your pencil and place the measurement against the width.

In that manner you can prove for yourself whether the proportions of your drawing are right or wrong.

The reason why we close one eye and extend the arm is this. By closing one eye we concentrate our vision. We see one object, minus all its distracting surroundings. When the elbow is straight the arm is extended at its greatest length. Without taking this precaution we might cheat ourselves and unconsciously alter the position of the hand, and confuse measurements.

By straightening the elbow we keep the hand at the same distance for all measurements.

Do not make a fetish of measuring. Use it merely as a check, as a corrective. Draw first, measure afterward. The obnoxious habit of measuring first, and ticking off the measurement on the paper, is a trick unworthy of an artist. Moreover, it is a trap. The more we measure the less we prove. It is quite possible to measure until we stupefy ourselves.

If you are in doubt—measure.

Ask yourself, " Have I made the nose too short ? " Take a measurement of the nose and compare it with the length of the face. " Have I drawn the house too tall in comparison with the poplar-tree, or the fence too high for the barn ? " Measure the house against the tree, or the height of the fence against the height of the barn.

Possibly the proportions of the house, tree, fence, or barn are fairly satisfactory, but you are not quite satisfied with 116

Measuring and Perspective

the lines that run parallel with your eyes, the top of the roof, the top of the wall.

Then put up your pencil or ruler, holding it at one end and

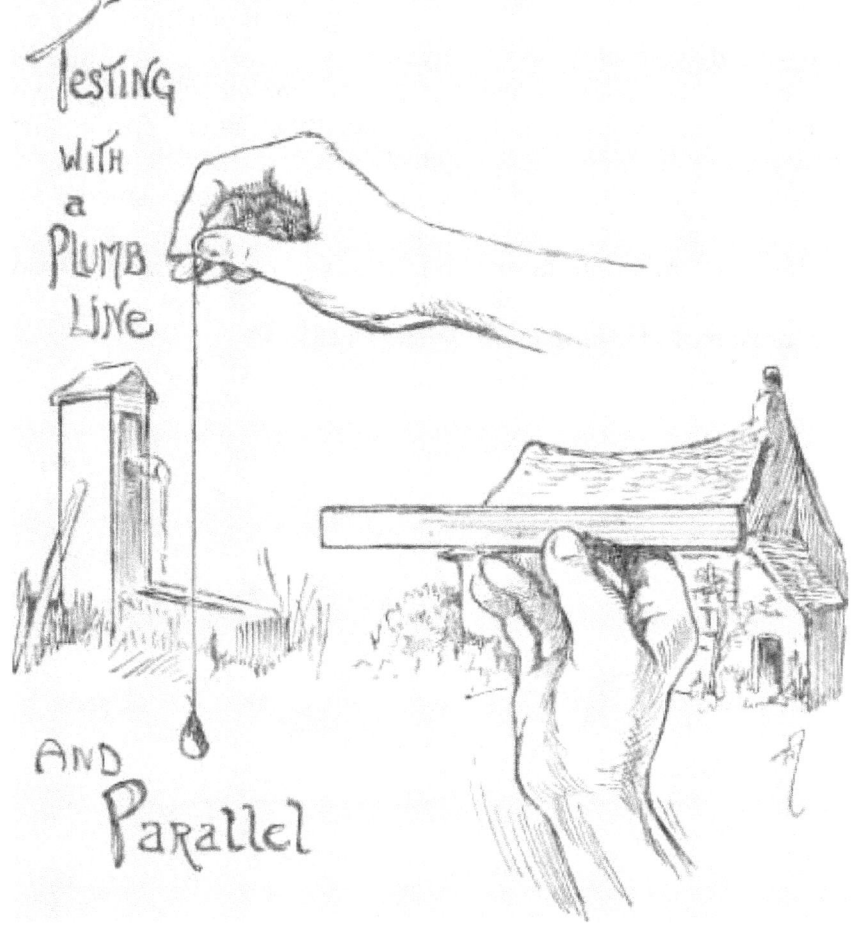

Fig. 45

parallel with your eye, and at arm's length. Close one eye. Raise or lower it until the roof or wall is almost but not quite covered. The pencil or ruler has a smooth unbroken edge, and every divergence from the straight line will be apparent.

Drawing for Beginners

Parallel lines of roof, wall, box, or house can thus be easily corrected. But what of the upright lines—the lintel of the door, the frame of a window, the sides of a wall ? How shall we prove whether we have drawn these correctly ?

Take a piece of thick silk or cotton, preferably of a dark tint, and weighted with a lump of lead (or some similar heavy substance), and you have one of man's oldest tools, the plumb-line.

Hold this at arm's length and between the finger and thumb and before the object of your drawing.

The plumb-line will prove whether the door or window is perfectly upright (or perpendicular). Pull your drawing-block, or drawing-board, forward and let the plumb-line hang before the doubtful line of your sketch. The plumb-line always finds the true perpendicular.

When, however, you are drawing complicated subjects such as a large box, pieces of furniture, a portion of a room, house, or a street, you are faced with greater difficulties.

" How are things in a drawing made to go back ? " is a question that requires a little more elucidation.

Probably as a small child you began to appreciate that as objects retire or recede, so must they become apparently smaller—a first rule of perspective.

Did you not sometimes play at the game of hiding from your sight a house or a tree by putting your fmger, or even a single hair, close to your eye ?

You must have noticed that the boat becomes smaller and smaller as it nears the horizon; that a man climbing a distant hill or mountain is reduced eventually to a mere speck ; that a huge aeroplane looks no larger than a tiny fly among the clouds ?

Therefore you have fully convinced yourself that objects must become smaller as they recede.

In other words, as objects retire, or are farther from the eye, they occupy less space upon the field of vision.

The objects in the nearest part of your picture—that is 118

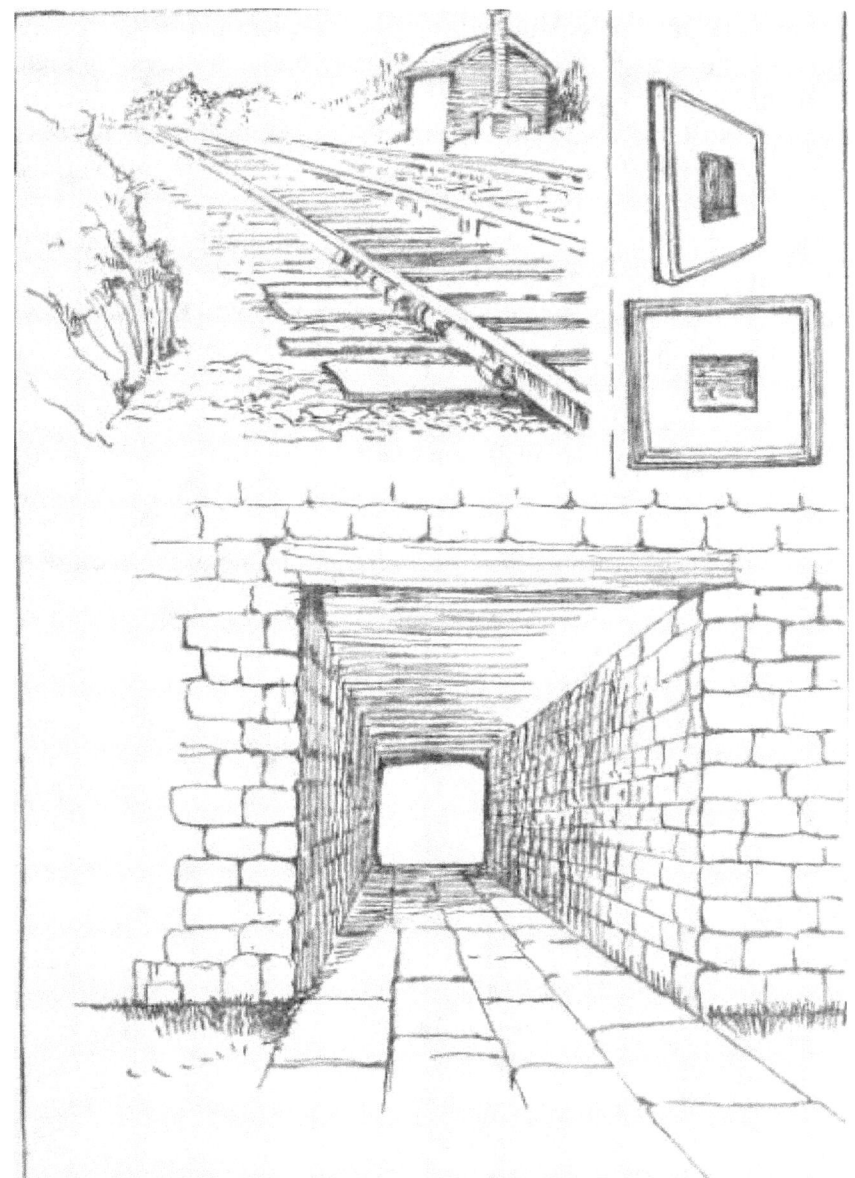

Fig. 46. Objects become Smaller as they Recede

Drawing for Beginners

to say, in the foreground—are largest; the things in the middle, or middle distance, are smaller; and the things in the far distance, or background, are smallest. And to explain these apparently simple facts we must exercise our wits.

You know that when you stand on the seashore and look seaward the extent of your vision is bounded by the meeting of the sea and sky, which boundary is called the horizon. The horizon is the line that follows the line of your eyes, the boundary line. The word is derived from the Greek horos, a limit or boundary.

When you stand on the beach and look at the sea your position is low, and your horizon is low, because it is on a level with your eyes.

But climb the cliffs and turn seaward; the horizon is the level of your eyes.

Ascend to the very top of the cliffs. Now you are high indeed. Look again toward the horizon ; it has extended; again it is the height of your eyes.

The line of the horizon is not always visible because of intervening objects, but as the horizon is the height of the artist's eye its position must be clearly understood, and indicated—for a time at least—in your drawings.

It is possible that you are still unconvinced. Perhaps you live in a city where roofs and houses block a distant horizon from view. Then we may apply another illustration and explain matters differently.

Suppose you descend to the street in a lift and look up at the buildings. What do you see ? Every window, every cornice and roof, coming down to the level of your eye.

Now take the lift to the top story of your tall building. What do you then see ? Everything reversed. The eaves of each lower building, the roofs and cornices, rising to meet the level of your eye.

And the level of your eye is the height of your horizon.

" Is the thing below the level of my eye, or is it above the level of my eye ? " is the inevitable question. 120

Measuring and Perspective

You sit in a chair and look at the cornice, the beading, the top hne of the picture frames, the mirror over the fireplace—

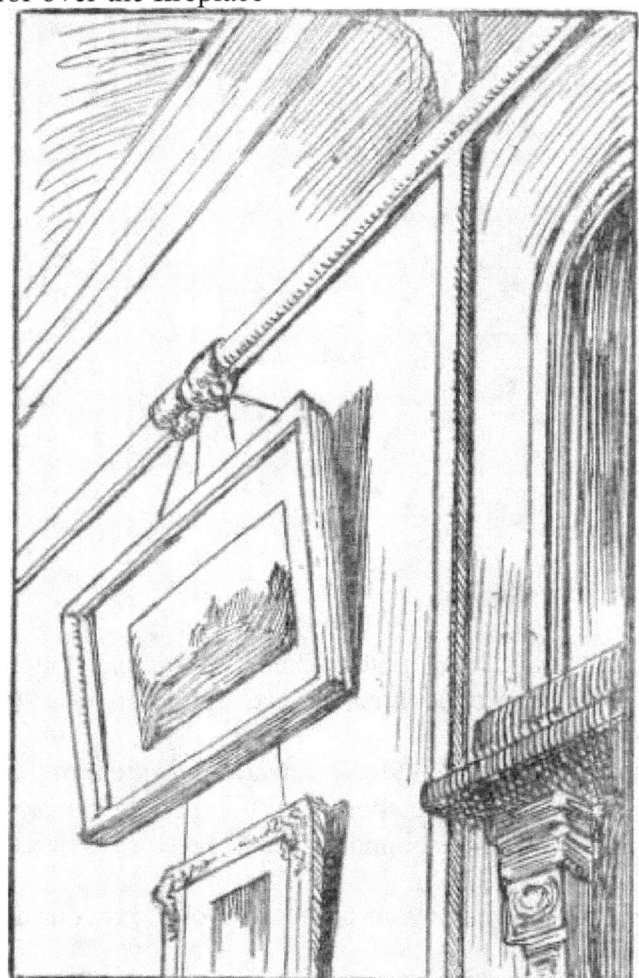

Fig. 47. Above the Eye-level

are they not above the eye-level and do they not come down to the level of the eye ? Cast your eye downward, still sitting on the same chair.

Drawing for Beginners

What do you see ? The outer edge of the carpet, the rug,

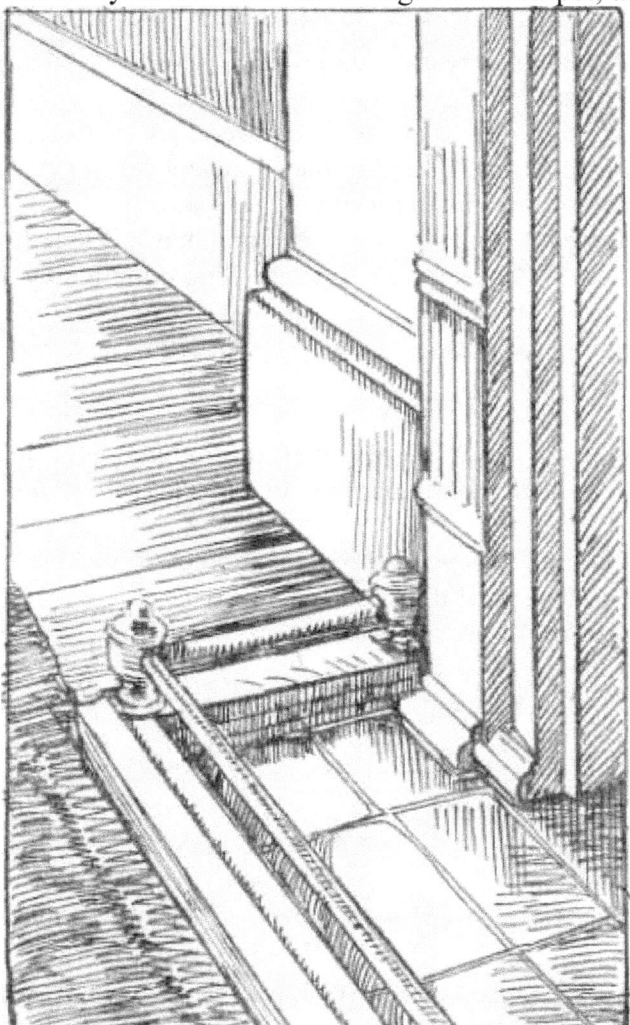

Fig. 48. Below the Eye-level

the wainscot, fender, the rail before the fireplace—all rise to the level of your eye.

You stand on a railway bridge and look at the long level 122

Measuring and Perspective

stretch of the lines and you note that the rails—wide as they are below your feet—seem to narrow down to a point in the far distance on the horizon. That point is called (what else could it be called ?) the Vanishing Point. And perspective says : All retiring lines have vanishing points.

Have you not observed the long straight street and its rows of lamp-posts or electric-light standards and noted that they diminish in size as they recede, though you know for a fact that they are all uniform in size ?

As the lamps lessen in height, so does the pavement narrow, and the houses on each side of the street diminish. For all lines that lie parallel disappear to the same point on the horizon — the vanishing point.

The lines of the long esplanade by the sea, of the long buildings, of the long passage or tunnel, all recede, and if continued in our imagination meet at the level of the eye, which is the horizon. For the vanishing point is that point on the surface of the picture where retiring lines if continued would meet.

A large picture in a frame is perhaps the easiest example of parallel lines diminishing.

You are well aware that the sides of the picture are parallel. They are equal. Measure with an inch measure if you have any doubts on that point.

Now hang the picture on a wall; stand aside and at one end, several paces away, and make a quick sketch of it in its frame. Does not the near end of the frame appear larger than the far end ? In other words, the picture-frame appears smaller as it recedes.

Measure the farthest end against the nearest by holding the pencil at arm's length. Continue the diminishing lines until they meet. Again we get the vanishing point resting on the (imaginary) line of the horizon at the height of our eye.

Let us procure a cardboard-box, and placing it on a table, three-quarter view, and about the height of the eye, take up our pencils and proceed to sketch it.

Drawing for Beginners

In all probability you will say, " I can't tell whether the lines are running up or down."

Can you see the top of the box ? If you sit about the same height as myself, you will say, " Yes, I can see a little bit of the top."

If we see even a small portion of the top, the eye is above the top, and if the eye is above the box, what must the lines do but rise to the level of the eye ?

The top of the box is nearest to the level of the eye, and

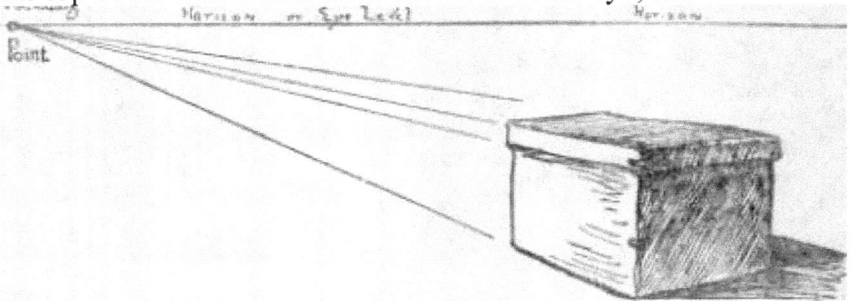

Fig. 49. Can you see the Top of the Box ?

the lower part of the box is farther away (the depth of the box is between). Therefore the top lines of the box rise a little, but the bottom lines rise a great deal.

If we have two lines which go gently on, one at a slight angle and one at a stiff angle, what must be the final result ? They will meet at the height of your eye, or at your horizon.

The higher you sit on your chair, the more you can see of the top of the box. The lower you sit, the less you can see.

Place the same box on the floor, sit on a chair, and make a drawing of it.

Then place the box at a height—say on the top of a cupboard about 6| feet high—and draw it again.

In the first drawing, up come the lines to meet the level of your eye. In the second sketch, down come the lines to the same level. In other words, your horizon in the first drawing 124

Measuring and Perspective

is higher than your object, in the second drawing it is lowfer than your object.

Some things have more than one vanishing point—for instance, this same cardboard-box. A box Horizcrv ov hei^hto^eye is an angular object.

y^

It has two sides which,

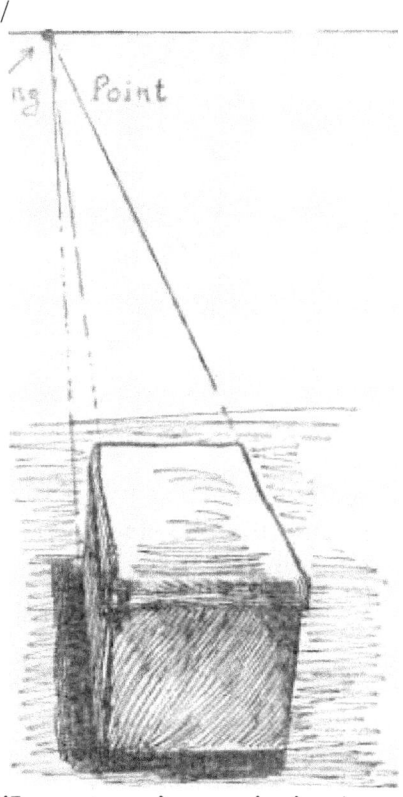

iL nas two siaes wnicnj . , '
11 1 1 ^ vaiiish.ia§
run parallel, and two o
ends which also run parallel one with another.

Place the box so that two sides can be observed, and sketch it lightly and without measuring. Roughly sketch its position, and decide whether the eye is above or below the top of the box, i.e., whether the horizon is low or high. Then draw the line of the horizon right across the paper, because hoth vanishing points must be on the same level — at the same horizon.

Young artists find it difficult to accept this

fact. They are exceedingly prone to provide a different horizon for each different angle.

The horizon at sea runs straight across the line of vision ; as you know, it runs level with the eyes. Then why try to reach several horizons in the same picture ?

In other words, it is not reasonable to assume two horizons in drawing one object.

125

Fig. 50. The Rising Lines

Drawing for Beginners

If more of one side of the box is seen than the other, then the side of which we have the broader view will have its vanishing point farther away. The side of the box presenting a more acute angle will have its vanishing point nearer.

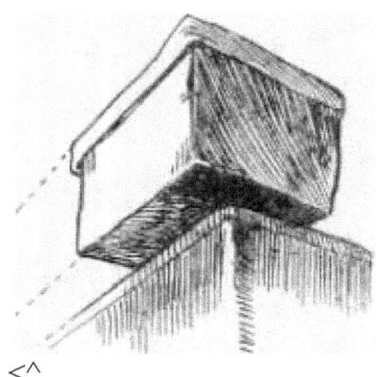

<^

J^

Hortz-of\) ov hei^h't o^ c^e

Vanishing voi'fl-t

Fig. 51. The Falling Lines

The vanishing points will be near or far apart according to the angles.

The farther the vanishing points are apart, the farther we are from the object; and the nearer we are to the object, the nearer together are the vanishing points.

We may now feel justified in drawing something a little more ambitious and a little more interesting than a box. If we select something the shape of which bears a general resemblance to that of a box and place it in the same position, 136

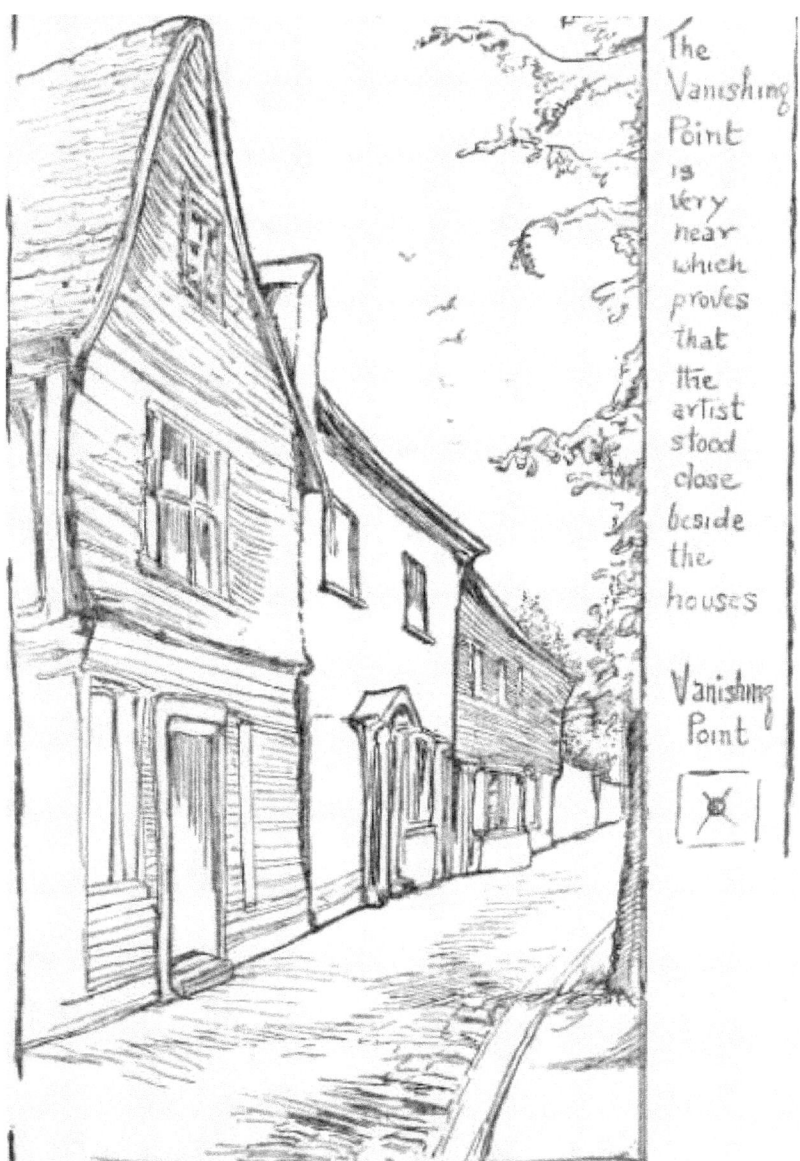

The
Vanishing
Point
is
very
near
which
proves
that
the
artist
stood
close
beside
the
houses

Vanishing
Point

Fig. 52. VAJitsHiNG Point close to Spectator

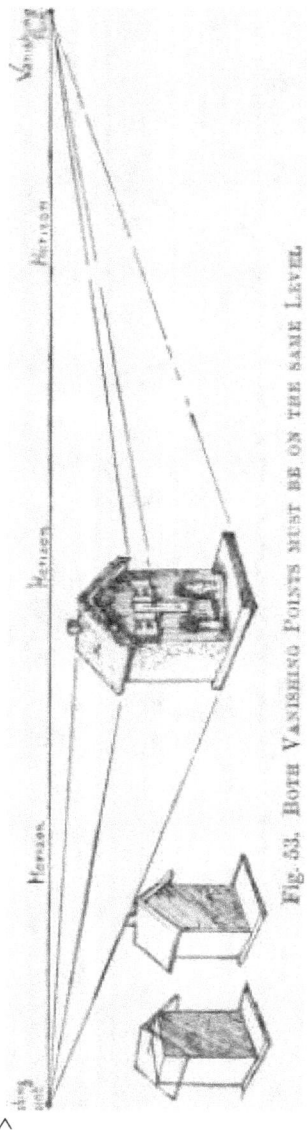

Fig. 53. Both Vanishing Points must be on the same level

Measuring and Perspective

we shall have the same perspective. A toy house standing on a little platform will serve our purpose excellently. The parallel lines of the projecting chimney-pot, the upper line of the roof, the lower line of the roof, the lower line of the roof on the far side of the house, the near line of the platform, and the far line of the platform—these all run parallel and meet on the horizon, the eye-level on the left of the diagram; while the front angles, the two overhanging points of the eaves, the base of the house, the front base of the platform, the windows, shutters, and doorways, all lie parallel, and disappear at the other vanishing point on the right of the diagram.

When you are sketching houses, boxes, or other objects that demand clear perspective, do not begin by drawing a mere plan of the lines. Remember you are trying to be an artist.

Sketch your house first, then puzzle out your perspective. Check the drawing by the perspective, never the perspective by the drawing. You will find, as time goes on, that you will rightly register the perspective with more and more ease.

Rules for perspective might be cited without end, but a few diagrams well studied will obviate many questions.

Receding lines that are not parallel to the earth, says a perspective rule, do not meet on the horizon, but either above or below.

The sloping lid of a box, the sloping flap of a cellar, and the sloping roof of a house do not lie parallel with the earth. This rule is clearly demonstrated in the diagrams shown on pp. 130 and 131.

The student often meets in examination papers the statement : " The drawing of a direct front view, or a full side view, will disqualify a candidate."

" Why is this ? " students invariably ask.

Think for a minute.

A box, a table, a wall, that faces your vision exactly has lines that lie parallel, and never meet. They cannot meet because they do not recede from you.

A full front view, or a full side view, has no vanishing point right or left.

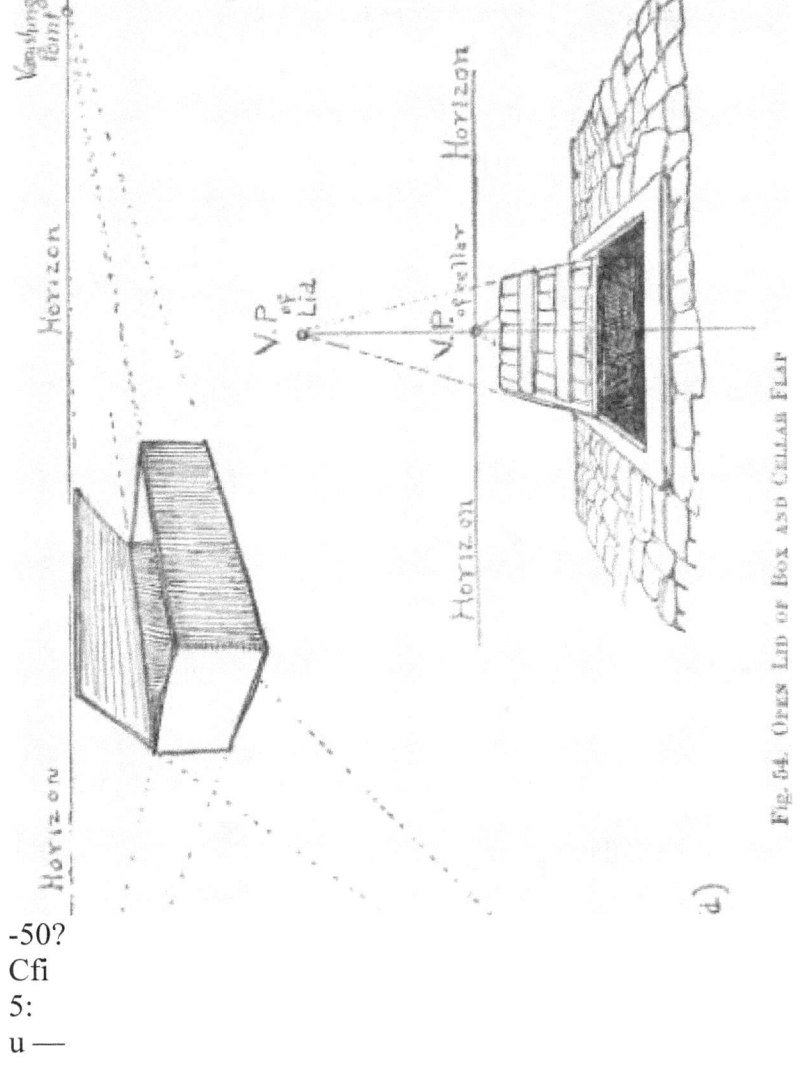

Fig. 64. Open Lid of Box and Cellar Flap

-50?
Cfi
5:
u —

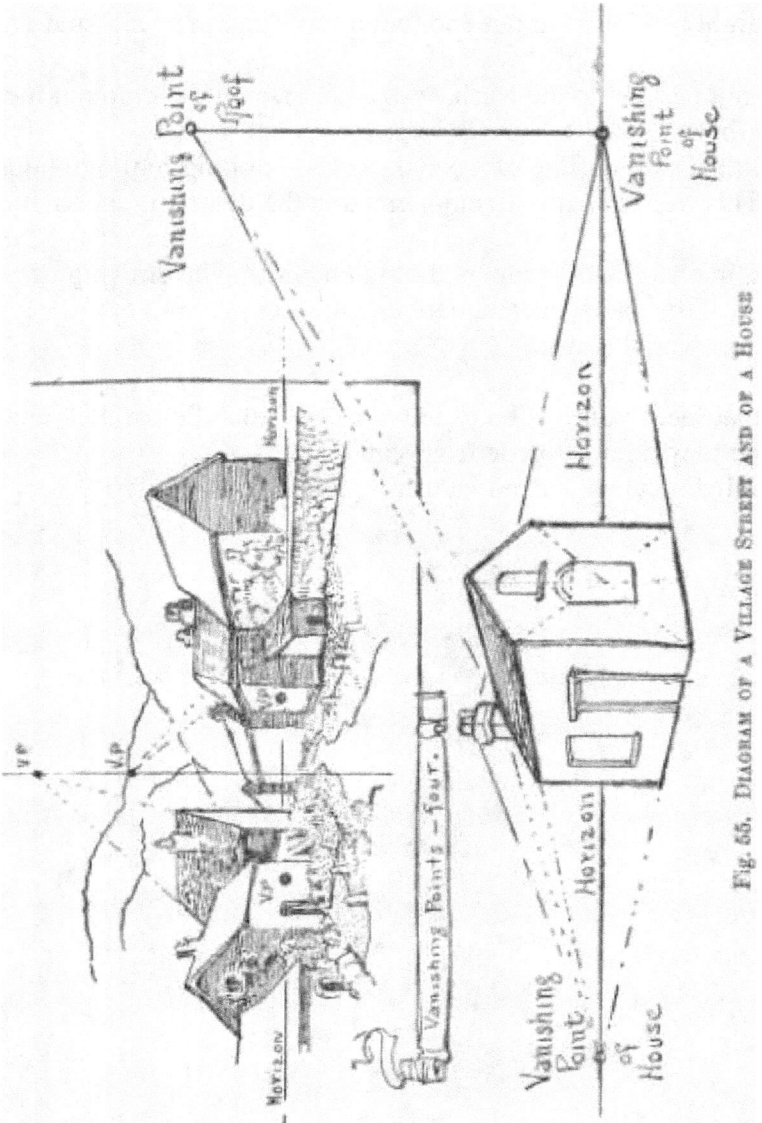

Fig. 55. Diagram of a Village Street and of a House

Drawing for Beginners

Therefore it must be crystal-clear that such views offer no test of accurate perspective drawing.

Then we have this rule :

'Parallel lines that do not recede never have the appearance of meeting anywhere.

Look at the diagram of a village street.

The nature of the ground prevents the building of a long straight street, and the houses are dotted about. Although they present a diminishing effect (they are receding from the vision), yet they diminish to the horizon at four different points. Observe this well; it will demonstrate that:

// there are ten retiring lines and all parallel, there will he only one vanishing point for all; hut if among the ten there are not two parallel lines, there will he ten vanishing points.

Perspective comes to our aid when we are perplexed with curves of arches, bridges, and doorways—beautiful objects that tempt the pencil and deceive the eye.

First sketch the arch or window, marking the direction of the base, the thickness of the wall; then, if you are in doubt about the rightful position of the curve, and the highest point of the arch, enclose the base lines in a square, drop a line from each corner, and at the intersection (or meeting-place) draw an upright line ; that should find the centre of the arch.

In other words, enclose curved shapes in rectangular shapes.

Although a single arch, or even a couple of arches, might be sketched fairly correctly without such aid, a cluster of arches presents a more complicated problem, and we should feel justified in using this method of checking perspective.

Circles, we know, are exceedingly difficult to draw correctly. An artist, of course, should draw circles without resorting to mechanical means, but a beginner, on occasion, may wish to check his drawing of a circle by enclosing it in a square.

In Fig. 57 we have an upright circle in a square, also a circle enclosed in a square and in perspective— i.e., receding from the spectator.

Strictly speaking, many perspective problems belong to geometry and not to art, and provided that we understand a 132

Measuring and Perspective

few simple rules, we need not worry ourselves with intricate problems.

But there is one deduction to which we must pay attention.

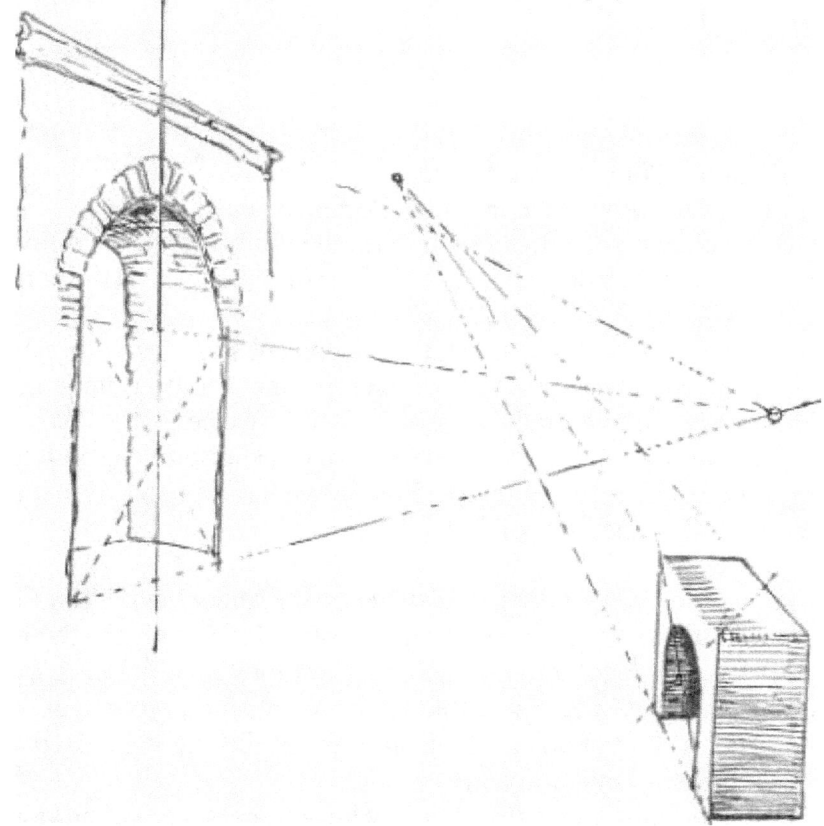

Fig. 56. The Fobeshorteking op Curves and Arches

Every receding line or surface must necessarily be foreshortened.

What is foreshortening ?

A coin seen upright and straight in front is a perfect circle ; a coin seen lying down is a coin diminished and a coin foreshortened. In the first example the circle is complete. In

Drawing for Beginners

the second example the surface of the coin is receding and the coin appears to be thicker in the part nearest the spectator. It does not appear to be a perfect circle.

Every object or thing that advances toward the spectator is foreshortened. For instance, some one points a finger directly at the artist. What does the artist see ? He sees the tip of the finger, the tip of the thumb, the width of bent fingers, knuckles, palm, and arm, but the planes or surfaces that recede—such as the shaft of the finger itself, the fore-

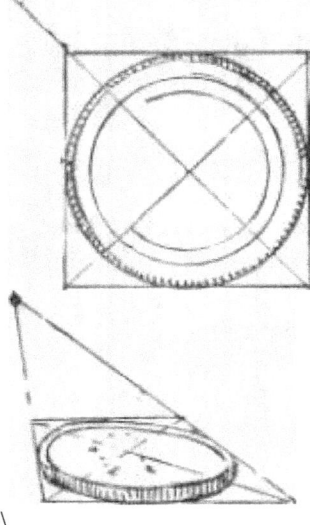

Fig. 57. A Coin Upright and a Coin Foreshortened

arm, and the upper arm—all these are seen in a foreshortened state.

Put up your own hand and clench your fingers, but with the thumb erect. Now lower the upper part of the thumb, inclining it away from your vision. Your thumb is now foreshortened, the upper part is receding.

The human figure, being a rounded object, must always present some parts foreshortened.

In the head, the width of the shoulder, the width of the hips, the smooth rounded limbs, the curves of foot and hand —nowhere do we find an absolutely flat surface.

If you wish to find the human figure depicted without any foreshortening, you must refer to the drawings and carvings of the ancient Egyptians, In Fig. 58 we have a copy from a carving produced about the year 1490 B.C. (For the laws of 134

Measuring and Perspective

perspective were all but unknown until the fifteenth century.) And what do you find ?

The head in profile, the shoulders squarely and flatly presented (front view), the legs apparently tacked on to a flat surface instead of a rounded body, for they do not recede one behind the other, but present knee against knee-joint, ankle against ankle, and foot against foot. And to add to the peculiarities of early Egyptian art, the front view of the eye is inserted along the profile view of the forehead, nose, mouth, and chin.

Does this not bring home that unless you absorb a few laws of perspective, proportions, and foreshortening, you will find yourself heavily handicapped ?

You can provide yourself with a good deal of amusement and useful instruction by searching for perspective, not only in your own paintings and drawings, but in the work of other people.

Study pictures in books and magazines, and photographs in the daily papers, and you will find endless examples of perspective.

By tracing parallel lines and finding vanishing points of planes and surfaces, much that bewildered you in the past will become clear and reasonable.

Planes, horizontal planes and perpendicular planes, are terms constantly used with regard to perspective.

A horizontal plane is a plane parallel with the earth ; a perpendicular plane is one perpendicular to the earth. The top of a table and the ceiling of a room are horizontal planes ; the walls of the room are perpendicular planes.

It might, very reasonably, be concluded that in using the words " tracing parallel lines " I intended to convey that lines should be drawn across the pictures. But that certainly was not my intention. There is no necessity to commit the

135

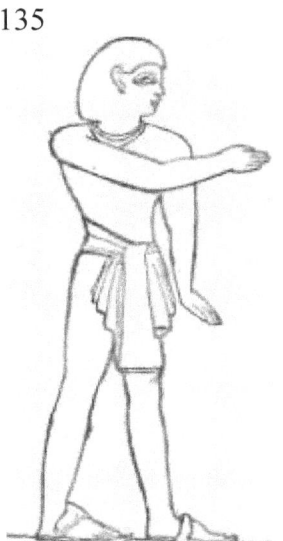

Fig. 68. Egyptian
FiGUKE
Drawing for Beginners

crime of scribbling with pencil or ink on the printed pages. A thread of white or black silk or cotton laid upon the surface will serve your purpose.

To explain more clearly. Lay a thread of cotton on one of the perspective diagrams, hold one end on the vanishing point, and from that angle swivel the thread on to the various parallel lines. Remove the thread to each vanishing point.

Test any of the perspective examples in this way by merely laying the thread on the paper, holding the right thumb on the thread at the vanishing point. An old reel with a small quantity of cotton is, perhaps, easiest to handle, then the thread does not slip out of the left hand.

Use black thread if the drawing is lightly sketched on white paper, and white thread if the picture is in a dark tone.

Let me presume that you wish to analyse the perspective of the accompanying photograph of a picture-gallery, which is a very simple example.

Lay the thread first against the lowest line of the left wall, and find the inclination of the floor; then lay it on the top line near the ceiling. You will easily discover the point where these two lines meet. Hold the thread on that place and test the right-hand side of the picture by laying the thread first against the base and then against the summit of the pillars.

By careful adjustment you will soon fix the actual position of the vanishing point, which lies, does it not, between the two dark frames on the facing (far) wall and the light frames of the two adjoining pictures.

All the pictures on the left-hand wall lie parallel with the wall and diminish as they recede. All the pillars on the right side diminish both in height and bulk. Is not the nearer pillar a great deal larger in girth than the next, and the second pillar larger than the third ?

Although the pictures are grouped at different heights from the ground, yet they all diminish to the same vanishing 136

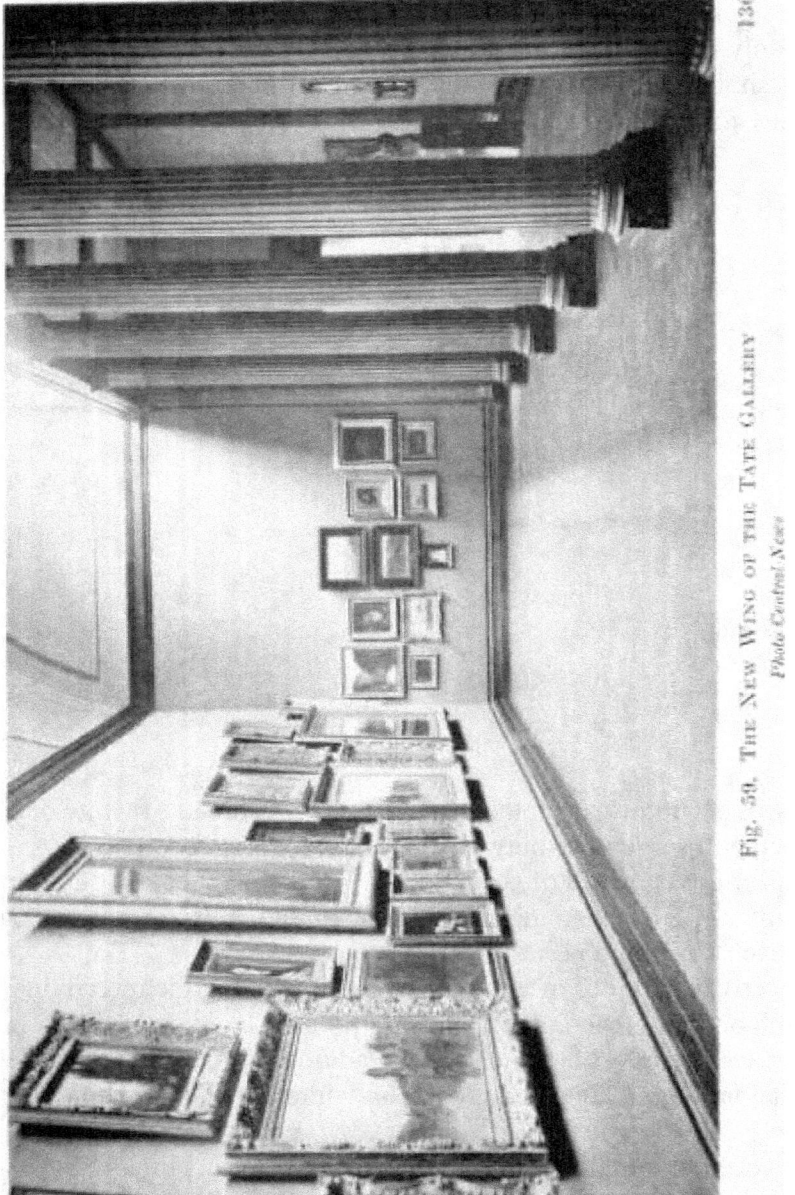

Measuring and Perspective

point—the vanishing point which Hes on the horizon, this being the height of the camera lens.

The pictures on the far wall exactly face the spectator, therefore they do not diminish.

You were told to lay the thread first on the floor, then on the ceiling. This is always the wisest plan. If you find the boundary lines correctly, then all within those lines falls into place.

When you are drawing from Nature always check the outside lines. If sketching the whole of the house, find the top line of the roof, and the base of the walls ; then the rest of the roof, the windows, doorways, lintel, and porch will all fall into place and save you an enormous amount of needless bother. If the outside lines are correct, then it stands to reason that everything within those lines will agree.

It matters not whether it is only a box or a house, a barn or a chair, a boat or a book—always, always check the extreme limit.

By the very simple aid of a thread you can discover many things. You can trace the low horizon of pictures that represent the low-lying ground. You will also discover that the low horizon gives ample space for the sky, and that clouds also conform to the laws of perspective and disappear as they recede.

Pictures of interiors of houses are extremely interesting. There you note that the walls, floor, and ceiling (or rafters of the roof) diminish to the same vanishing point (because they lie parallel one to another), but that the chairs and tables, unless they are arranged parallel with the walls, have each a separate vanishing point, though each vanishing point must, of necessity, meet on the same horizon. (See Fig. 53.)

By making a friend of perspective and interesting ourselves in its various little problems, looking not only for the perspective in our own drawings, but for the perspective in others, we shall soon acquire a useful amount of knowledge.

Drawing for Beginners

Shadows and reflections both bow to the law of perspective. Reflections in water, we are told, are geometrical but not pictorial. Objects are repeated in water geometrically.

All reflections of lines parallel with the surface of the water vanish on the horizon at the same point.

For example, we sketch two upright posts supporting a beam of wood.

The beam diminishes as it inclines toward the horizon; carry on these diminishing lines till they meet on the horizon.

The lines in the beam of wood reflected in the water are parallel with those in the actual beam above; these too must incline to the same vanishing point.

If a bridge is sketched with the curve of its arch reflected in the water, the reflection must incline toward the same horizon and the same vanishing point.

It is quite possible that you are a keen observer, and that your quick eye has already noticed these facts. Nevertheless there is no harm in impressing them upon you. Water is exceedingly deceptive. The rippling play of the winds on the surface and the break of the waves are apt to lead the eye astray. Which point was realized by many of the Old Masters, who safeguarded themselves by omitting reflections and painting sky and water with the same colour and the same brush.

Now for a final observation ; perhaps you have not noticed that the reflection of the sun and moon, the stars and the clouds, are the same distance below the horizon as the originals are above.

It is by no means uncommon to find a young student neglecting shapes and proportions of shadows; and here perspective holds out a helping hand.

The extent of the shadow is ruled by the position of the source of light.

When the sun is high in the heavens the shadows are comparatively short. When the sun is sinking the rays elongate. That is a matter of pure observation. Even a baby will 138

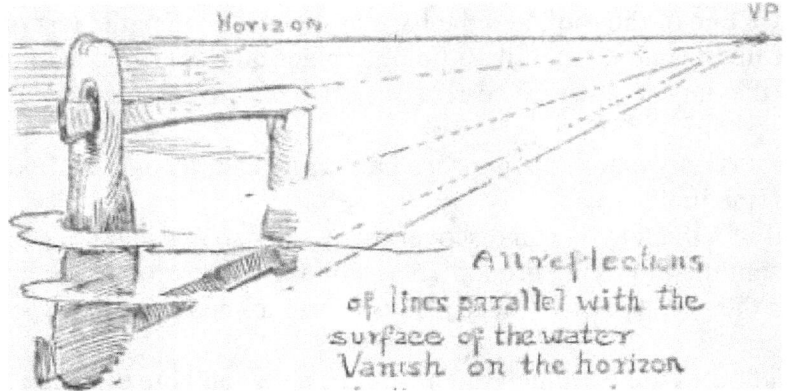

of. lines parallel vutfi th^
Vanrsh, on the iioi'J7or\. ■to the- sawe poLfii

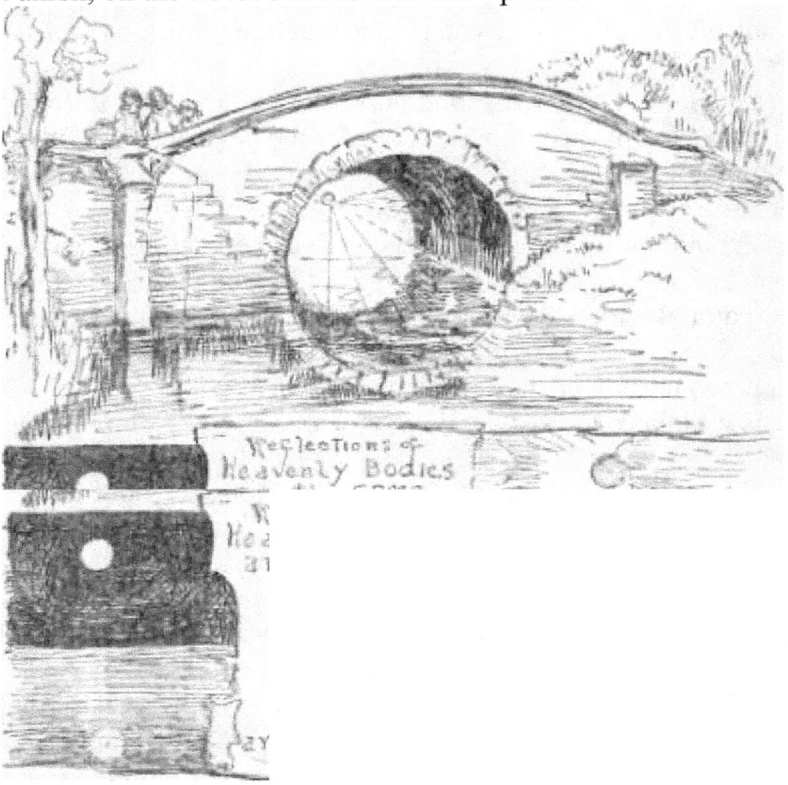

a re the, -""-
below
-The.
boruo
as.
the.

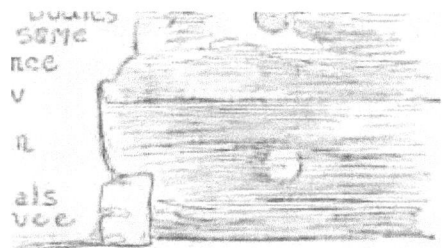

Fig. 60. Reflections

sometimes notice the long shadows cast by a stone, the flickering ribbon of shade thrown across its path when the sun is low on the horizon.

By comparing diagrams of sun and shade you can make your own deductions.

The sun is so far removed from the earth's surface that its rays are 'parallel. But the rays from lamp or candle radiate on all sides and cannot be considered parallel.

CHAPTER XII

Sketching Out of Doors

To the keen, enthusiastic young artist there is nothing more fascinating, more enthralHng, than sketching out of doors.

A walk abroad among foreign scenes and strange people or a walk at home among one's own familiar haunts can be equally fruitful.

There are one or two points which need explaining, and one or two pitfalls of which the novice might be warned.

For the ardent young sketcher frequently digs a pit for his own feet. He begins a ' sketch,' but he pursues it into a finished study.

A sketch, it must be remembered, should he a sketch and nothing more. It is a trifle, an impression.

" How unfinished ! " remarks some one, looking over the young artist's shoulder. Do not let the remark influence you against your better judgment.

Did you begin the sketch as an impression of a particular thing—the wind swaying a spray of flowers, a branch, or a tree, a cloud passing over a distant hill and blurring its contour, a scrap of rugged masonry, a sunny portion of a terrace, a garden seat, a toy flung on the grass, a fragment of a flower over which a bird or butterfly hovers ? Then do not try to finish it. All the spirit of the sketch will vanish if you ' finish' one tiny portion at the expense of another part.

Experience, that hard taskmaster, and experience only, will teach you how far to carry your sketch.

But the main thing to remember is this. If you wish to sketch— sketch. Leave the finished study for other times.

, %

Drawing for Beginners

And never, never tinker with your sketch when you take it

home.

Now, having given fair warning, let us proceed to details. The secret of successful sketching is to arrive at your

chosen place fresh and eager for work.

If you burden yourself with a lot of sketching paraphernalia,

you will arrive with aching arms, hot and tired, and possibly cross. " Travel light when sketching" is a good motto. Take with you only essential sketching materials. A block or a book, and, if the book has limp covers, a piece of board or stiff cardboard on which to rest it, a pencil, india-rubber, paint-box, brushes, and a bottle of water are necessities. An easel, a camp-stool, a sketching umbrella, personally I should regard as superfluous. It is usually possible to hold your book in such a way that

your paper is shaded by your shoulder, your hat, or the opposite page.

A stile, fence, stone, stump, or bank more often than not offers a convenient resting-place and saves you the trouble of carrying a camp-stool.

If the weather is damp, an ordinary newspaper carried under your sketch-book and folded and used as a cushion is a good precaution against catching colds ; should the weather be very hot the same paper, folded and held fan-wise, shields the page from the glare of the sun.

142

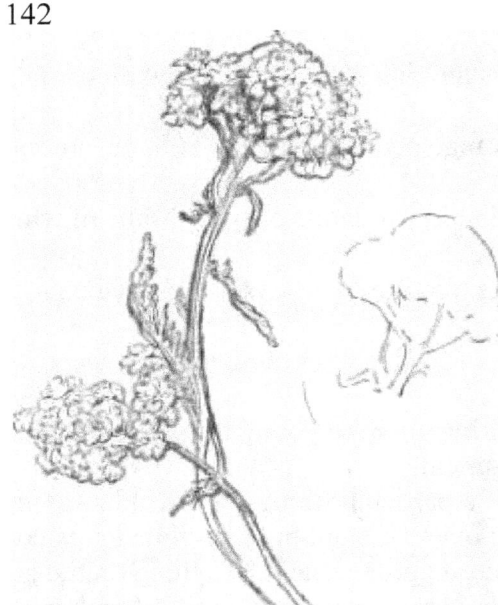

Fig. 61. An Impression
Sketching Out of Doors

A great point is gained by starting in a business-like frame of mind. It is a mistaken idea that an artist drifts into painting a picture as a cloud drifts across the sky. To obtain practical results you must start with practical intentions. You must be firm with yourself. You must choose your subject quickly and settle down determinedly, and you must not he too ambitious. Young people balk their efforts by attempting subjects that are so ambitious that they might well make a practised artist hesitate.

" I should love to paint a field of corn, with poppies and convolvuluses . , . and perhaps a little dip of the sea— and a glimpse of the village church beyond," one will exclaim.

And another will say :

" Let's go on the beach and sketch the harbour, and the boats, and the cliffs. It would be simply topping ! "

I admit the attractiveness of such subjects. The very suggestion quickens one's pulses. But the difficulties !

Once upon a time there was a man of most eloquent tongue who wrote about art, and more especially about pictures. He advised artists to take a stone and study that. There's something very interesting in the drawing of an old lichened stone, though it is far from easy. A wise principle of selection, however, is—choose one simple subject rather than a dozen complicated ones.

From the field of corn choose a blade of wheat with perhaps the tendril of a convolvulus creeping up its stalk ; a cluster of poppies, a tall grass. If a butterfly flutters near, watch intently the angle of his wings, the exquisite poise of his body, the clutching, delicate strength of the tiny legs, and draw your remembrance of him.

In a meadow-land of gold and silver, where cows are " forty feeding like one," choose a spray of buttercups, a single fine marguerite ; take one cow under your observation ; make a sketch of a portion of a tree, a gnarled branch, or some twisted roots with an over-curling plume of a fern. Sketch the stile, or the fragment of a paling round which a spray of ivy is climbing.

Drawing for Beginners

Should you wish to sketch a cottage, be careful not to sit too near. If you do, your perspective will be very violent

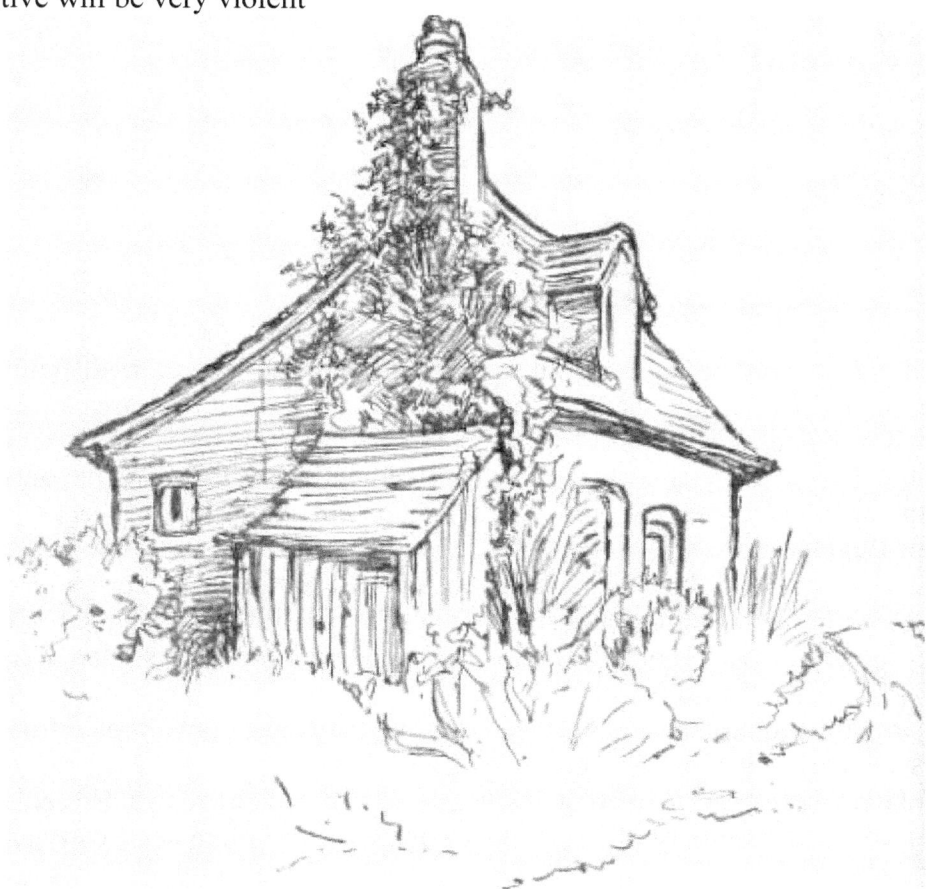

Fig. 62. When sketchinq a Cottage do not sit too near
and look exaggerated. Sit half a meadow away rather than at the front gate.

And if the cottage is complicated (that is, filled with detail, the thatch deep and overhanging, the creepers thick and concealing the shape of the wall, and the little lattice-windows nearly hidden from view), draw a portion of the cottage—a 144

Sketching Out of Doors

corner of the eaves and one window, a portion of the roof and the queer old chimney, the porch with its potted plants and window-seat, or the well-head with its dripping rope and

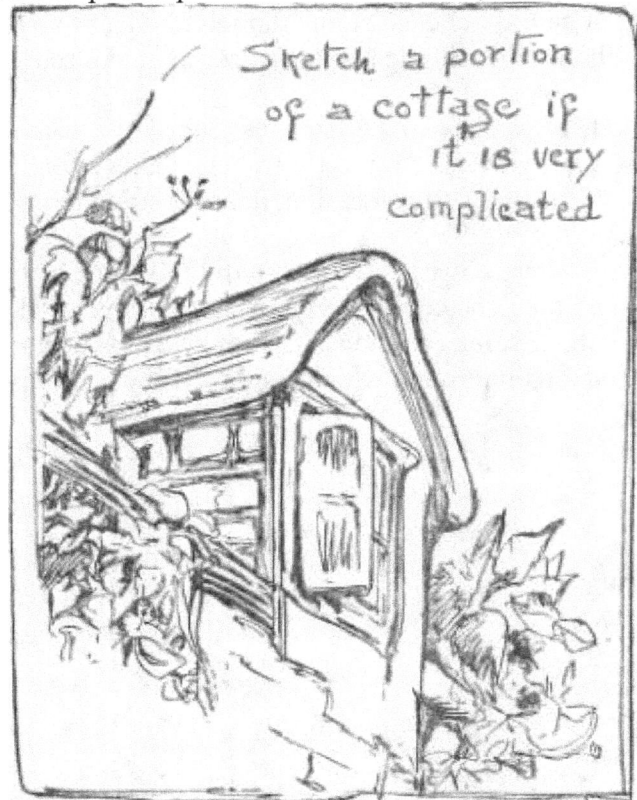

Sketch a portion of a cottage if it is very complicated

Fig. 63

shining pail. And a word of advice about a garden. There is nothing more difficult than garden scenes. The subjects are many, the lights are often broken, the shadows are confused. Content yourself with a woodshed, or portion of a summer-house, a few mossy steps, a garden roller, a corner of the terrace, a wheelbarrow, or a cluster of pots and a trowel. At the outset ask yourself whether the object you intend to draw will best fit an oblong or upright sheet of paper.

Drawing for Beginners

If you wish to draw a tall subject, such as a tree, a narrow building, an upright flower or figure, hold your sketch-book in an upright position. If you intend drawing a long-shaped subject, a reclining figure of a person or animal, a wide-spreading building, a stretch of low-lying ground, hold the book open at the full width of the page.

Beginners are prone to dash at a subject, and, finding they have drawn it on a smaller scale than they intended, add other details until the page is filled.

But why fill the whole page ? An artist's sketch-book is a book of scraps. He seldom carries his sketches up to the margin of his paper. One page may, and often does, carry an amazing variety of subjects.

If you decide to do

Fig. 64. The Well-head nij.ii .

^ a small sketch keep to

that intention. Should you feel unhappy because a wide margin surrounds your small sketch, frame the sketch with a lightly drawn pencil line.

It is astonishing how important are these apparently trivial matters, how much they influence the sketch for good or ill.

We will presume that you have arrived at your destination and are sitting in a shady place, faced with a bewildering number of beautiful things. After fixing and unfixing your mind many times you at length decide to draw something 146

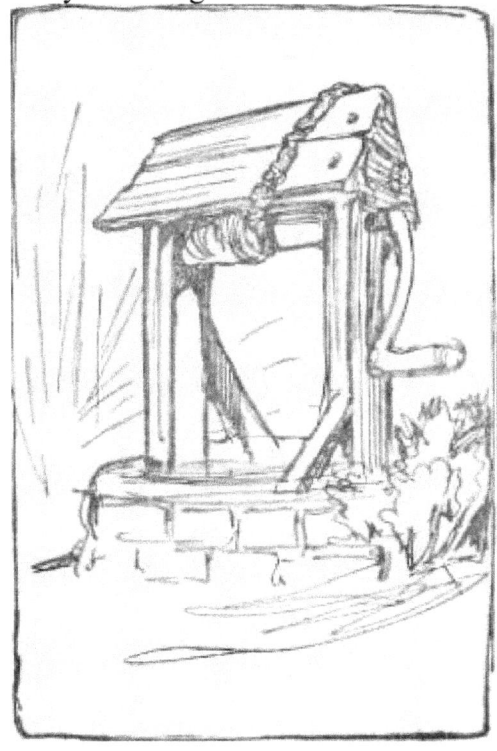

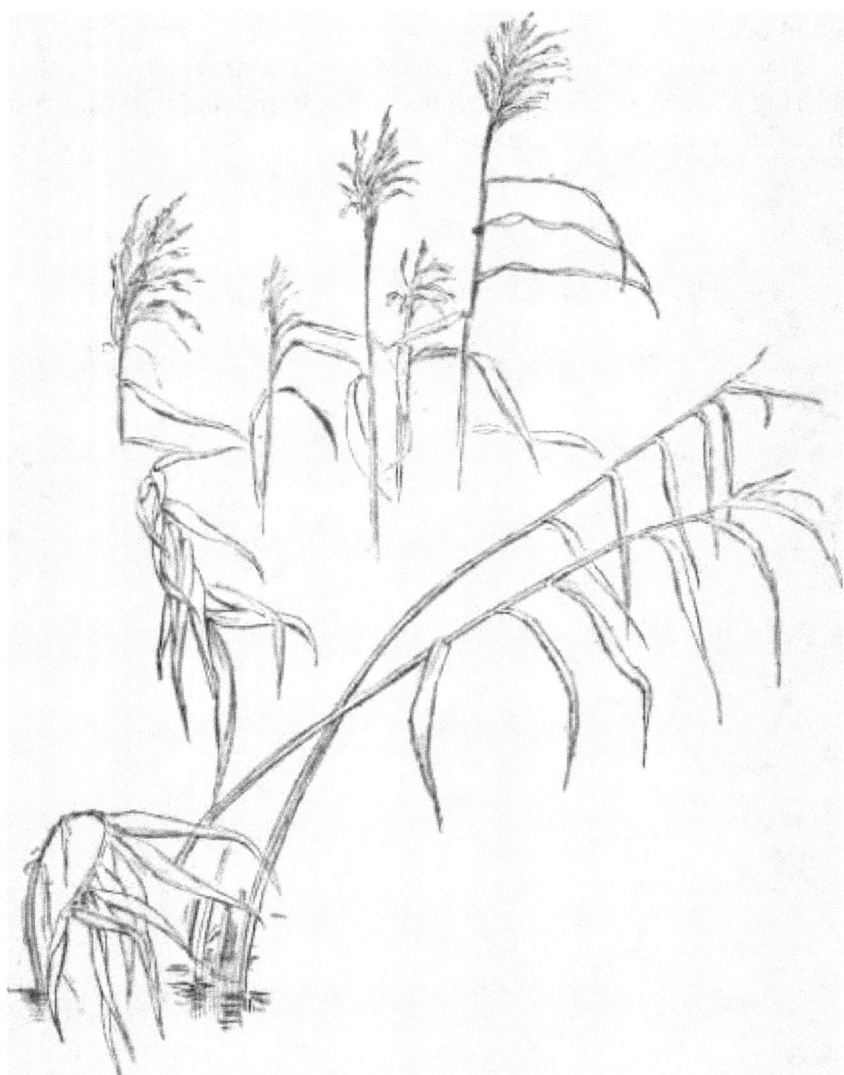

Fig. 65. Flowering Rushes
Drawing for Beginners

that is close at hand—a tiny clump of white flowers with feathery foliage, golden disks, and silvery petals growing humbly near the shorn stubble of the cornfield. It is a wise selection. Being of a lowly habit, the flowers will not be tossed and stirred by the wind, and so worry you at the very outset of your task. Moreover, the flowers have simple forms. They resemble tiny umbrellas with long handles. Draw first the shape and curve of the slender stem, then the circular gold centre, then the ' mass ' shape of the petals, dividing up each petal later, noting their wayward manner of growing.

After this your eye probably will be attracted by the gorgeous berries of the woody nightshade twisting its jewels round the ash stump and fence.

Draw the post and paling before the entwining tendrils and stalks. Wide-flung circles and rampant growth such as these lead the eye astray. But if the upright post and the cross-piece are once fixed on paper, then we have two simple and solid shapes lending contrast to the delicacy of the twining stem. If you began by drawing the stem of the plant, your eye might be misled by its strength and sinews. The foliage is vigorous. There is no feeble indecision in the sweeping curves and twisted heart-shaped leaves. Sketch the looping curves of the stem, then place the leaves, drawing from tip to tip on the outside edges. The berries gem the post in fanciful clusters, hanging from thread-like stems. Make the post firm and strong and shade it broadly. The richest tone, however, is reserved for the berries, and the leaves have a high polish.

It is undoubtedly a tempting subject for the brush. Mix your colours clearly. The berries will probably attract your first attention. Try to get the rich tints glowing and bright, then the colour of the leaves, allowing for their transparency by laying the paint freshly and broadly, and, when dry, adding some of the deep greens and browns of the background.

In all probability you will be disappointed with your first 148

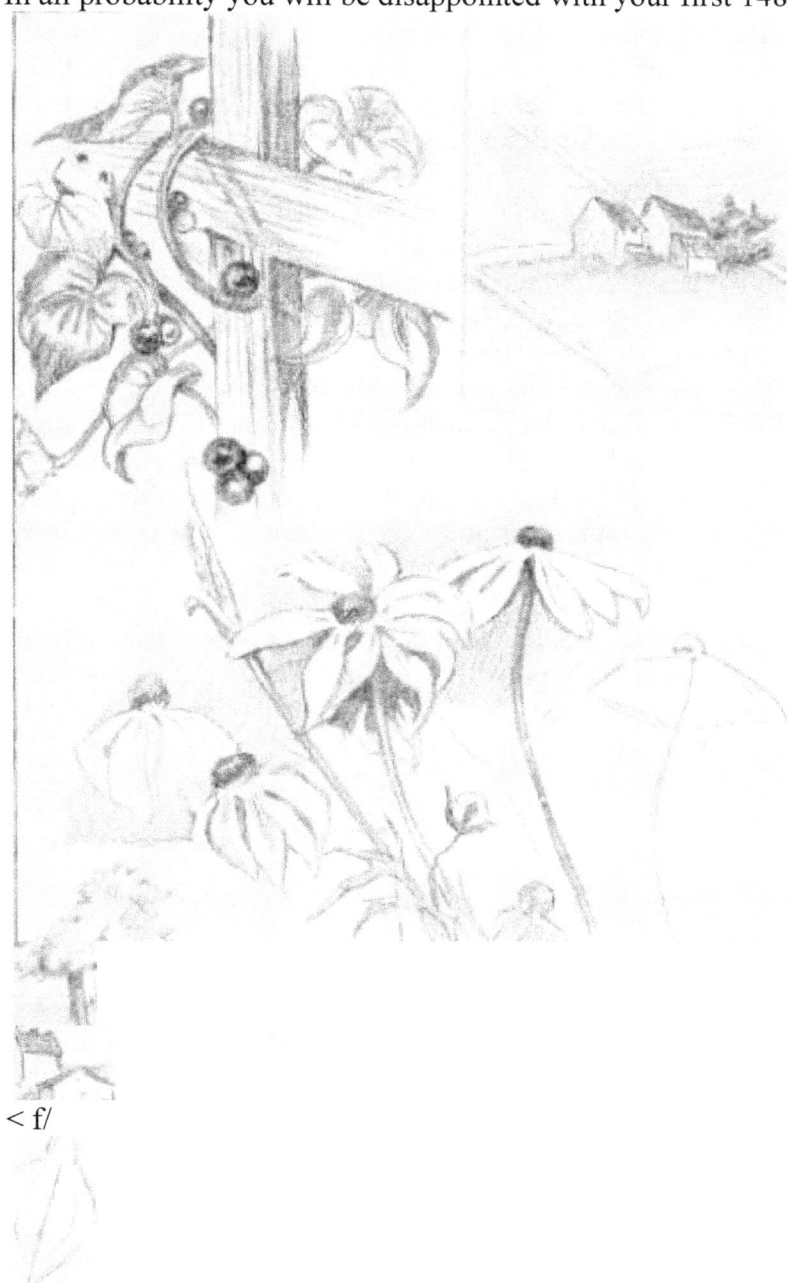

< f/

Fig. G6. Sketching Plants. Thumbnail Landscape Sketches
Sketching Out of Doors

efforts. The open air is one of the most exacting of conditions. The pure clear atmosphere reveals every blot and blemish. Your model challenges your poor attempts with its incomparable beauty.

Nevertheless, do not be discouraged, for you have this great encouragement, that if the painting or drawing looks at all passable out of doors it will look infinitely better within doors.

A clump of brilliantly coloured fungi is a delicious subject for pencil or brush, and one that is often found in the woodlands on a summer's day. What could be more simple in form than a toadstool, with its curved top and ridged surface beneath, and the bulbous-shaped stalk ? Being a rounded surface, one part will be lighter than another. Try to place the shading correctly. The edge of the fungus may be broken, chipped, splotched, or stained. Do not neglect any of these happy accidents. Dame Nature springs the most extraordinary surprises upon those bent on discovering her secrets, and if we are lax in small matters we shall miss the beauties in larger objects later on.

A trailing spray of blackberry is a charming subject for brush and pencil alike. Sketch the direction of the spray, then the mass of each spray, then the direction of each leaf in the spray.

When the sun is high in the heavens and the colours are faint and sickly, use your pencil instead of a brush.

A bit of a fence overhanging a piece of rock or sandstone, or a fence topping a grassy bank, or a stile dividing two fields, are equally interesting subjects for a sketch.

And here I must repeat myself at the risk of appearing wearisome. In no case do I wish you to choose necessarily the subject that I have discussed. My examples are chosen, first, because they are simple and direct; secondly, because they are within reach of the majority of young artists ; and, thirdly, because they represent variations of themes found over a broad area.

Draw the nearest upright post, get the direction of the

Drawing for Beginners

farther ones, and the bars that link the three. If you are in doubt about the angle of the bars hold your pencil at arm's length and then you will note their direction. If you desire to check the perspective, lay your book on the ground and seek for a long piece of slender grass. Hold one end of the grass on the right of your drawing and above the top bar—

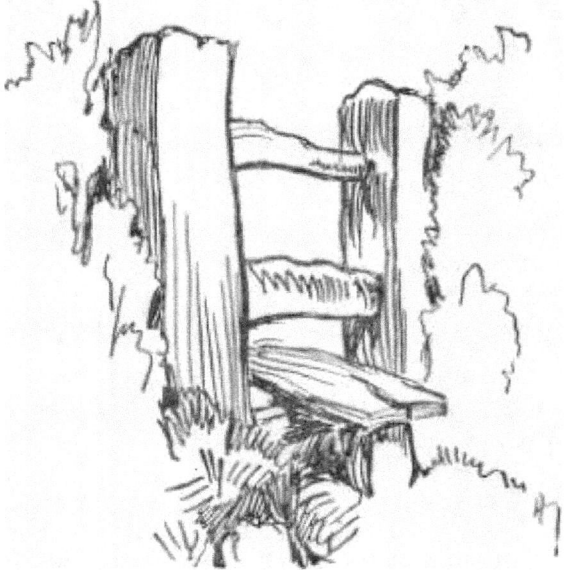

Fig. 67. Choose Simple Subjects

for that is the height of the eye in this little sketch (Fig. 68). The palings are curved and bent, and overhang the rock. The rock is a thick crumbling substance, its rounded edge projects, and its flat surface is slightly cleft and cast into shadow. Always draw the largest and most important parts first, such as the fence, and the rock, then add the grass tufting the summit, and the bramble swinging down into space. An oak-tree stands close by. Its roots have become welded into crevices of the rock, and it rears a twisted and graceful trunk bending slightly backward in its efforts to reach the sun. The rock and tree have characteristics in common. Sketch the mass of the projecting boulder, then the root of the tree, 150

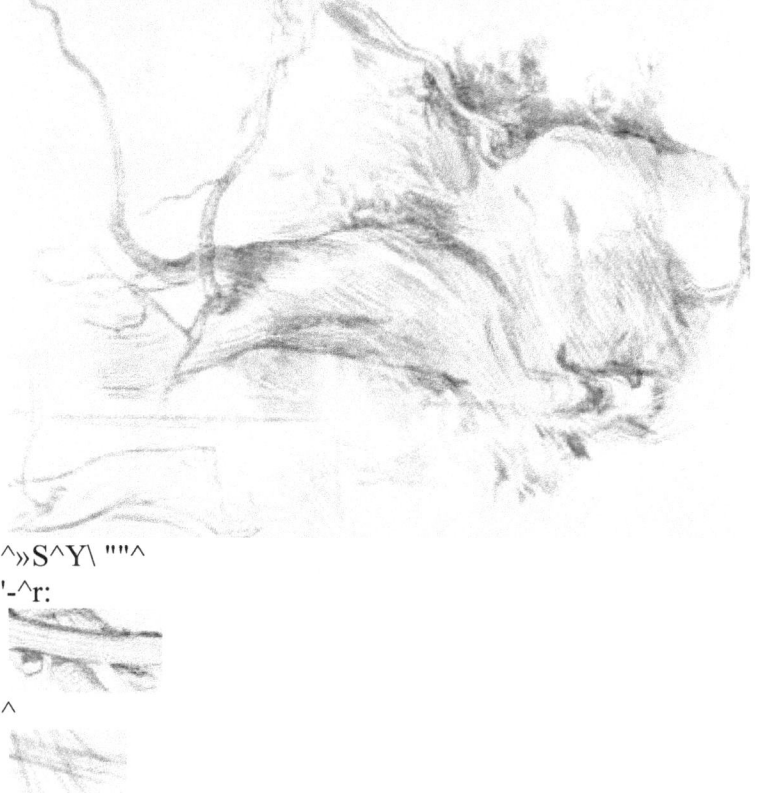

^»S^Y\ ""^
'-^r:

^

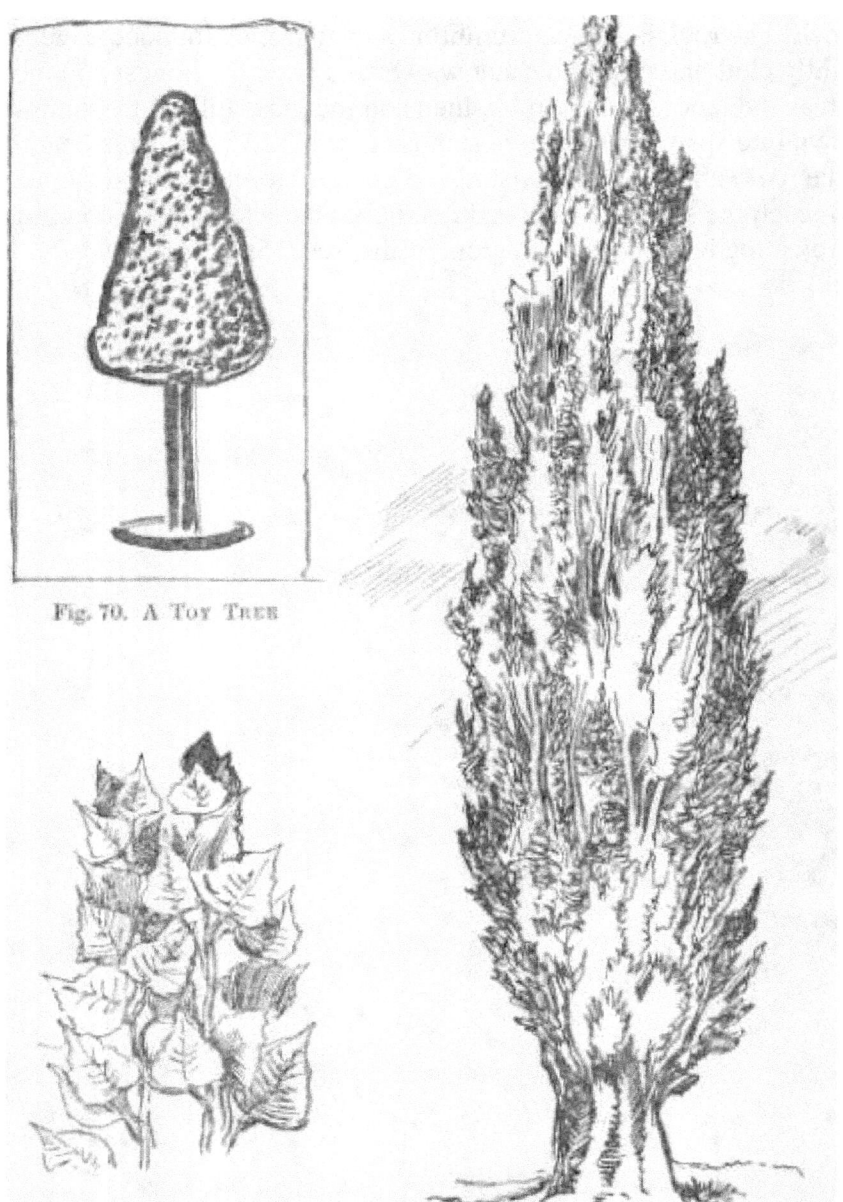

Fig. 70. A Toy Tree

Fig. 71. The Twig of a Poplar
Fig. 72. A POPLAK-TREE
Drawing for Beginners

mark the girth of the trunk, and draw the tree, building up with big curves, and noting the snake-hke twist of the slender branches. Mark the richest and deepest shadows, how the shadows break into shadow shapes of twigs, leaves, and grass.

Trees are difficult—that much is admitted even by Ian, who is devoted to his pencil.

" Oh, yes," said Ian, " I can draw horses, and men, and houses—but trees " and he paused thoughtfully.

To draw a tree from life, we must aim at the main structure. First draw the trunk, then the biggest branches, lastly the leaves.

There is a curious fact about trees that is worth recording, for it is often helpful when we are faced with the difficulties of grasping such a big subject. A branch of a tree will have all the characteristics of the tree itself.

Examine a small branch of an oak-tree—just a spray of leaves. Are they not sturdy, stout fellows ? Does not each twig strike out in an independent fashion—spreading strongly ? And is not the branch from which the twig is broken gnarled and twisted, stubborn and strong ? Walk some distance away from the oak-tree, then turn and observe it carefully.

Has not the tree the same characteristics as the branch, as the twig ?

Compare a twig of the poplar-tree with the tree itself. Is not the twig the same pyramid shape as the parent tree ?

It is a good idea to draw some twigs of a tree before trying to draw the tree itself. And this is an excellent subject when the weather is too cold to stand out of doors. Gather some bare twigs and carry them home and make careful drawings of the twigs. When spring is approaching you will find delightful little subjects in the swinging green and red catkins and the soft down of the pussy willows, and autumn provides us with a wealth of clustering nuts. Which studies will help you with your drawing of the tree.

When drawing the branch of a tree look from one side to 152
sketching Out of Doors
another side, from one angle to another angle. Build up the tree, as if it were growing under your pencil, with its roughness, nodules, and irregularities. Do not draw it too smoothly.

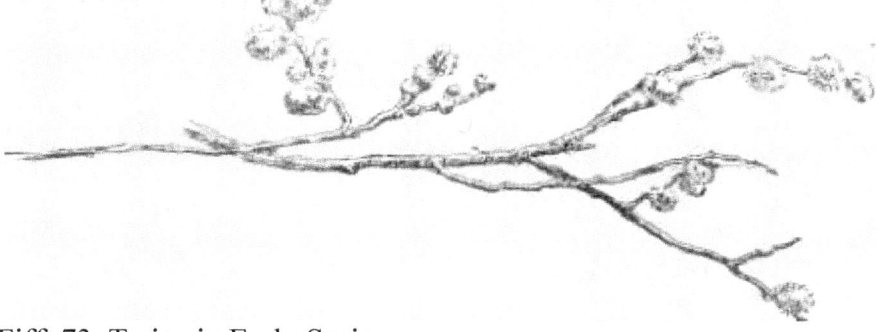

Fiff. 73. Twigs in Early Spring
like the polished leg of a table, but try to give it a natural sturdy growth.

Trees of a striking peculiarity are easiest to draw, as are people with strongly marked features. Such are Scotch fir-

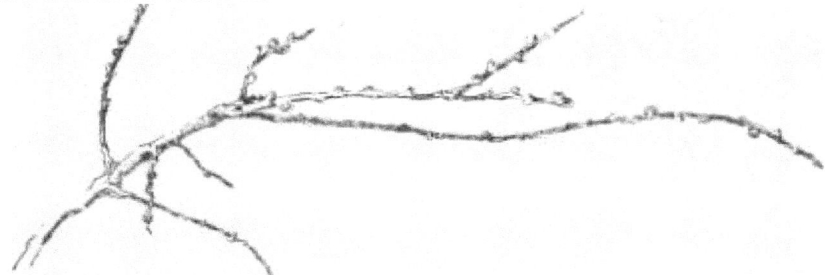

Fig. 74. Twigs of Trees without Leaves
trees with spiky needles, bony branches, and spiked trunks ; thorn-trees, small and twisted with the winds; oak-trees that have braved many a storm, with lopped branches and thin foliage.

You will find it interesting to sketch clumps of trees with the brush, either in black or white or colour—a few tall elm-trees in a distant meadow, or a fringe of fir-trees against
Drawing for Beginners

the sky. This teaches you to observe trees as a whole, and also impresses upon you the varied silhouette of each type of tree. Before we embark on the subject of landscape — for our horizon is broadening rapidly — we might spend a few moments discussing the sketching of ruined castles and old houses, which so often form an excuse for an excursion or a picnic, and of which we usually desire to carry home some little memento in the shape of a sketch.

Do not attempt complicated subjects. If the ruin is large and there are many turrets, many towers, flights of steps, and long passages, choose a modest fragment.

An angle of a wall against which twist the bony stems of ivy, one little window framing a patch of blue sky, a morsel of broken masonry, or a few steps—any of these will give you the materials you need.

154

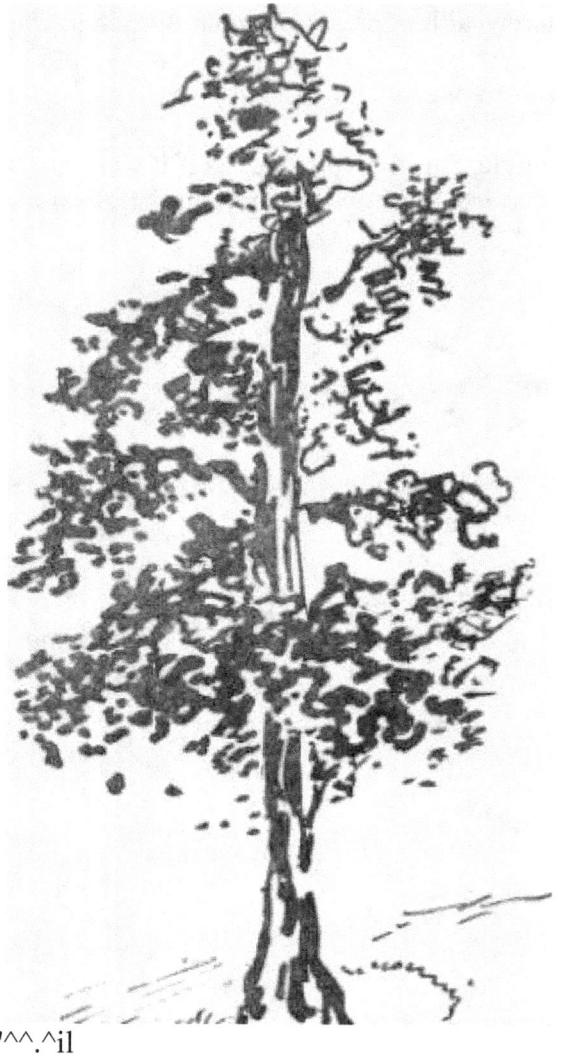

'^^.^il

Fig. 75.

A Tree drawn with a Tv/ig

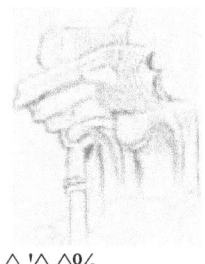

^.'^.^%

Fig. 76. A Silhouette of Treks. Sketches of Ruins 154

Sketching Out of Doors

A ruin invariably presents a crumbling, and softened, and somewhat elusive outline.

Rough in the whole mass, the general structure. Look for the highest point, compare the position of each thing with that point, then, having settled on the principal forms, look for the darkest dark and brightest light. Try to give an impression of the roughened surface. Draw the near shapes with care. If you sketch the masonry in the foreground with accuracy, then the parts that lie farther away can be more slightly drawn. The little bit of knowledge acquired by sketching something with care has a very solid value. Young sketchers faced with picturesque ruins are often tempted to try a tricky way of drawing.

We have all seen ruins ' touched in ' with sharp and telling bits of light and shade (apparently with ease and quickness), and we are fired with a desire to do likewise.

Believe me when I say that this is yet another pitfall for the unwary. The tricky methods of drawing never advance us one step. We must sketch only what we see, and that with care.

Look also for the perspective (another thing that is often ignored when sketching out of doors), check the top angle, and the base of the arch, also the fragment of carving, and the window in the wall with the near and projecting masonry.

Once we are fairly embarked on the subject of ruined buildings and trees, we feel more capable of trying real landscapes on a larger scale.

As an introduction to this more ambitious task, try your hand at thumbnail sketches. By thumbnail I mean tiny impressions of fairly large things, small houses, small trees, and the broadest indication of the curve of the ground, of fields, hills, and hedges. Not scribbles, but honest though minute sketches marking the chief characteristics : the lie of the ground, the position of the houses, the shape of roof (whether pointed or flat), the comparative size of the trees or shrubs, the tint or tone of trees, grass, roof, and walls. (See the examples in Fig. 66.)

Drawing for Beginners

Needless to say, distance does lend enchantment to the view in these thumbnail impressions, and they are far easier to draw when seen from a long distance. They are useful, too, for the few minutes' wait at a railway-station, or the short space of time spent at places when motoring. We can seize on a few of the salient or chief characteristics of the landscape and jot down tiny little pictures of houses and trees, hills and valleys, cliff-end and sea. The concentration necessary for these sketches will help us to grasp the chief characteristics of larger sketches.

A barn on the top of a sloping field, with a horse cropping the turf, and a morsel of a fence is as simple and direct a subject as one could find. Begin by sketching the slope of the ground, on which erect the shape of the barn, with its pointed roof, then the upright palings and short bushes, the horse with bent neck and the barrel shape of its rounded body.

Then as to the colour. A soft yellow light pervades sky, barn, grass, and horse, and on this float the rounded misty shapes of the grey clouds. The golden-brown roof is touched with cooler grey shadows on the near side, and the grass mingles with the reddish soil, something the same tint as the barn. The hedge is olive deepening to brown, and the flank and neck of the horse is a richer brown and olive sharpened with darker tints.

Light and shade out of doors is often most bewildering to the young student. The light is suffused, the air is clean and penetrating, shadows flicker and change.

Before beginning a sketch try to decide on the most definite bits of light and shade. Make a thumbnail sketch in the comer of your book if you will, in pencil or charcoal. Say to yourself, " The sun was out, the rays shone from that particular angle." Should you find the shadows and rays vanishing before the approach of large clouds, wait till the clouds pass. If, instead of passing, more clouds appear, then begin another sketch, for those clouds change the whole effect of the landscape. And how much they 156

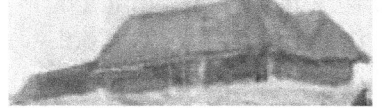

Fi^-. 77. A Si-\iri.K La.mi.-m'apk

Sketching Out of Doors

change it can be proved by referring to your thumbnail sketch.

Sketching on the seashore raises a fresh crop of difficulties and delights.

Boats are not easy things to draw when lying on the

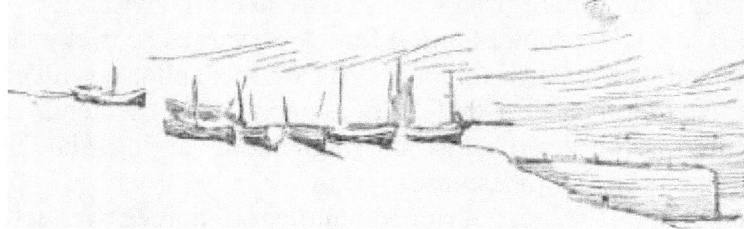

Fig. 78. On the Seashore

beach. " And that is the reason," Audrey explains, " why I prefer to draw them in the water."

Audrey is wily, but she doesn't altogether avoid her difficulties. If we are spared drawing the curve of the keel seen

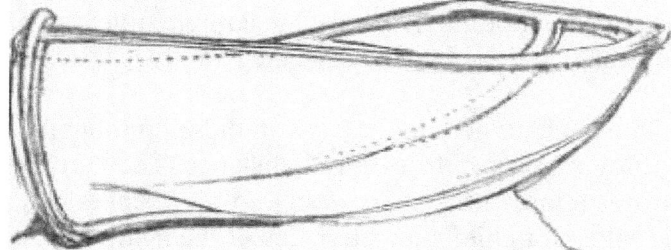

Fig. 79. The Shape that is hidden by the Waves

when the boat is exposed on the pebbles, there is all the rigging to lead us astray when the boat is in the water.

Moreover, we must know something about the shape that is hidden by the waves. As it is necessary to know the shape of the limbs covered by the clothes, and the branches covered with the leaves, so is it essential that we should know something of the build of the boat.

Should our artistic eye be attracted by the rich tints of

Drawing for Beginners

the sails of fishing smacks or long-shore boats, we must be careful not to neglect the rigging and shape of the sails.

I have a distinct remembrance of five drawings by five little ladies of a fishing smack with sails exactly the same shape fore and aft. Compare one sail with another sail. Begin by drawing the long sweeping curves of the hull, and then the angle of the mast. With these two facts carefully noted you won't go quite so far astray.

A beach, however, has a lot to offer besides the boats.

There are the capstans, and the high black houses where

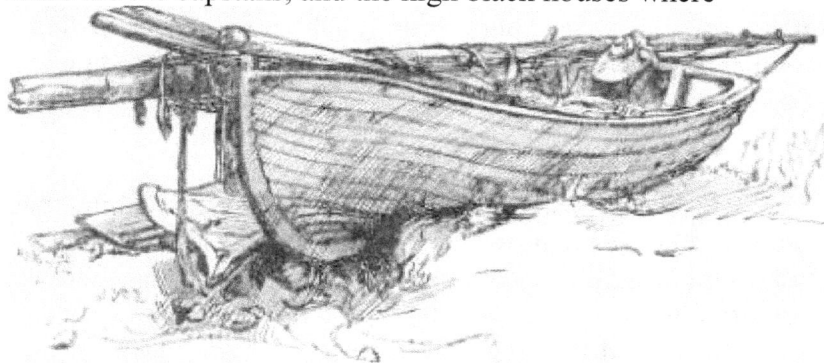

Fig. 80. Study of a Boat

the fishermen store their nets and tackle, and the lobster pots, and the heaps of coiled ropes. There are the rocks with their brown and mossy sides reflected in limpid pools ; crabs; shells of all descriptions; starfishes most obligingly lazy and quiet; sprays of deliciously coloured seaweed; sand castles, wooden spades, and scarlet buckets.

The beach is full of interesting little colour subjects. The air is clear, and the water reflects the light; bright caps and frocks, sails and seaweed, and the striped tents and scarlet buckets are all most attractive.

All our former discussions, our thumbnail sketches, pencil and chalk studies, and small landscapes in colour will render sketching by the seashore easier.

If we wish to sketch people sitting on the beach, or children 158
h^

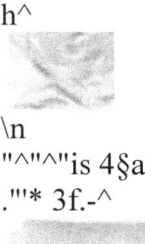

\n
"^"^"is 4§a
."'* 3f.-^

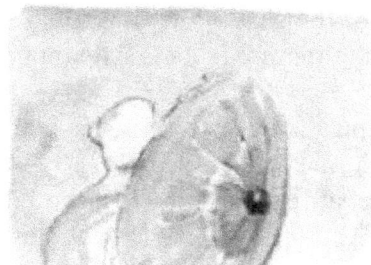

Fitf. si. On tiik Hkach
Sketching Out of Doors

playing, we shall have to be very rapid. It is wisest to sketch the stationary things first. If we desire to sketch Mollie or Rosemary by their tent or climbing the breakwater or rocks, do not let us waste time waiting. Sketch a bit of the tent, the breakwater or rock, then when Mollie or

Rosemary appears you will be prepared. Also, and I speak feelingly on the subject, they may dart away before you have painted the colour of their shoes, belt, or even dress—if so, write the colour tint in the margin.

But with the distant promontory and the glossy procession of rocks stretching into the sea, you will happily find something at rest. Only, remember this, never begin a sketch in the morning and finish the same at night. The light will be wholly different. Sketch a morning scene by morning, a noonday scene at noonday. If you have not done all you desired to do during those periods of time, put the sketch away until those hours recur. It is highly improbable that you will see the same effect again, for that is at once the bane and delight of sketching—its never-ending variety.

CHAPTER XIII

How to Catch a Likeness

THE word ' portraiture ' has an awe-inspiring sound. Portraiture is something that we may possibly attain in the far-off days when we are grown up.

Granted that the art of portraiture may be too ambitious for our humble pencil, yet there is every reason why we should train our eye, hand, and brain in the devious ways of catching a likeness. It will be a big help to the portrait-painting of the future.

The gift of catching a likeness, of transposing a recognizable drawing of a face to paper, is a very wayward gift. It does not follow that because we are artistic we shall have a jiair for portraiture.

There are some people—far from artistic—who can catch a likeness.

There are many amateurs (by which I mean those artists who do not take the artistic profession seriously) who have a wonderful facility for drawing a likeness ; also there are very clever artists to whom the gift of portraiture is denied. All of which demonstrates that this peculiar gift lies apart from other branches of art.

Whether we have this gift, or whether we have merely a feeling that we should like ' to try our hand ' at sketching a likeness, it is our plain duty to make a few efforts, for it stimulates three very valuable qualities: it promotes carefulness, accuracy, and reasoning.

Now we might consider a few methods by which we may become proficient in this very elusive art.

Possibly at some time of your life you have amused yourself with sketching the shadows of your friends. You placed 160

How to Catch a Likeness

a candle or some other light at such an angle that the shadow of the profile was thrown on a sheet of paper pinned on a wall; then by tracing the outline of the shadow with a soft pencil, or piece of charcoal, you secured an outline sketch. The size of the picture is its disadvantage. Who wants a life-sized outline of even their dearest and their best ?

But in a sizable, careful little outline drawing of a friend's features filled with black ink or paint we have an old-fashioned method of portraiture—the silhouette.

Silhouette drawing is not such a difficult art as it might at first appear. It is, moreover, an excellent stepping-stone to the broad highway of portraiture. And it has two very popular advantages: it is quickly done, and it is pleasing when done.

Armed with a smooth card or a firm-surfaced paper, a pencil, a fine brush or pen, ivory black paint or black drawing ink, we have all that is necessary.

Ask your model to move his head aside till he presents his profile, then take up your pencil and lightly sketch head, face, features, neck, and hair.

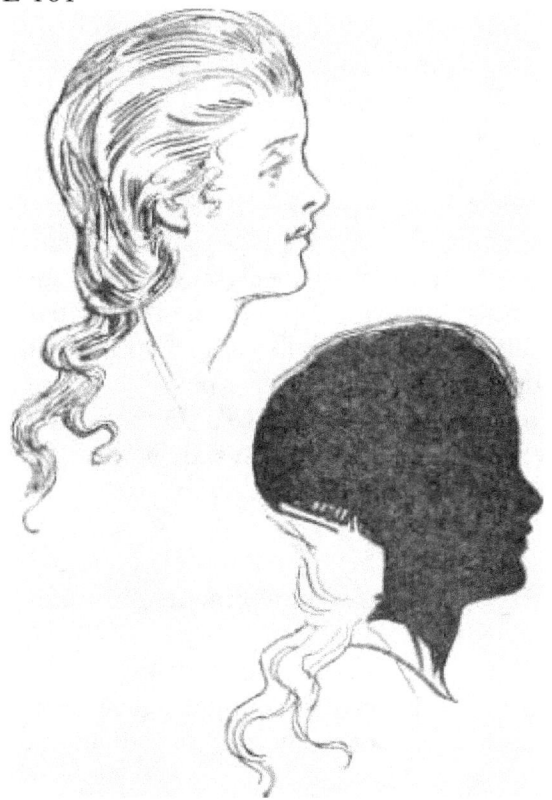

Fig. 82. A Light Sketch and a Silhouette

Drawing for Beginners

Look critically at the proportions of your drawing. Compare your sketch with your model. Is the face the right size ? Does the forehead creep too high to the crest of the head ? Examine the curve from the brow to the bridge of the nose. Is it sufficiently indented ? Carefully note the length of the nose, the shape and projection of the upper and lower lip, the curve of the chin, and the moulding beneath the jaw.

Do not make the neck too thick. You can add bulk to your silhouette, but you can't take it away. Carefully note the shape of the head.

There are various methods of ' finishing ' the neck. For our first essay the neck may be finished in a sloping curve beginning at the nape of the neck and sloping thence in a sharp curve downward to the forepart of the throat.

Always sketch the shape and position of the eye, also the nostril, ear, jaw, and corner of the mouth. This will help to check proportions and keep the features in place.

Having drawn the general shape of the coiled, floating, or clipped locks, the stubby moustache or beard, we shall find it easy to indicate the shape and character by the fine hairs projecting beyond the outline.

When the outline is ready to be filled with ink or paint (and supposing that paint will be your most likely medium) mix a good quantity of ivory black or sepia on the palette, and lay it on smoothly and evenly.

The silhouette filled and the outline firm and clear, you will note any projection of hair, frills, collar, lace, and ribbons. Draw these with a delicately fine line.

A word about the size of your silhouette. Do not make the drawing too large, but, on the other hand, do not aim at making it minute. If you sketch it no larger than a postage-stamp you will find it difficult to correct in the early stages ; and if you draw it very large you will lose the dainty effect that is the chief charm of the silhouette. One and a half inches high is a fairly reasonable size.

If you are not satisfied with your first attempts at a 162

How to Catch a Likeness

silhouette, do not despair, try again. Make another start— sketch a fresh model. Do not expect to succeed without practice, for remember you are up against a difficult problem. You are not merely trying to depict ' a nose,' ' a face,' ' a head ' ; but a very special nose, face, and head.

Moreover, there is another excellent reason for many attempts. There is no satisfactory method of correcting a silhouette. If we make a false step and give too long a nose, too thick lips, too square a jaw, we cannot afterward amend our mistake. It is of course possible to take a brushful of thick white paint and fine down our outline. We can also use a scraper (a very sharp knife) and scrape at the surface of the paper. But neither method will be satisfactory. The pure, hard, sharp outline is the hall-mark of a good silhouette. The one unforgivable sin is the ragged edge.

It is a thrilling moment when we can trace a likeness between our model and our silhouette. And I can truthfully say that, given a little patience and intelligent application, there is no reason against, and every reason for, that happy result.

The drawing of likenesses in silhouette (for there are many other subjects to which we can apply this fascinating little art—sprays of leaves, birds, or fluffy animals, grotesque and quaint figures, landscapes of fantastic description, to quote but a few) has this advantage. It hides defects.

The double chin, the dragged lines of eye, mouth, and nostril, the wrinkles of forehead and face, the untidy head of hair—all are softened and veiled with the kindly brush.

163

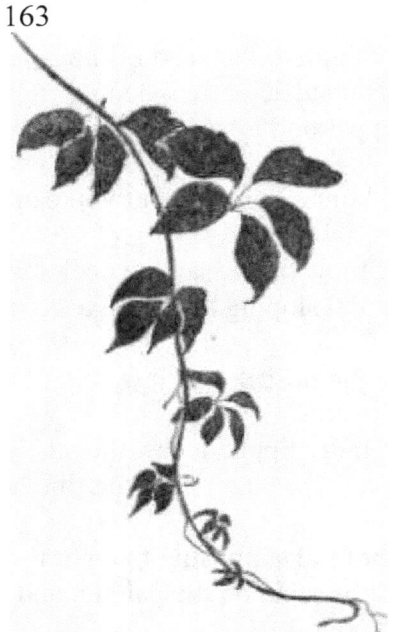

Fig. 83. A Spray of Leaves IN Silhouette
Drawing for Beginners

Once your interest is aroused in portraiture the art of the silhouette will not wholly satisfy your cravings. It is a charming but, it must be admitted, a limited art.

Now we are prepared to pass on to more ambitious subjects, and here I must offer a word of advice, for I do not want to make this difficult business of portraiture unnecessarily more difficult. We must go warily. The fascinating task of drawing likenesses is sometimes apt to give offence.

" That— my portrait! " said an old lady, ruefully regarding a drawing of mine. " Ah, well ! "—following up with a sigh—" I was considered rather nice-looking in my day." The sad result was that the old lady refused to pose again, and the rest of the holiday was wasted, so far as further endeavours at sketching a likeness were concerned.

It is just as well to bear in mind what was written of Sir Joshua Reynolds, the great portrait-painter of the eighteenth century:

His pencil was striking, resistless, and grand ;

His manners were gentle, complying, and bland ;

Still born to improve us in every part.

His pencil our faces, his manner our heart. ■<*

Compare our beloved Sir Joshua with the Chinese painter who, like most Chinese artists, was excellent at copying a likeness, defect and blemish complete, and to whom one of his sitters objected that he had not made him handsome enough. The painter replied, blandly but firmly :

" No hab got handsome face, how can hab handsome picture ? "

Supposing that it is your intention to sketch the likeness of a person who has what is sometimes called an unfortunate profile, you should not pitch on the particular position of a profile for choice.

The pencil says that my model has a small eye, snub nose, receding chin, and it records these facts remorselessly. It may not mean to be unkind. But the outline is such and down it goes.

164

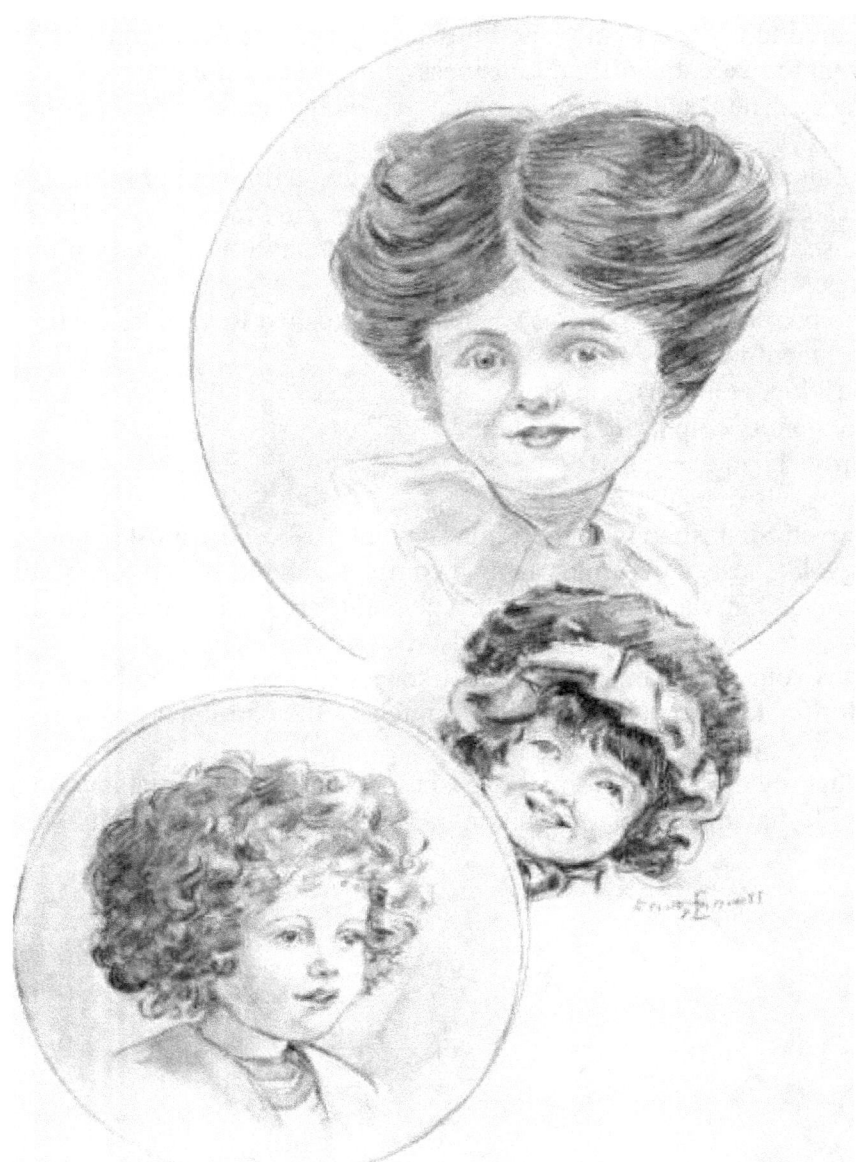

Fig. 84. Expression in Portraits

How to Catch a Likeness

In such a case a three-quarter view, or even a full face would be wiser—and kinder.

Some people run away with the idea that portraiture is merely seeking out defects and exaggerations—but that is caricature.

We should look for the pleasing characteristics. We do not, it is true, wish to draw the ' pretty pretty ' face—the chocolate-box style of beauty—but there is no reason against recording pleasant rather than unpleasant facts. It takes a very big man to rise above facial defects, and an Oliver Cromwell to wish to be painted ' warts and all.'

We will presume that a group of girls and boys are waiting primed ready to sketch portraits. And one has been selected, or very good-naturedly volunteers, to sit as a model. Some one remarks, not very politely and a little despairingly, " There's absolutely nothing in Rachel that isn't just ordinary! "

Ordinary ; what is ' ordinary ' ? ' Common, customary,' says the dictionary (among other things).

Is Rachel ' ordinary ' compared with the rest ?

Look swiftly from Rachel's lips to those of Patricia. Rachel's upper lip is ' ever so short' compared with Patricia's rather pouting mouth ; and her eye—she has a fine-lidded eye, with clear, open pupil. John's eye is slightly hidden by his brow, and his iris is dark. And compare the three pairs of eyebrows. Rachel's extend thickly from the nose to the outer edge of the eye, Patricia's are thin and silky, and John's are queer little dabs of hair, one of which gives a humorous twist and expression to his face.

Expression, ah !—now we are getting to the root of this portrait business. . . .

Let us break off for a moment.

When we have seen a portrait by a famous artist—or the reproduction of one—what lingers most clearly in our minds ? Does not the expression haunt our memories ?

To quote a few of the greatest portraits in the world: Think of the gentle austerity of Titian's Doctor, the shy grace of Velasquez's Baby Princess, the demure questioning

Drawing for Beginners

of Reynolds' Strawberry CHrl, and the tragic dignity of Rembrandt's Old Woman.

I doubt if you could give the faintest description of the features of one of these portraits.

And now let us look at our portrait of Rachel or Margery.

That may be Margery's eye, nose, mouth, chin, hair, and ear, but if we have missed Margery's mischievous look, the wicked twinkle in her bright eye, the twitching curve of her lips, and the jaunty tilt of her glossy head ; in short, if we have not captured her expression, Margery's portrait is no portrait at all.

When we draw likenesses we must not labour first with one feature and then with another, but try to grasp everything together.

We begin by noting any peculiarity, such as the poise of the head on the shoulders, afterward roughing out the angles of the features, or the arrangement of large masses such as a woman's hair or a man's beard; then we confine ourselves to the drawing of the features.

There is no sense in racing along if by nature you are a plodder. We must all ' gang our ain gait.'

Personally, however, I have a feeling, or rather a conviction, that if I cannot capture something of the likeness in the earliest stages it will always elude me.

From the very first attack the angle of the head, the placing of the neck on the shoulders, the cock of the eye, the droop of the lip.

There is another point to bear in mind. Do not get too easily discouraged. Don't be depressed if your efforts do not gain immediate success. You must try many times before you can hope to be proficient.

After all, you do not expect to play a sonata of Beethoven's, or to write a thesis on an abstruse subject, or to compose an exquisite lyric—without practice.

And remember too that you are in search of the unexpected. It is your business to find and record facts usually unnoticed by persons who are not artists. 166

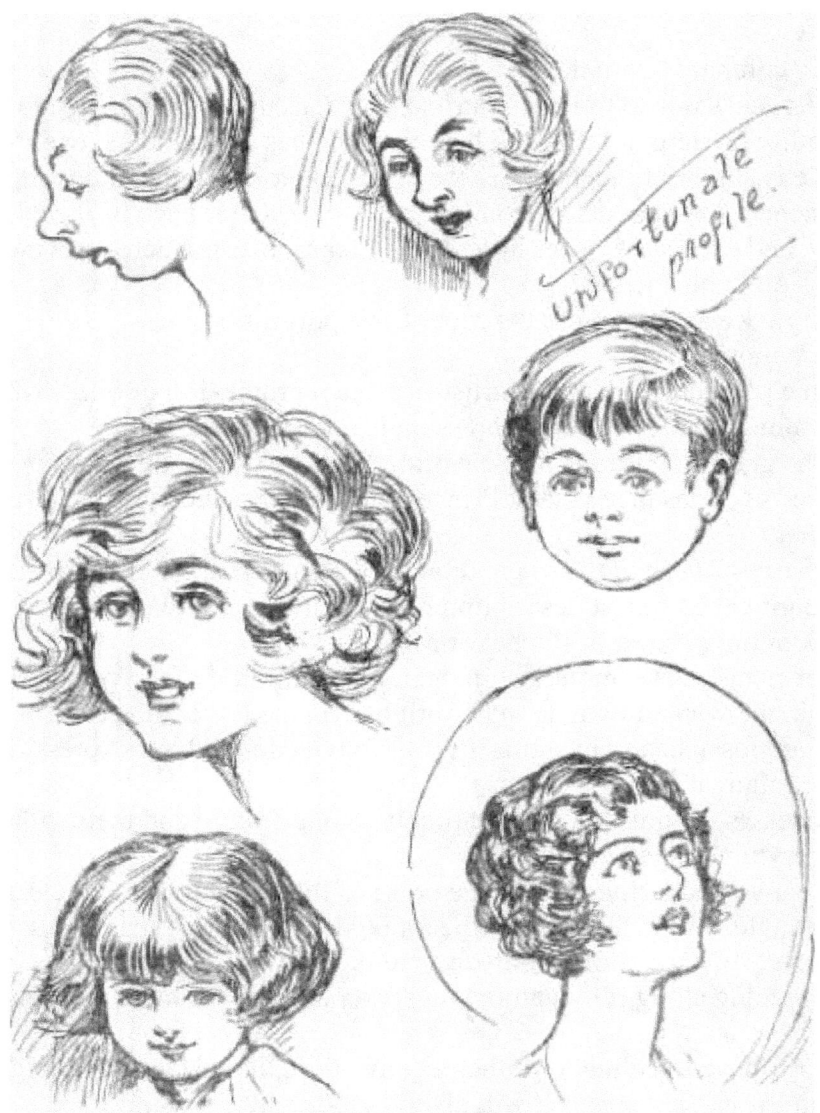

unfortunate profile.

Fig. 85. Likenesses

Drawing for Beginners

Naturally some people are more easy to draw than others. Those with marked characteristics are the easiest of all. If you have any choice in the matter, choose some one with striking features, the drawing of which you cannot miss.

Take your subtle and more delicate studies later.

When I was a child I was very fond of copying photographs of celebrities from papers and magazines —not such a bad method of training the eye and hand in the curious ways of catching a likeness. And I remember copying a charming profile of a certain little princess (her daughter is now as old as the picture to which I refer), and her Royal Highness's ear was of a prodigious size. If ■^ " some one looked at

Fig.86. PEX-POKTBAiTO^LomsAM. Alcott ^^^ drawing without

recognizing the subject I would say indignantly, " Oh, but you must see who it is by the ear! " That I knew to be right. I was quite annoyed when a friend said with an air of surprise, " But I have never noticed the Princess's ear was so large; surely you are mistaken."

You must be prepared for that sort of criticism. If you make it your business to observe things that are out of the way, you are certain to meet with such remarks.

It is not only with eyes, nose, ears, mouth, expression that 168

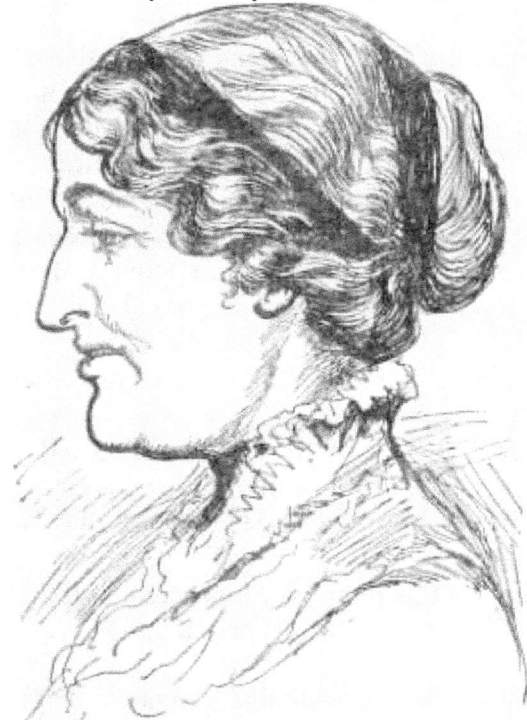

How to Catch a Likeness

we must be observant, but we must note and compare the little unobtrusive characteristics and traits which distinguish individuals.

One sits erect, another lolls in a languid manner, another slouches into awkward attitudes. Some perk up their chins, or incline their heads slightly to one side. All of which are valuable helps to the getting of a good likeness.

It will lessen your difficulties if you remember to leave a space between yourself and your model. It is a sheer impossibility to see such a large object as a human being in proportion unless we remove ourselves a good many paces away.

If you place yourself close to your model, as young artists often do, you will see the top of the head, the top of the shoulder, the upper part of the body, and the feet. You will have the curves of the features very much accentuated, and it will be exceedingly difficult to get the whole picture ' in drawing.'

Artists when painting full-length portraits invariably pose their models a good distance away from their easels, and sometimes the models are placed on a low platform. We can dispense with platforms, but we cannot dispense with distance.

Naturally, when drawing the head you can sit near your model with safety. But when the object is large then you must move away until you get a good and comprehensive view.

I would not discourage you from drawing people who happen to be near if you feel a strong desire to attempt it. Do not resist the impulse to sketch some one who is bending over the same table as yourself, for example, but bear in mind that you are close to your model and make allowances.

It may be that you are not able to procure many sitters, that you live where there are very few people, and your opportunities of observation are therefore very restricted. That need not prevent you from drawing portraits. You must study the few. Even the greatest artists have contented themselves at times with a moderate range of subjects. And

some of the finest portraits are the portraits of the artist's relations and friends. Gainsborough painted his own daughters. Some of Rubens' best portraits are those of his wife Helena ; Rembrandt was for ever painting himself, and his clever rubicund face eyes us shrewdly from many a canvas ; and there is the painting of Van Dyck himself with the sunflower.

And so we narrow our portrait-drawing down to ourselves. If you are driven to the drawing and painting of yourself (and it is always easier to draw other people, because one cannot back away from one's self and so get a good ' general' view), and you are presumably standing before a looking-glass, remember this—you are drawing yourself not actually as you are but a size smaller.

A mirror reduces and makes us appear smaller, and this reduction forces the little things upon us at the expense of the more important.

It is very easy to prove this. Stand a few paces away from the looking-glass and ask some one to dab with a colour-brush the reflection of your head, the crest of your head and the tip of your chin, and measure this space with the brush against your own face. You will find that the looking-glass face is about a third the size of your own.

The art of catching a likeness, then, brings us to this point. We must first of all have good ground-work. We must practise drawing faces and features of various people in various positions.

We must draw with knowledge, not guessing at things, sketching at random and trusting to luck.

We must be prepared to catch the fleeting look; we must hold ourselves, as it were, on the very tiptoe of expectancy for the smile, the glance, the pout, the thoughtful or mirthful expression.

A line well expressed will send our hopes soaring high, and a line faulty and wrong will dash all those hopes to the ground. Never be daunted by mistakes, but take your courage in both hands and persevere. 170

CHAPTER XIV

Action and Composition

WHEN I was very young I cherished intense admiration for a certain httle friend who was fond of drawing birds—not single studies of birds, but birds in flight. Flicks flick, flick —so many swift touches of the pencil and the birds sprang into sight, crowds of little

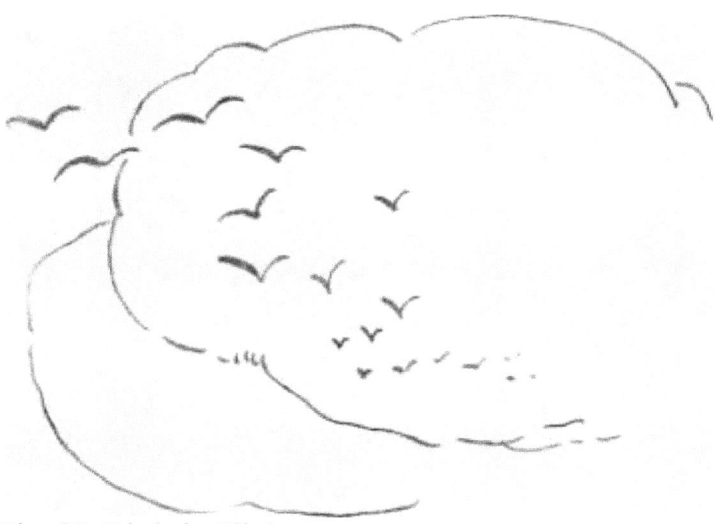

Fig. 87. Birds in Flight

birds with curved wings against solid chunks of rolling clouds. Have you not drawn them yourself ? Have you not sometimes watched the birds crossing the sky and tried to follow their flight with a pencil ?

Fishes are not so easily studied, but sometimes they can be observed in tanks, or in the wonderful Nature pictures of

Drawing for Beginners

the ' movies,' and fishes swimming in water bear resemblance to birds flying in the air. We are inclined to neglect our opportunities of studying

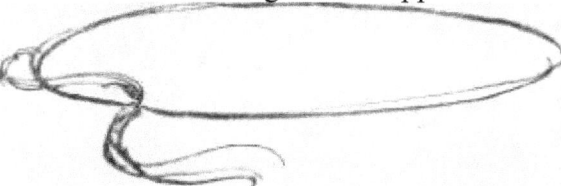

Fig. 88. Pattern formed by Children playing a Round Game

things in action. Now that most of us can see in the cinematographs things moving as they never (seemingly) moved before, we should be all the better primed for this very

fascinating study. ffi \ When crows caw and circle round tall trees,

I /'I or pigeons rise in great sweeps and eddies

from the ground, it seems as if they were weaving patterns against the sky, and if each little beak held a gossamer thread there would be an exquisite pattern floating against the clouds.

Given sufficient motives or reasons for gathering groups together, then the result must be patterns shaping and reshaping.

Consider—from this particular point of view —a group of children playing a round game, a ring of swaying bodies from which one or two units separate and dart to and fro, inter-Patte'rn FORMED wcaviug aud making another variation of the BY A Country same shape.

Or old country dances and games in which two long rows of people face each other, and become linked by individuals coming from opposite ends and meeting and dancing in the centre.

Or again : a crumb dropped in a bowl of water containing fish, and tiny glistening bodies moving in star-like shapes. 172

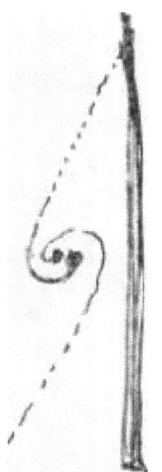

Fiff. 89

<rr\

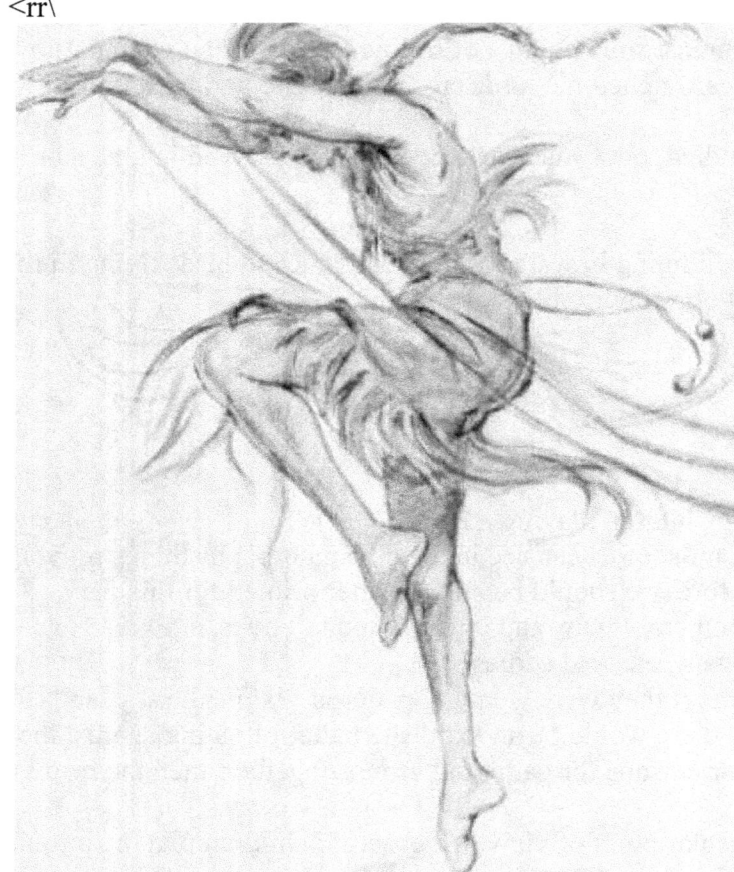

Action and Composition
Birds in the air and fishes in the water form shapes by the grouping of their bodies.
Children chasing a butterfly or a ball; children playing

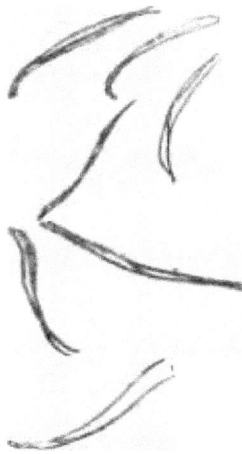

Fig. 91. Pattern formed by the Movement of Fish in the Water

with kites ; children rushing along a flat surface bowling their hoops ; a flock of startled geese rising from a marshy mere; a cluster of grubbing sparrows among the puddles of a muddy street; a flock of sheep chased by a dog; a slow procession of cows moving along a lane—all and each move in a certain pattern.

You will ask, is it possible for anything to move without making some continuous pattern ? The answer is that there is no end to movement. We dance, and our arms and legs follow the curves and actions of our body. We run, and the same thing happens in a different degree. The dog wags his tail, not in one, but in many continuous movements.

173

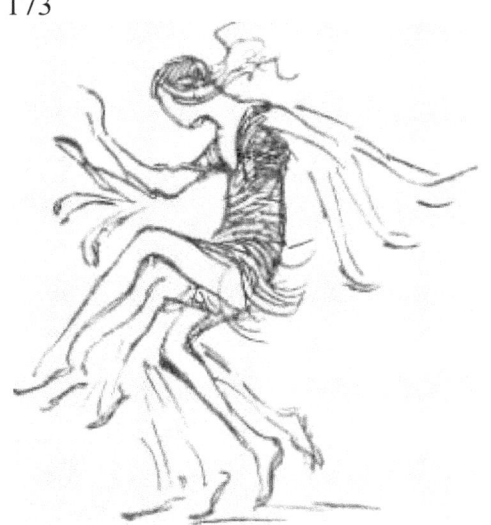

Fig. 92. We Dance

Drawing for Beginners

When we wish to plan a drawing or painting we must put

this sense of movement into our picture. Obviously our

figures and objects will be stationary, but there must be a sense of movement that carries the eyes pleasantly throughout the whole. We must make patterns, and evolve action or rhythm between each object.

If we pick up a book, attracted by the first page or the first few chapters, and we find that there is nothing further to hold our interest, what do we do but discard the book ? So it is with a picture. We must arrest the eye. But we

must also hold the interest pleasantly within the picture.
We must not put something down which says " Stop ! " and
then treat the subject in such a barbarous manner that
the eye wanders dissatisfied out of the
picture. We must,
like the writer of the
book, give something
more than a first
attraction. Take as
an example the
simplest instance,
that of a sheet of
paper containing an
upright line.
If we have one

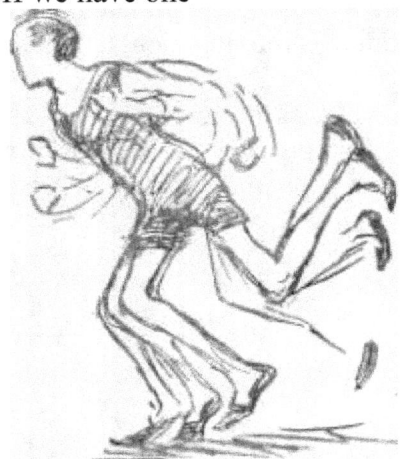

Fig. 93. We Run

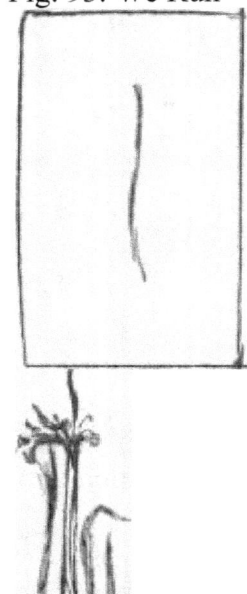

Fig. 94. Improving an Empty Space

sharp line in the centre and no more, the space appears empty on either side, but add a few natural lines and the space is pleasantly broken. 174

Action and Composition

If we sketch a cottage on a plain and put it down squarely on our paper, the cottage in the centre with a tree on either

side and a stretch of _

flat country beyond, how foolish and empty the flat plain appears !

But shift the cottage to one side, and search for some little ' incident' (or action), though it is but a pathway, to impart an interest Fig. 95. An ' Empty ' Picture

to the larger space.

Then the sketch becomes at once more satisfactory—it holds the eye. Firstly, we are attracted by the cottage and trees massed pleasantly together; secondly, by the

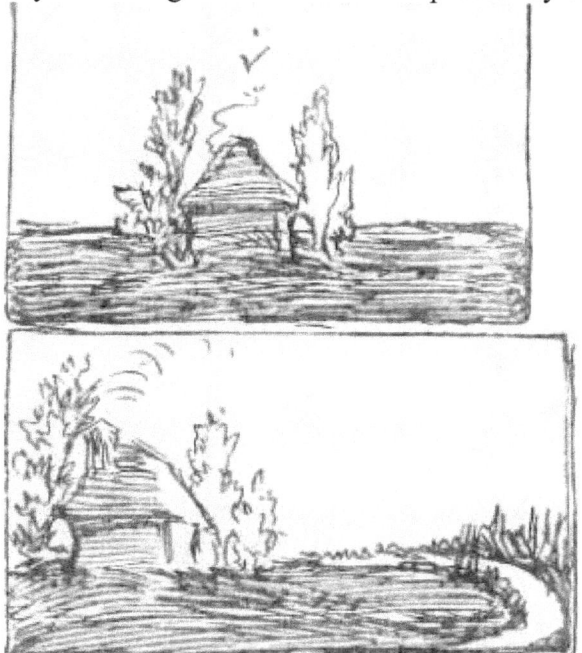

Fig. 96. An Interesting Rearrangement

pathway, which brings the eye back again to the centre of the picture.

Nature has her compositions; we merely select from them with a little care. We do not aim—the Fates forbid !—at rearranging Nature. But we do aim at choosing a happy time, or, rather, sketching a good subject at a happy moment.

Drawing for Beginners

Landscape, figure, domestic pictures, historical scenes— whatever the subject demanding our attention—this problem

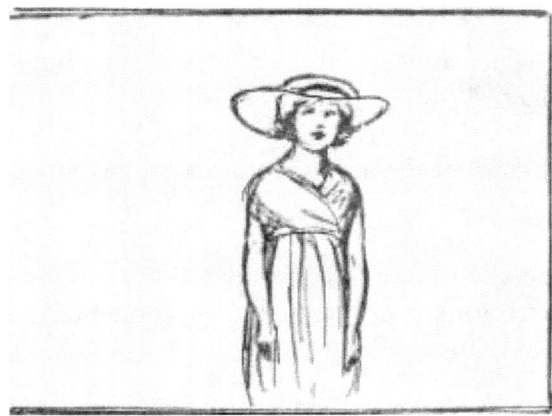

Fig. 97. A Single Figure Poorly Composed

arises—^what arrangement, plan, or movement will you give your picture ?
Let us assume for the sake of argument that you wish to

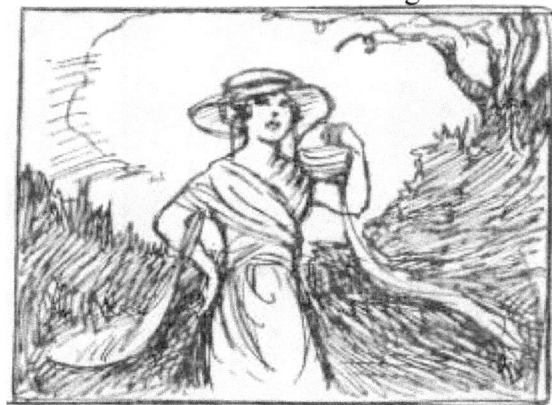

Fig. 98. The Effect of Composition

draw the single figure of a girl. We sketch her in a simple position, standing with her arms to her sides, and more bulk at the head than the base ; how silly she looks—how meaning-

176

Action and Composition

less! But give some reason for this particular picture— the flowing of a scarf, the widening of the design at the base, an uplifted arm holding a basket, clouds floating behind her head, and sloping banks on either side. Then the eye is caught first by the central figure, next by the shawl, arm, clouds, and led at last to the banks and trees.

Possibly you might object to that particular pose. You want something quieter and more restrained; in fact, you wish to keep to the original pose of the slim upright figure. Very well; but would it not be wise to place your figure in an upright space, and introduce either a misty effect with delicate lines, or else something that will help your figure ?

I have seen it stated that arranging ' pictures' is a very different affair from arranging simple studies of ' ordinary' subjects; that one could not possibly apply the same ideas to both.

But this is a false notion, and precisely where many people go wrong.

After all is said and done, your so-called ' ordinary' subjects, your pots and pans, your flowers and books, may be the subjects in which you excel. For everything to which we direct our attention should result in a picture, must result in a picture. It may be a bad picture if we do not take the laws of Nature into consideration, but a picture nevertheless it will be.

We will take the subject of three pots, one large and two of a medium size.

These we place in a row, the large pot in the centre and the two smaller pots on either side (Fig. 100).

You can see for yourself that this is an unsatisfactory M 177

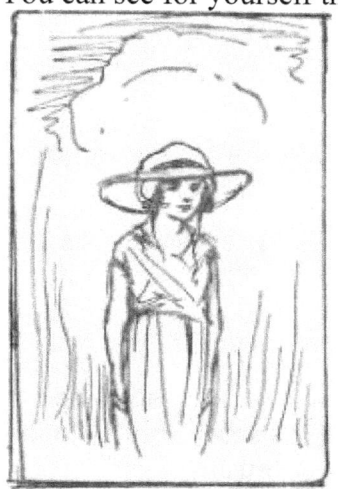

Fig. 99 Another Arrangement
Drawing for Beginners

arrangement. The eye lands on the central object and then slides out of the picture. Better to group the pots together

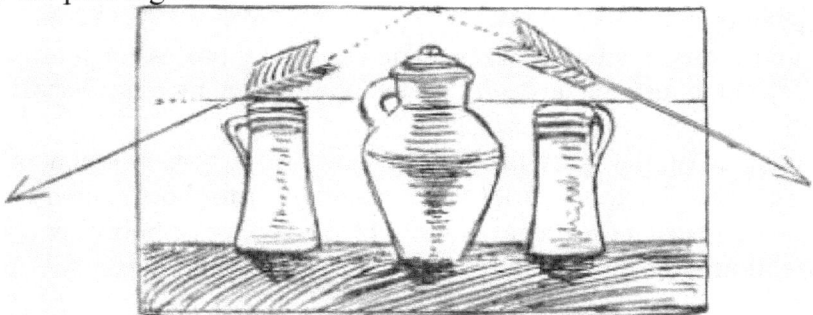

Fig. 100. A Group of Pots

in a less mathematical manner, making a more irregular pattern (Fig. 101).

Had the two small pots been of different heights, the first arrangement would have balanced itself better.

Or, if we strongly desire an oblong instead of an upright composition, we could place two of the pots together and the third a space apart, linked by a fragment of ribbon, a feather, a spray of leaves (Fig. 102). The study of a simple subject, such as a flower with some leaves, is an easy introduction to composition. First choose an oblong, circular, or square space, and say to yourself that in that space you will sketch the flowers or the leaves. Try to fill the space pleasantly. The word ' fill' must be taken with reservation. I do not mean that you should aim at crowding a varied number of flowers or leaves together, but at arranging a spray, a very slender spray with a few leaves, and selecting its characteristics, 178

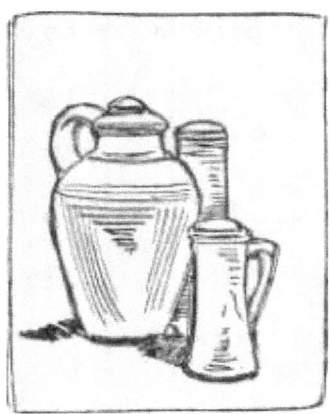

Fig. 101. An Upright Composition

Action and Composition

Having sketched your study with pencil or brush, consider it well. Is the composition lopsided ? Have you crowded too much into one place ? Have you left a space crying aloud for some attention, though it l)e but a few short strokes of the pencil or brush ?

Turn your drawing upside down. Look at the picture as a pattern, regardless of other interest, and try to consider it as such. Or, again, collect a number of small objects, a few vases, ornaments, shells, ribbons, books, hats, balls, gloves, candles (and candle-shades), and, arranging those which harmonize together in groups, make swift sketches merely for the sake of arranging patterns, of practising composition.

Whether we wish to push on our studies and become eventually professional artists, or

whether we only intend to amuse ourselves by sketching now and again, we shall certainly have to give attention to these considerations.

If you are a professional artist, the space that you intend to fill with pen or pencil bulks very largely on your horizon. If you illustrate stories for magazines, or for books, then the arrangement, or composition, demands a great deal of thought. The editor or publisher specifies the number of square inches allotted for your picture, and it is by no means an easy task to fill that space satisfactorily.

If portraiture is your special forte, then it is essential to arrange the composition so that it fills the canvas and paper pleasantly. Sometimes I have seen portraits arranged with so little care that the unfortunate subjects seem to be slipping out of the picture.

179

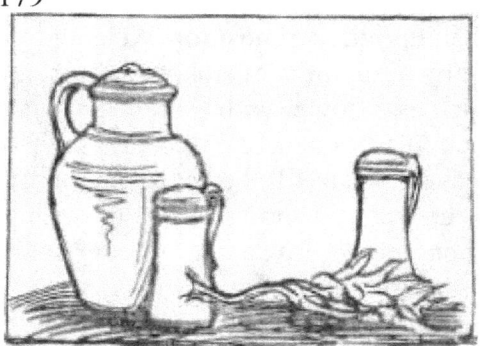

Fig. 102. An Oblong Composition

Drawing for Beginners

The biggest spaces should be given to the most important part of the picture.

Several young artists gathered together would find it helpful to enter into a friendly competition in a particular subject to be drawn in a specified space. They would work independently and would eventually compare their sketches and discuss the various points.

It is remarkable how seldom similar sketches agree. Our neighbours' interpretation of the same thing often arouses great astonishment in us, and gives us much food for thought.

As time goes on our minds will naturally incline toward good composition.

Nature's beautiful ' arrangements,' her ' composition,' her ' rhythm,' her ' action,' will strike your eye at every turn.

A group of tossing elm-trees against the clouds and a few dark wings streaking the sky; a tumble-down shed round which cows are grouped, standing or lying, lazily chewing the cud ; a shuffle of chimney-pots against a city sky and a trail of smoke ; a boy flying down a long, narrow wet street, with a bundle of papers beneath his arm ; a swan ' floating double ' past a tuft of reedy grasses ; an old man leaning on a thick stick or with a bundle on his back and climbing a steep path ; a woman sitting under the light with her sewing grouped at her elbow ; boys and girls gathered about a game, or fire, or a gate—all these are natural ' compositions,' and charming ones.

You might turn your attention to advertisements, for these are arranged with a view to attracting the eye and gripping the attention. Look at them as so many patterns, and ask yourself if the allotted spaces have been filled pleasantly.

Look at reproductions of the Great Masters. The wonderful way in which these painters grouped their subjects is an education in itself. The extraordinary simplicity of the arrangement, action, and composition will often surprise you.

The shapes of some pictures have given rise to quaint legends, and probably the most famous of all is that of Raphael's Madonna della Sedia, or Madonna of the Chair, 180

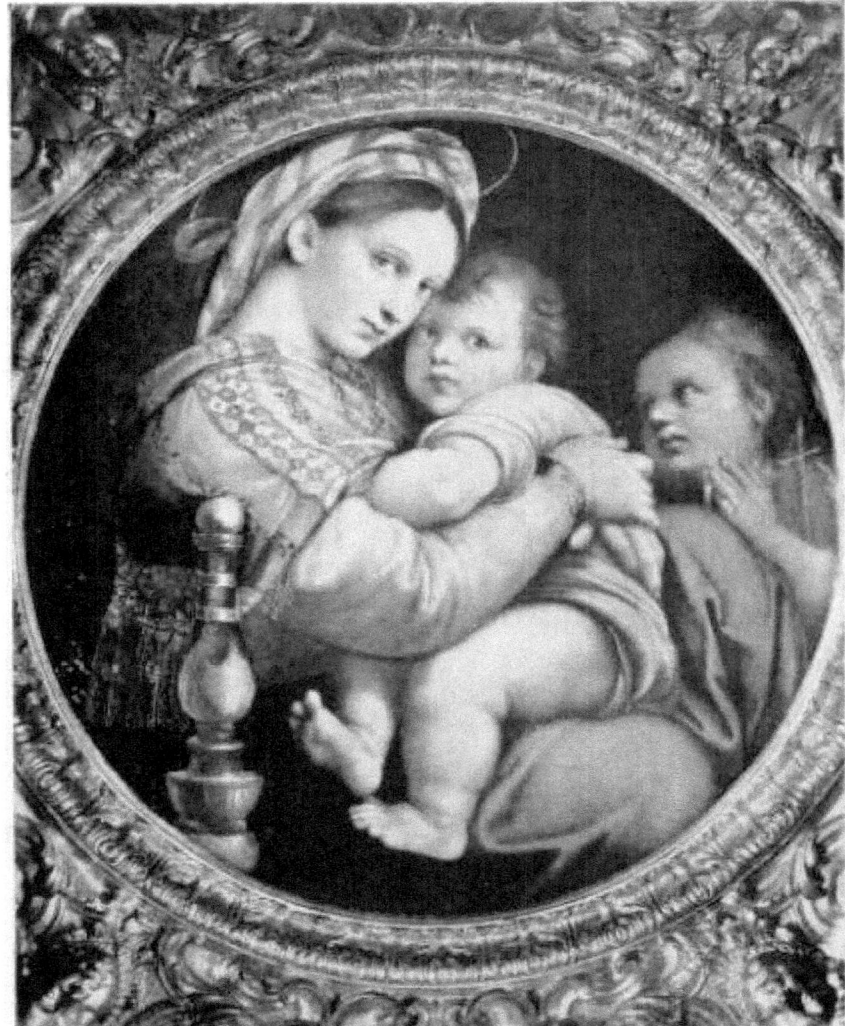

103. Thk Madonna uella Sedia Raphael

Photo Anderiion

Action and Composition

The story goes that Raphael was passing through a village at vintage time, and seeing a mother and child sitting in a doorway was filled with a desire to paint the beautiful group. The only materials to hand were empty wine-vats. On one of these Raphael seized, and began this picture on the upturned bottom of the vat.

Then Raphael snatched a half-charred ozier stick, And on the wine-cask at that moment drew That Child and Mother, just then glorified By the last sunshine's deepest, softest hue.

The picture is treasured as one of the world's most beautiful paintings, but whether the wine-vat legend was invented to explain the peculiar shape we shall never know. As a composition pure and simple, look and judge for yourself.

CHAPTER XV

Light and Shade

WHAT constitutes light and shade ? " is a question more easily asked than answered. Briefly, all objects on which light falls present light and shade.

Twist a piece of paper into a cone and look at it with half-closed eyes. What do you see ?

One side is light, one side is dark, where light and shade mingle there is half light and half tone.

In Nature all tones and tints are gradated. Light blends into half light, half light into half tone, half tone into shade, dividing and subdividing indefinitely.

There are no outlines in Nature. ' Outlines,' or ' edges,' are merely names for the particular parts thrown into prominence by light and shade. Certain parts present sharply defined shapes ; but shadows dissolve into light, and light dissolves into shadow.

An outline drawing is a drawing that represents the outside or extreme edge of a person or object, as the contour line in a map is the extreme outline of a country. There is no visible outline to a leaf, vase, or hand.

Outline drawing merely represents a shape without shading.

Therefore when we speak of ' drawing light and shade' we mean drawing broad masses of light and shade, giving the right balance—neither too much nor too little value to each light, each shadow, each cast shadow. Drawing objects in light and shade with a pencil point is a tedious business. It is best to adopt some means by which we can cover the ground quickly.

There are many methods of tackling this very interesting 182

L.ight and Shade

subject, but I should advise (at any rate as a beginning) drawing with black and white chalk on a tinted paper as the quickest and most straightforward manner of drawing broad masses of light and shade. Besides, it has one great advantage over ordinary stump or chalk, charcoal, pen and ink, or wash : it reverses the usual style of drawing. The method of drawing with light and dark chalk upon tinted paper exactly reverses the method of drawing with pencil, stump, and charcoal on a white ground. Then we draw middle and darkest tones and leave the white paper to express the light. But if we draw on brown, grey, blue, or otherwise tinted paper, we draw the lights with white chalk, the shadows with chalk (or charcoal), and leave the tinted paper to express the middle or general tones. By these means we build up the shapes quickly. We look for the shapes of the lights—which are too often undefined—no less than the shapes of the shadows.

As it is easier to draw broad, simple, and strong masses of light and shade, choose several simple objects of a uniform colour and place them on a table and in the bright and concentrated light of lamp, candle, or (shaded) electric bulb. Bring the light fairly close to the level of the table. A small piece of candle or a low lamp will give a better, because a less diffused, light.

Choose a white ^gg, a table napkin in a white ring, a white paper-covered box, a white paper flower, or other such things. A newspaper folded in a white wrapper, a white cup, or cup and saucer, white enamel bowl, white glove—all these will be equally suitable.

First ask yourself where is the brightest light, and draw the shape of the light with white chalk. Then look for the darkest shadow, which will naturally be the part that is farthest away from the light, and probably where the object rests on the ground. Draw the shape of the dark shadow. Next look for the middle (or binding) tone and blend with white chalk if in the light, and shade with black chalk if it forms part of the shadow.

Drawing for Beginners

When the surface is highly polished, as, for example, on the curve of the napkin ring, there will be a ' high light.'

The general colour of the tinted paper will give the general prevailing tint of the background and the middle tints of the models.

Keep a wary eye on the shape of the shadows cast by the various objects. Beginners find it difficult to realize that cast shadows bear a resemblance to the objects by which they are cast.

Not only do objects project their shadows in a major or lesser degree according to the distance of the light (as we have already noted in perspective diagram. Fig. 60), but they reflect their chief characteristics. For example, the ^gg, you will observe, casts a smooth, even, oval-shaped shadow. Beneath the shaded objects the box and napkin are roughly sketched with white chalk, giving a slight indication of the position of the shadows.

When we have absorbed some of the lessons to be learned from drawing objects in a bright and artificial light, we should proceed to draw objects in the more subtle light of day.

A few ordinary models, such as a couple of books and an old silver candlestick, placed on the edge of a table will serve our purpose very well.

The books, one bound in light cloth, the other in dark red leather, the unlit candle, and the candlestick present three different tones.

Note first the brightest lights and the darkest darks.

Seen through half-closed eyes the silver is a shimmer of lights and soft reflections, and requires a few careful strokes of white and black chalk, following the shapes as closely as possible, making good use of the definite lights and shades on the rim, the barrel, and the twisted support. The light catches the edges of the dark book ; also there are slight reflections on the polished table. You may now suggest the middle lights, leaving the paper itself to express the middle tones.

Other articles will, of course, serve the purpose. Choose 184

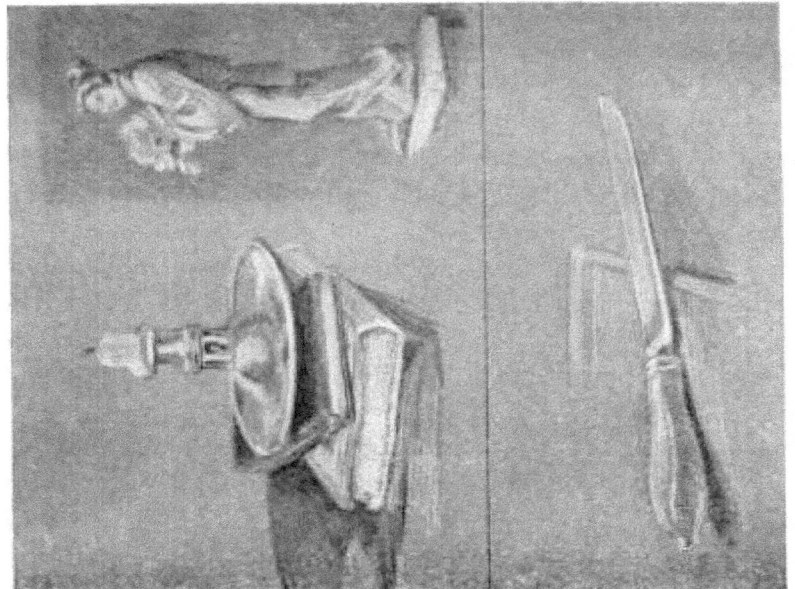

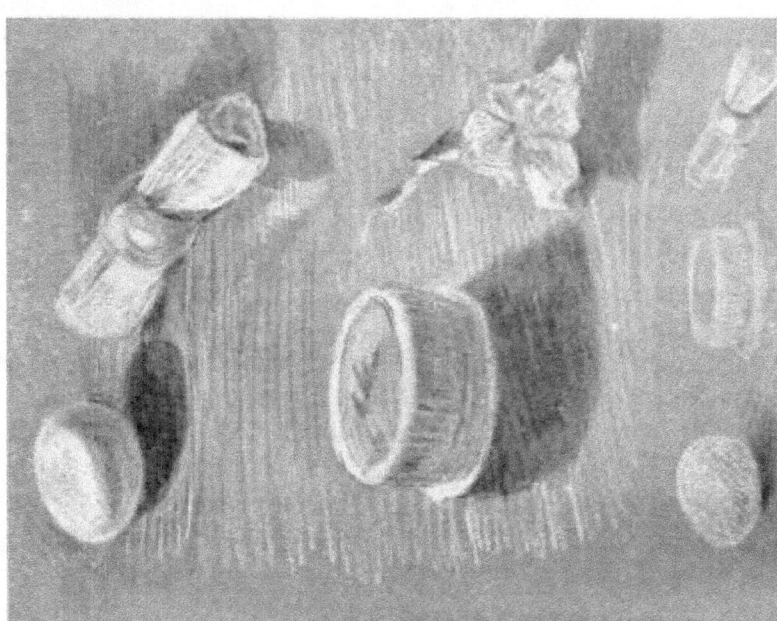

a few near in shape and in three shades—hght, dark, and middle—and place them in a simple light and clear of their surroundings.

If you have not the ordinary bread-knife depicted in my drawing, choose another, but let it be a large knife rather than a small one, and do not select a clasp-knife. The latter is not so simple in form, nor so shapely, as an ordinary cooking- or carving-knife. The French cooking-knife is an excellent study for light and shade, for it has invariably a straight, smooth, and pointed blade, and a shapely handle.

The bread-knife presents a simple plane, a flat blade and a rounded handle. The brightest lights leap at once to the eye from the edge of the blade and the square-shaped hasp. The rounded handle throws an oblong shadow; the blade also throws a de-cided shadow on the tray.

The wooden handle shares the tone with the background. It is a middle tone, and only requires a few slight touches to ' lift' the light shape away from the background. The shadows on the rounded handle are strongly moulded (or shaped); the groove in the wood catches both light and shade, and can be drawn with a dark streak against light strokes of chalk.

The little Japanese figure of papier mache in my drawing (Fig. 105) has a face almost as white as the white edge of the stand. She turns to the light and presents a narrow upright shape. The glossy hair has dark shadows, not quite so dark as the dark folds behind the sleeve and sash. A broad white shadow lies over the upper part of the back.

There is little variety of colours and tints in these groups. They are neutral, with the exception of the lady's grey-blue dress, and the mauve silk flower in her hand, and the small book with the dark crimson cover supporting the candlestick.

And the objects gathered beneath the bright artificial light are all of a uniform whiteness, chosen for this very reason.

Colour confuses the consideration of tones. Whether colour represents dark tones or light tones depends to a great extent on the light which falls upon it.

185

Drawing for Beginners

Naturally, however, rich colours retain the shadows and lighter colours reflect more light.

Look through half-closed lids (not for colour, but for pure light and shade) at a large armchair upholstered in one uniform and unpatterned material. Note how the colour varies under the play of light and shadow. Cannot you see the difference between the colour in the shadows and the colour in light ? And a contrast between the back and the seat of the chair, the tops and the sides of the arms, the edges of the arms and seat and the edges of the back ? The sofa, settee, and table covered with a plain piece of material offer the same object-lessons of light and shade.

Observe—in a bright light—a cream-coloured jug or cup decorated with a broad band of pale colour. The pink, blue, or yellow band merges into the shaded side of the jug, and becomes almost indistinguishable from the cream surroundings.

Place a pale blue, pink, or yellow enamelled mug, or tumbler, upon a white plate and in a strong light. Do you not find that the mug or tumbler—though a shade darker than the white plate—mingles with the cast shadow thrown on the plate ?

The contents of a small table—a man's smoking table no less than a lady's toilet table— ^will offer innumerable objects for the study of pure light and shade. A cigar-box with its gilt and gaily tinted labels is a very good object-lesson in light and shade, and seen in a shaded position the light label blends with the polished dark wood on the shadow side.

A cigarette, like a cigar, presents a tubular shape, light on one side, dark on the other. The gold or cork tip of the cigarette merges into the shadows of the shaded side ; the crimson and gold band of the cigar mingles with the rich brown shadows of the cigar itself.

If you arrange several objects of contrasting colour closely together and in the same light, the contrast helps to force the effect.

Draw a cluster of purple grapes and light green grapes 186

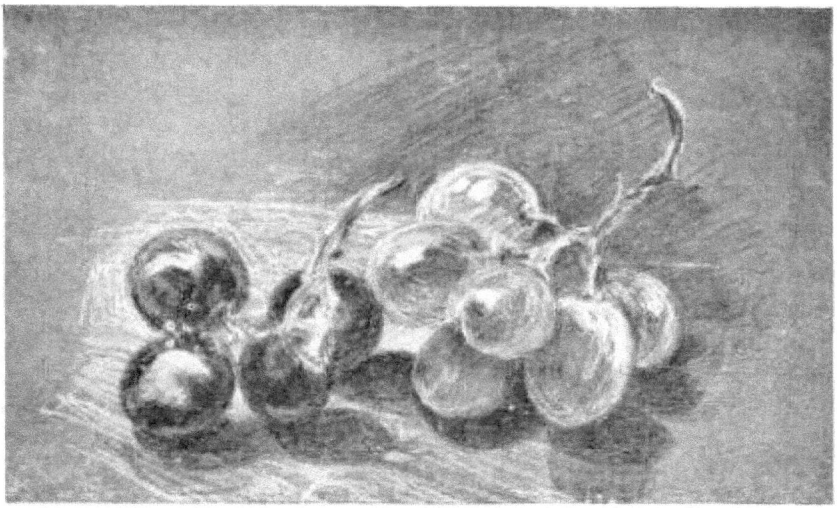

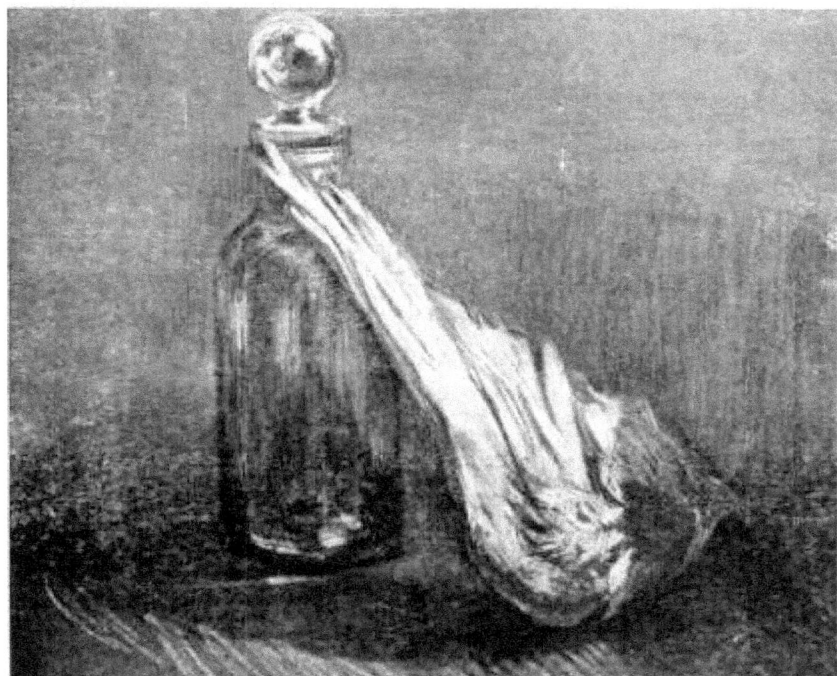

Fig. IOC). Light and Shade on Coloured Objects

side by side. The purple grapes catch the hght and hold rich shadows. The light grapes should be as firmly but more delicately drawn; they require light touches of chalk, and shadow-shapes drawn with a gentle hand. The depth and shade of the grapes vary very little. There is a slightly heavier tone beneath the dark round globules.

A white or cream bird's wing leaning against a dark green bottle with a shadow projecting over the feathers makes a very interesting contrast of light and shade. Only the stopper of the bottle reflects pure light. The rest of it is submerged into shadow, and, half closing your eyes, you will find that the bottle loses itself in its own shadow cast on the ground.

The whole of the wing is a light tone, the lightest portion being that which is nearest. Draw the triangular shape with firm touches of white chalk, then shade down with black chalk where the shadow lies. There is a rich shadow in the foreground. The wing, though deeply overshadowed, still remains many shades lighter than the ground.

If the bottle and wing are a thought too difficult, draw something a little less complicated.

Arrange several objects of contrasting tints in a strong light, either with or without a cast shadow (which is easily arranged by intercepting the light with a few books, or a piece of cardboard). If it be a woman's hat with a contrasting plume or wing, either the hat should be dark and the feather light, or vice versa ; or you may place together a man's black hat and a pair of light kid gloves, or some yellow and white flowers in a dark vase. A sunshade of brilliant colours lying open on the grass, half in shadow, half in light, provides an excellent model.

A coat, a cloak, and a hat, or three hats, all of a similar colour, placed on chairs several paces apart, present a more fascinating and more difficult study of light and shade.

The reason why the separation of the articles makes the study more interesting and a hundred times more difficult is that there is space between each object. And this

187

Drawing for Beginners

introduces a new problem which requires very careful consideration.

If you had three red apples of a bright and more or less uniform colour and shape and placed them one on the near end of a form, one in the centre, and one at the far end, and you took up your pencil and drew the light and shade of the three apples, would you draw each apple with the same degree of light and shade ?

If you put the apples on the ground in the playground, or garden path, or open field, five, seven, and twenty paces away, and tried to draw or to paint them (the question of light and shade applies with equal force to drawing and painting), would you draw them exactly the same ?

Would you not give the near apple more distinct light and shade, more accent, more strength than the apple farthest away ? Of course you would ! Even if you drew without thought you would instinctively draw something a good distance away in a broader and simpler manner.

For the sake of argument let us presume that we are painting a picture representing three ladies in black velvet. One in the foreground, another in the middle distance, and a third in the far distance. If we painted the black velvet dress in the far distance as richly, as strongly, as definitely as the black velvet dress in the foreground, we should paint an untruth.

Things in the extreme distance must not be as strongly depicted as those in the foreground or middle distance, as I demonstrated when stating the first rule of perspective.

If we draw or paint a picture of a street with its diminishing houses, railings, lights, pavements, drawn correctly in perspective, but ignore the air that intervenes and blots details from view, then we shall draw something that is not true to Nature.

The policeman on his beat at the end of the street is merely a dark uniformed figure ; as he approaches we note that he wears a high helmet; nearer still, we see his silver badges and buttons and shiny boots ; as he passes under our window 188 we distinguish the tint of his complexion and the shape of his features.

But it would be untrue to Nature if we painted or drew details in his face when he first appears. His face is a blur —because of the space that intervenes.

Things in the distance cannot be as strongly drawn as those in the middle distance. For between the artist and the distant object floats a veil of atmosphere.

Some young artists will argue that they have seen pictures drawn with firm lines and details even to the very horizon. This is perfectly true. But we must bear in mind that we are discussing the subject from the point of view of pure light and shade. It is quite correct to say that details can be drawn with firm outlines and the effect of space more or less ignored. That represents a certain style of drawing or painting, a conventional kind of art. But, if we are honestly trying to draw light and shade, if we are drawing varied tones, painting not merely flat washes of colour, but gradated tints to represent the light and shade of colour, then we cannot ignore the truth. And it is by these observations, and the recording of these observations, that our work becomes artistic or otherwise.

Such facts, like all simple laws of Nature, we cannot avoid even if we would. The newspaper with its photographs of ordinary events confirms them daily. Look, for instance, at a photograph representing crowds gathered together in the open. In the foreground are large strong masses of light and shade, broken up into details—clothes, hands, faces, and features ; in the background are misty effects, either of trees or other details of a landscape ; in the middle distance are groups of people, some sitting and some walking, their clothes of dark or uniform tint, their faces misty blurs, their features indistinguishable.

The clearer is the atmosphere, the more distinct is the distance. The more brilliant is the sun, the richer and deeper are the shadows. The rich shadows of a tropical scene will be richer in the foreground than in the distance. It is purely

Drawing for Beginners

a matter of degree. From simple objects grouped on a table to complicated scenes in a landscape, all will present their own peculiar and fascinating problems of light and shade.

No doubt you will wish to try other methods of drawing light and shade than drawing on tinted paper with chalks of black and white.

There is the much vaunted method of rubbing on powdered chalk with a stump of twisted paper or kid in varying tints upon a white paper. With this method we can obtain very subtle gradations by erasing with rubber or bread and by stippling in with the stump. Provided that we attack the study with vigour, sketching it in the first place with charcoal, and rubbing on the chalk speedily, and not spending too much time smoothing the surfaces, it may help us to learn a good deal about light and shade. Nevertheless there is a very great danger of expending too much time over the surface at the expense of the structure. It is quite possible to stipple in a head or an arm with such beautiful shades of light and tint that the essential shape of the nose, head, and arm is forgotten. In other words, the drawing is lost.

Have you not seen old-fashioned stipple-drawings of bygone days so lacking in definite shape that the gentlemen and ladies are dropping into a sugary, boneless state ? And that constitutes one great danger of drawing with the stump.

There is another method. By covering a sheet of Michelet or other grained paper with charcoal lines lightly rubbed to a fairly even tint, wiping out the lights with rubber or bread, and drawing the shapes with charcoal, one can achieve a very artistic study of light and shade.

Another method strongly advocated by one very famous art teacher is drawing with pen and ink on a smooth white surface. It is certainly a very direct method. Pen and ink, however, is not for beginners a very good method of drawing light and shade. In the first place, it is an 190

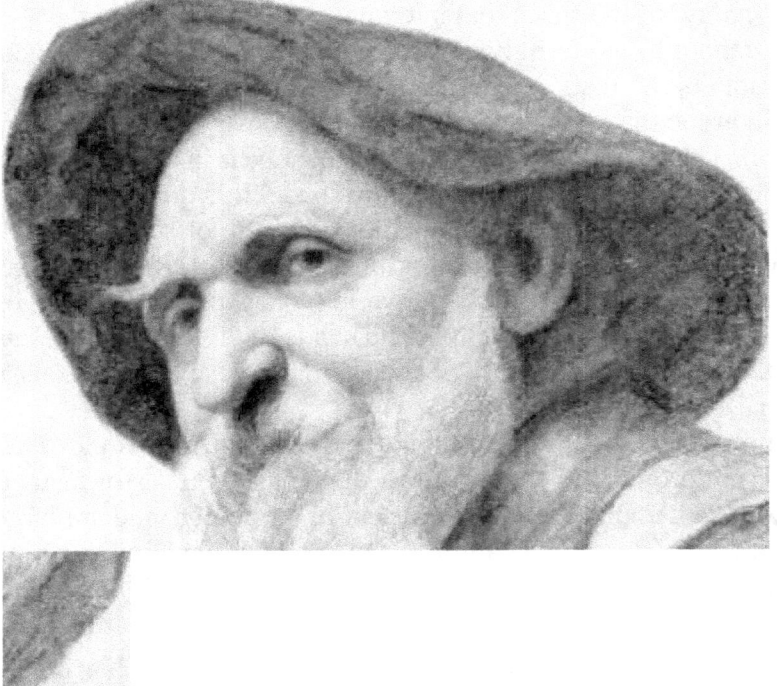

Fio;. 107. Stump-drawing of Old Man's Head

extremely difficult medium because it requires a considerable amount of experience to alter and correct a false bit of tone

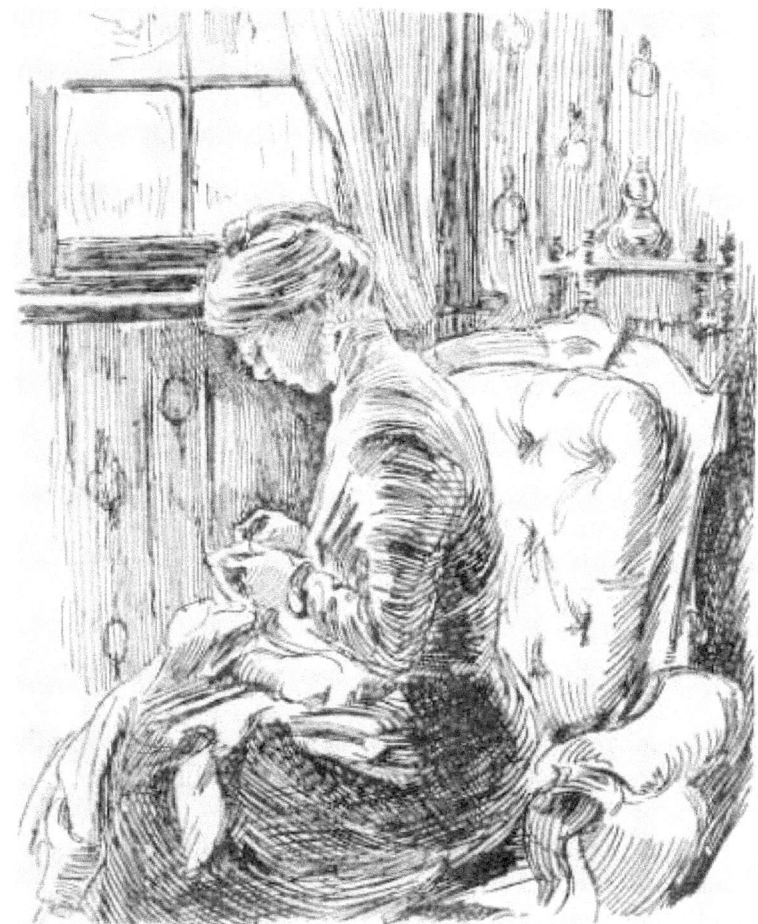

Fig. 108. Light and Shade drawn with Pen and Ink

satisfactorily, but, above all, broad smooth masses of light and shade, unless done by an experienced hand, have a very mechanical effect.

Light and shade can be studied with the brush by mixing sepia and flake white, ivory black and white, or charcoal

191

Drawing for Beginners

grey and white. This method is more akin to pen and ink, inasmuch as it requires a practised hand to apply clear fresh washes of colour.

For the beginner a ' dry ' method is certainly the wisest, and he will gain valuable experience by constant experiment with it.

Vd\

CHAPTER XVI

Correcting our Drawings

How many times do we cast our pencil down and exclaim, " Oh for a little help ! " Or we take up our drawing and despairingly rend it in half.

If we have landed in a hopeless morass of difficulties, we had far better tear up our drawing or fling it aside—and begin again. To begin again, however, on the same object, round which clings the flavour of defeat, is disheartening. Personally I prefer to start on quite another subject.

On the other hand, if you are pluckily determined to discover your mistakes you should put your pride in your pocket and seek out your nearest available friend, who, though ignorant of drawing, may detect the something that is wrong. He or she will probably laugh (how easy it is to laugh at the mistakes of other people !); but try to find the reason for that laugh.

" Why laugh ? "

" Oh, I don't know why, but it is so screamingly funny."

" Where does the scream come in ? "

" I don't know."

" You must know. Is it the face, or the eyes, or the hand ? I am sure the hand is quite good."

" N-no, but, oh ! "—another explosion of merriment— " oh, dear ! did you ever see such a leg in all your life ? "

And in all probability you have taken more care with the drawing of that leg than with the rest of the drawing put together.

Now that your attention has been drawn to the leg, look at it carefully; something may strike you as peculiar. It may— you possibly concede—look a trifle ' out,' but where is it

Drawing for Beginners

wrong ? You may pounce on the doubtful drawing, but how will you correct it ? You might even make matters worse.

Hold up your drawing before a mirror. The picture will be reversed, and seeing the unfortunate detail from an entirely different point of view sometimes—if not always—flings the mistake in your face.

Should you find it to be so in this instance, try again. Put down your drawing and erase it gently. Never use the rubber viciously or revengefully, as you may be tempted to do, for you must always treat the surface of your paper with respect.

Supposing, however, that you are still unconvinced ; that you believe your drawing to be right and your critic wrong. Try another test.

Hold up your drawing to a strong light—of a lamp, or at a window—and look at the back of it, when your drawing will be seen reversed. Can you now perceive anything wrong ?

He-who-cannot-draw sometimes fancies things are wrong —^that I will admit; and he-who-cannot-draw can be just as obstinate in his opinions as the artist.

Should you honestly feel that your drawing is a correct interpretation, stick to your opinion. But try to keep an open mind, and never despise advice because it is humble.

Some of the greatest people have sought the advice of simple folk. Wasn't it Moliere who read his plays to his cook ?

Try to get an expert's opinion. ' An expert' does not necessarily mean an expert artist—that we cannot often hope to find—but one who is expert in the particular subject that is engaging our pencil.

For instance, if I made a study of a cow or sheep, I should preferably take that drawing to a butcher or a farmer for a criticism. The criticism might be shattering, but there is this to be said for it. The man who is familiar and more or less an expert with such animals will instinctively pounce on glari g mistakes.

A doctor has a sound working knowledge of the human 194

Correcting our Drawings

frame, and I shall never forget the laugh of a doctor when his eyes lit on my first attempt at drawing the figure with the surface muscles exposed. I learned a lot from that laugh, or rather from the remarks with which he tried to excuse his merriment.

A builder might let fall a few helpful remarks concerning the drawing of the steeple of a church. " Rather a steep steeple," said one when looking at a sketch of the village street made by a young friend of mine.

And the carpenter might possibly remark that there was something very peculiar with regard to the chair on which the lady (of your drawing) is sitting.

When drawing a vase on a table, the glass round which a model has clasped his fingers, the tankard on the sideboard, the porch under which mine host is welcoming or dismissing the guest, turn the paper upside down and regard it from an * upside down ' point of view. This is a most useful way of correcting things with two sides alike, and probably you will notice that the vase bulges rather lower on one side than the other, that the glass veers to one side and its stem is not quite straight, that the handles of the tankard do not balance, that the posts of the porch are leaning acutely in two different directions.

Another method of correction. If you have drawn a vase and feel that it balances badly, draw a line down its centre and measure from the central line to the outside edges, then note whether the measurements agree.

Bear in mind, however, that these are corrective devices. Never begin drawing with mechanical aids of the kind. Always draw freely. Make your correction afterward. If you are not very severe with yourself on this point, you will find yourself depending on these measuring systems. And overmuch measuring maketh an artist brainless.

Another excellent corrective is to hold the drawing at arm's length, or, better still, place it near the model (on a chair or on the floor), then resume the position from ^ /hich you are making your study.

Drawing for Beginners

Glance quickly from your drawing to the model. The strong, and often cruel, contrast of drawing versus Nature ' does the trick,' and emphasizes faults of light and shade, construction (or framework), balance, and proportions.

In the drawing of the " human form divine " there are many things tp deceive the eye and make the task difficult. Clothes are the greatest offenders—skirts, wide trousers, full sleeves, thick leggings, large bonnets, baggy tunics, cloaks, robes, hats, wigs—anything, in short, which is bulky is deceiving.

How often do we see the lady's feet emerging from her pretty floating skirt in a position which is a physical impossibility !

The Tudor and the Early Victorian costumes are great temptations to the novice, who greedily seizes upon the picturesque ample robes and skirts to hide the difficult drawing.

They may save a little trouble in the small matter of drawing arms and legs, and even feet, but beware lest they plunge you into worse difficulties !

A young artist of my acquaintance loathed the drawing of hands. She used the most ingenious devices to hide the hands from view. Winds blew, aprons flew, cloaks floated and concealed, but if the hands had of necessity to appear then she was utterly lost, and found that she had no knowledge wherewith to inform her drawings. Dutch men, women, and children— what favourites they are ! And there again do we find the lure of the dress in the wide trousers of Jan, and the big sabots of Jan's pretty sister. The wider the trousers, the fuller the skirts, the less shall we see of the difficult legs, says the young artist. But no matter how thick and frilly are the petticoats and how wide are the trousers, those difficult legs are not to be ignored. They must be traced lightly beneath the garments.

We cannot disguise the fact that if we are drawing human beings, two legs, two arms, and a head and body of reasonable proportions are essential for each. 196

Correcting our Drawings

Should you have an uncomfortable feeling that there is something not quite correct in your drawing, that the feet do not come in the right position, that the hand protrudes from the frilled wristband at an angle not quite in harmony with the elbow, take your picture to the window, lay it against a pane of glass, and trace the head, hands, fee^, and all parts revealed on the back of the paper. Then return with your drawing to the table and (still with the back of it uppermost) connect your tracings by sketching in the rest of a human body.

Ere you have finished your sketch you will possibly appreciate that you have made the limbs play queer tricks ; it is highly probable that you will have made the farther limbs longer than the nearer ones. We have sometimes noticed in sketches of persons sitting with legs crossed that the limbs are inextricably mixed !

Should the paper on which you are drawing be of too thick a substance for this test, take a piece of tracing paper, or a smooth piece of ordinary tissue paper, and on this trace your drawing. Then remove the original drawing, and, laying the tracing paper on a white surface, link up the head, feet, and hands as suggested above.

In all these methods of checking ourselves, it is the fresh view of our drawing that reveals its weaknesses.

When painting, if you feel that your colours are not what they should be, that your tones are dark, or too uneven, that your highest light is not ' in tune ' with your middle light—take a piece of smoked glass and look through this at the reflection of your painting. Gone are the pretty colours, the subtle tints. Your painting will be merely a prosaic black and white affair, and with everything reduced to black and white, to high tones and low tones (light and shade), in all probability the wrong tone will shriek at you.

But if, after all these various methods, you still can see nothing wrong, though a horrid feeling prevails that all cannot be right, if neither advice nor the devices described give a clue—then, lock up your drawing, put it away for a

Drawing for Beginners

few days, or a few months, until you have entirely forgotten the circumstances in which it was drawn. When you again examine it the chances are that you will see at once what is wrong.

Either you will say, " How could I miss seeing that mistake ? " or (and, believe me, the chances of this are very remote), " Why ! there is nothing wrong—after all."

CHAPTER XVII

Materials

A LARGE stock-in-trade is a mistake. If you provide yourself with a lavish quantity of materials, you are probably handicapping, not helping, your studies.

Far better use a few tools, a few materials, than fly from one paper to another paper, from one pigment to another pigment, from chalk to charcoal, and charcoal to pastel.

To begin with, buying many expensive materials has the great disadvantage that it is likely to check your most valuable instinct for experiment.

If you stop to consider whether you are wasting good material, and the question arises, " Have you anything ' to show for ' the expensive paper and paints ? " the probabilities are that you will decide to finish a poor piece of work instead of flinging it aside in favour of a fresh start.

A few materials well chosen, a few tools well handled, are worth a whole shop-full used irresponsibly.

Buy a paper that will serve several purposes. Cartridge paper will ' take ' pencil, chalk, or water-colour. It is a useful all-round paper. Therefore, I would advise a cartridge-paper sketch-book. Do not begin at the wrong end of this, or on the wrong side of your paper. Lay the tip of your finger upon the surface; you will soon detect that the right side has a smooth and satiny surface. Michelet paper is suitable only for charcoal and crayon, and thick hand-made water-colour paper is rather unnecessarily expensive for the early stages.

If your mind is definitely settled on brushwork invest in a medium Whatman or O.W. paper, in sketch-book or block form. The block should not be smaller than 5| by 7 inches.

Drawing for Beginners

Nothing cramps the style more effectually than block or book of a minute size.

Buy pencils of a medium quality—HB, B, or BB. BBB's are useful for soft and sympathetic studies, for rich shadows and textures.

Rubber of soft crumbly substance is preferable to hard or gummy rubbers ; ink-eraser should never be used, it destroys the surface of the paper.

A sketch-book, a pencil, a piece of paper, and a knife— these are all that are required for a start.

If you wish to draw on a larger scale, you must buy paper by the sheet, which necessitates a drawing-board, drawing-pins, and an easel. Easels are stocked in every quality, size, shape, and description, and listed in all the colourmen's catalogues.

For water-colour painting you require a small colour-box (japanned boxes are lighter and more useful for sketching purposes than wooden boxes), a moderate range of colours, and a couple of good camel-hair or sable brushes.

Good brushes are essential. You can trim your pencil, your chalk, your charcoal to suit your various needs, but you must abide by the brush. A brush that spreads and splits, or that moults its hair over the paper, will be of little use. A large full brush and a small brush will suffice for every purpose. Or, if preferred, one full brush of a medium size (number five or six) with a fine point will do the work of two.

When choosing a brush dip it in a pan of water and roll the point on the hand, or on a piece of paper, to make certain that it has a good point.

The old-fashioned hard cakes of paint had many excellent qualities ; the colours were lasting and good, but the rubbing process was certainly tedious, and they are seldom seen nowadays. The half-pans of moist paint have taken their place ; they are not wasteful, provided they are used with ordinary care. On the other hand, tubes of paint—bearing in mind that we invariably squeeze out more colour than is necessary—are, most decidedly, extravagant. 200

Materials

We can trust any reputable colourman to fit a box with paints, and we strongly advise buying the best paints and leaving those of a cheaper grade alone. It is by far the best economy. The small boxescontain eight to fourteen half-pans. Group your colours together carefully. Nothing hampers a young artist more effectually than sprinkling paints haphazardly in a paint-box. When cobalt jostles vermilion and lemon yellow flanks ivory black your paint-box is unbusinesslike. Group together blues, reds and yellows, browns and black.

A box to hold twelve pans should contain the following colours :

Chrome yellow Vermilion

Yellow ochre Vandyke brown

Raw sienna Ivory black

Burnt sienna Prussian blue

Light red Ultramarine

Crimson alizarin Cobalt

For a box of fourteen colours the following is a good selection :

Lemon yellow Chrome No. 1 Yellow ochre Vermilion Crimson alizarin

Light red Raw sienna Burnt sienna Sepia Ivory black

Cobalt

French blue or French ultramarine

Prussian blue

A tube of Chinese white

For a beginner a small range is better than a large number of colours. A multiplicity of tints is apt to bewilder the mind. By experimenting with a few paints we can obtain a surprisingly wide range of tints. We must learn too the good as well as the bad qualities ; how one tint will permeate others, how the liquid brilliance of one will neutralize the dull opaque quality of another.

Drawing for Beginners

Now and again indulge yourself in a new paint.

Moist aureolin, cyanine blue, orange madder, are all a little dangerous—a little expensive and delicious to handle.

Before leaving the subject of water-colour paints I might mention the water-colours in tubes known as ' slow-drying.' These are recommended for hot climates.

One stipulation more.

Whether you have a lavishly stocked box, or whether you content yourself with a modest range of colours, you must always treat your box respectfully.

Keep the paints clean and dry, the palette clean.

It is a good rule to start a fresh painting with a fresh mixing of colours.

Before putting your box away see that no paints are submerged under water. Colours soon deteriorate, and it is astonishing how quickly mould will accumulate on certain tints. A tiny piece of sponge is useful, and pieces of soft rag, freed from fluff, are almost a necessity for cleaning purposes.

Chalks or pastels are often used as an introduction to colour-work, and an excellent beginning they are. They are not so messy as paints. They train the eye quickly. We must abide by the chalk or pastel; it is difficult to correct or erase.

Chalks are the cheapest of all colour mediums, and a box of twelve pastels costs a very small sum.

The large boxes containing a range of beautiful tints are necessary for more advanced work.

Pastels require pastel paper, but this is not expensive and it is easily procurable. As a substitute for pastel paper use brown paper, the ordinary packing paper with a not too smooth or shiny surface. This will serve excellently for chalk, both black and white.

White (unsized) sugar-bags are useful for water-colour painting. The inside of a thick white envelope provides a choice paper for pencil or black chalk.

Michelet paper, or imitation Steinbach, is useful for char-202

Materials

coal studies. A grained paper is more satisfactory than one with a smooth surface, for the latter tends to exaggerate the brown instead of the rich black shades of charcoal. Vine charcoal is sold in small cheap boxes and the Venetian charcoal in larger quantities.

Plain wooden easels last a lifetime. On the other hand, the hinged easels—of which there is an enormous variety— made to pack in a small valise or to carry in the hand, are equally serviceable for indoor and out-of-door study.

If an easel is not at hand a chair can be used as a substitute.

Sit on one chair and place another chair with its back toward your knees. Put your feet on the back rail of the second chair and the drawing-board will then rest on your knees and (at an angle) against the back of the chair. The seat of the second chair can be utilized for your various tools.

For charcoal studies a bottle of fixative and a sprayer are almost a necessity. Charcoal rubs with the slightest impact. Scent-sprayers can be used in place of the ordinary metal or glass sprayers sold for the purpose by the artists' colourman.

Once more I advise the young student to dispense with all unnecessary paraphernalia and buy only necessities.

Ponder well what the Scottish mechanic said when his eye fell on Turner's painting of Modern Italy :

" Eh, mon, just see what white leed and common paint can dae in the hand o' genius."

CENTRAL

•.T-'Pl"""'^ * ?

>»

www.ingramcontent.com/pod-product-compliance
Lightning Source LLC
Chambersburg PA
CBHW081453170526
45166CB00008B/2418